IMAGES of America

TOLEDO'S WOODLAWN CEMETERY

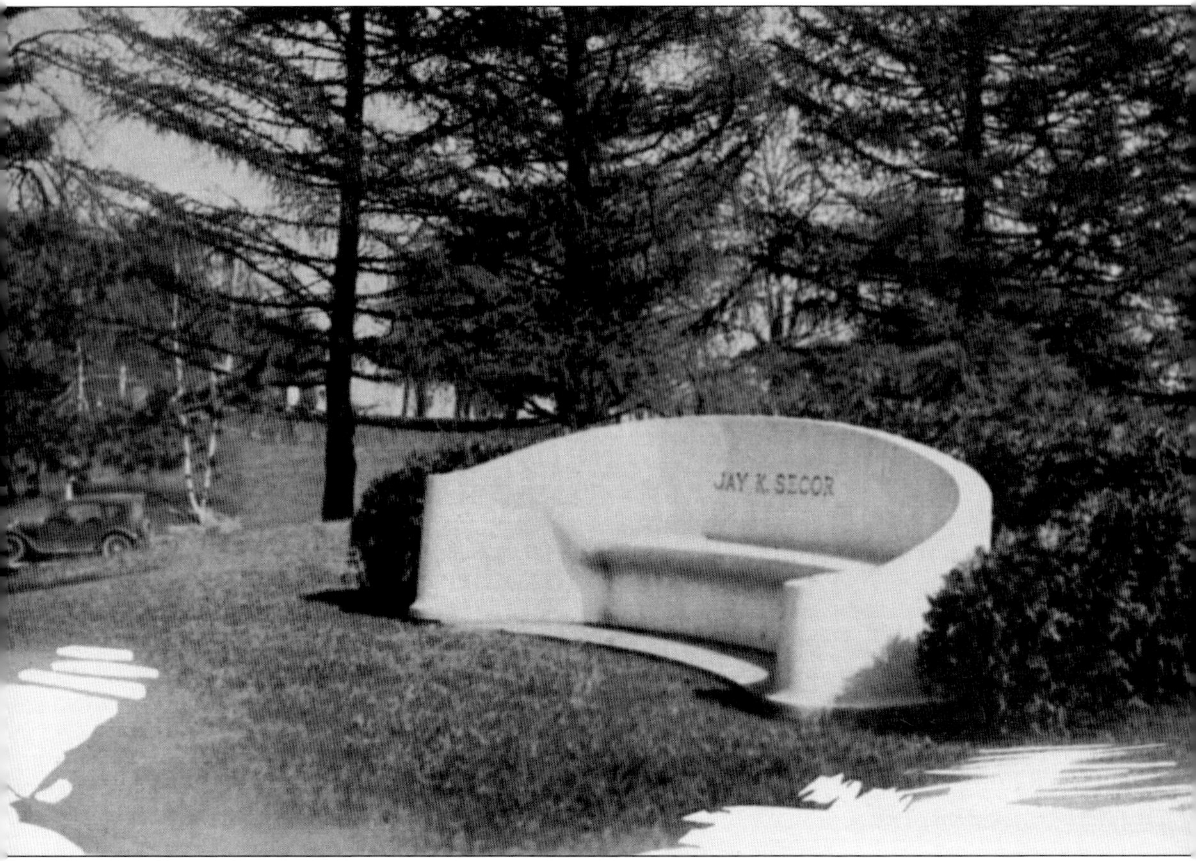

One of the many unique memorials found in Woodlawn Cemetery, this bench provides a quiet spot to contemplate the lives of the living and those who are no longer with us. (Historic Woodlawn Cemetery.)

On the Cover: Surrounded by newsboys, this pyramid was built in honor of John Gunckel, who dedicated his life to guiding the most undisciplined boys of Toledo onto the right path through his program, the Toledo Newsboys Association. For his compassion and remarkable achievement in working with these boys, he was sometimes referred to as the "father of the fatherless." (Billie Gunckle Iles.)

IMAGES
of America

TOLEDO'S WOODLAWN CEMETERY

Rebecca Deck Visser and Renee Ciminillo Jayne

ARCADIA
PUBLISHING

ISBN 978-1-4671-1295-6

Published by Arcadia Publishing
Charleston, South Carolina

Printed in the United States of America

Library of Congress Control Number: 2014941397

For all general information, please contact Arcadia Publishing:
Telephone 843-853-2070
Fax 843-853-0044
E-mail sales@arcadiapublishing.com
For customer service and orders:
Toll-Free 1-888-313-2665

Visit us on the Internet at www.arcadiapublishing.com

In memory of Robert Harden, Woodlawn executive director from 2009 to 2011, for his preservation, vision, and inspiration for the future.

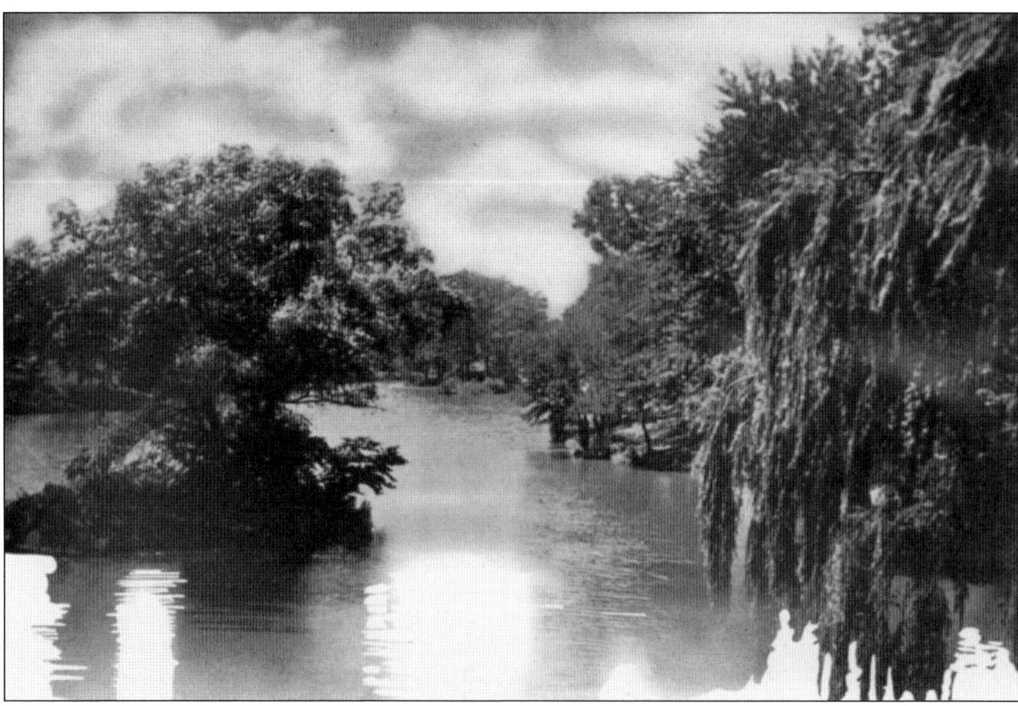

Large and small monuments surround this peaceful lake. Such monuments can reveal much about the deceased. Their name and the time they spent on earth can be easily detected on most. Other markings, carvings, epitaphs, and the design of the monument often reflect the individual's values as well as their degree of wealth, taste, and stature in life. (Historic Woodlawn Cemetery.)

Contents

Acknowledgments

Many thanks go to the following group of talented people and organizations. This book would not have been possible without their support and encouragement: David Bailey, Beckett Baither, Richard Baranowski, Don Bauman, Carol Bentley, Tom Boltz, Tina Mather Bothe, Bowling Green State University Center for Archival Collections, Browning Nursing Home, Jill Clever, Communica Company, Dave Cook, Davis College, Barbara Floyd, Fred Folger, Kay Foster, Gayleen Gindy, Jennifer Hart, Natalie Helm, Historic Woodlawn Cemetery board of directors, Ann Hurley, John Husman, Billie Gunckel Iles, Anthony Jayne, Veronica Jayne, Cathy D. Knepper, Cecelia Kinor, Kathleen Kuns, Rob Lamlein, J.B. LeBoutillier, The Library of Virginia, Ted Ligibel, Kate Bentley MacPherson, Irene Martin, Julie Mayle, Mary Mennel, Joan Moomey, Jean Moon, Becky Pegorsch, Dana Puga, Rutherford B. Hayes Presidential Center, Leslie S. Smith, Liz Storer, Peter Storer, Jodie Tienvieri, Toledo Firefighter's Museum, Toledo History Museum, Patty Toneff, Larry Sloane, John Swearingen Jr., Ron Visser, Laura Voelz, Jay Wagner, Mary and Dennis Wittman, and Mike Young.

Extra-special thanks go to Donna Christian, Gary L. Franks, Jack Kerin, and Gayle and Dale Floyd, whose last-minute contributions were immeasurable, and to Arcadia Publishing's Maggie Bullwinkel for her continuous patience and guidance.

The following persons and institutions provided photographs. The initials following their names will be used to credit each photograph: Andersonville National Historic Society (ANHS), Don Bauman (DB), Beckett Baither (BB), Fritz Bell (FB), Bentley Company (BC), Bowling Green State University Center for Archival Collection (CAC), Browning Nursing Home (BNH), Davis Business College (DBC), Donna Christian (DC), Flower Hospital (FH), Gayle Floyd (GF), Gary L. Franks (GLF), Historic Woodlawn Cemetery (WC), John Husman (JH), Billie Gunckle Iles (BGI), Jack Kerin (JK), Monclova Township (MT), Joan Moomey (JM), Rutherford B. Hayes Presidential Museum (RM), Secor family (SF), Storer family (STF), Toledo Club (TC), Toledo Firefighter's Museum (TFM), Toledo–Lucas County Public Library (TPL) Toledo Museum of Art (TMA), Toledo Police Museum (TPM), Library of Virginia (LV), and Mary Wittman (MW). Any photograph not credited is the property of author Rebecca Deck Visser.

Introduction

Show me the manner in which a nation or community cares for its dead and I will measure with mathematical exactness the tender sympathies of its people, their respect for the laws of the land and their loyalty to high ideals.

—William Gladstone (1809–1898)

Toledo's Woodlawn Cemetery tells a history of the cemetery and, to a certain extent, of the city of Toledo itself, highlighting the happy and sad times of the past and glorifying all who rest within its borders. A look at those who contributed to the cemetery's development, those who utilized it as a final resting place, and those drawn to it for other purposes reveal their expression of Toledo's culture, values, and ideals during the first 50 years of the cemetery's existence (1876–1926). The cemetery itself reflects the rural cemetery movement, which began some 30 years earlier at Mount Auburn Cemetery near Cambridge, Massachusetts. This movement was inspired by idyllic perceptions of nature, art, national identity, and the melancholy theme of death. While these cemeteries emphasized a natural state, the architectural styling of the monuments was characterized by diversity and a look as pleasing to the eye as the landscape. Some reformers believed that rural cemeteries could be culturally and morally uplifting for city dwellers and, at the same time, instill a sense of historical continuity and social rootedness. As the rural cemetery plan took hold throughout the country, local citizens interested in modern ideas in cemetery planning used it as the model for Woodlawn. A peaceful retreat, blending the characteristics of an elegant park with the pensive beauty of a burial place, was the result.

The book is partitioned into seven chapters, with the first discussing the development of the cemetery. Many of those involved in taking the idea of a new cemetery through all the necessary steps to open the gates of such a monumental venture are featured in this section. New burial customs that emerged throughout the 19th century, as well as changes to the cemetery and to the public's use of it, are also presented. Chapters two through six cover the lives of numerous people who left their mark on Toledo in various ways. Institutions, companies, and buildings still important to us today were first developed by many of the people buried here. In choosing Woodlawn Cemetery for their final resting place, these people are honored by the great and small monuments chosen to memorialize them. Each chapter has a focus, such as businessmen, soldiers, and politicians, reflecting the person's career and interests. However, several individuals transcended fields throughout their lifetime, creating a challenge for their placement in this volume. Each chapter is organized in a chronological manner based on the date of the person's death. This technique was utilized to highlight the significance of commerce, travel, manufacturing, and other important developments and events that occurred as Toledo evolved during these years. While each description is brief, additional information regarding these people can be found on the cemetery's website, www.historic-woodlawn.com.

Finally, the last chapter was reserved for a special Toledo company, Lloyd Brothers. The 19th century and early 20th century was a time when craftsmen could sculpt individualized monuments for a living, creating great diversity not only in architectural styles, but within styles. The Lloyd brothers were exceptionally skilled craftsmen in this area. They are responsible for many of the most elaborate and artistic monuments on the cemetery grounds as well as others both personal and public found throughout the country. Where known, Lloyd Brothers monuments are identified in each chapter.

As one flips through the book, a limited showing of women and low-income groups who lived and worked within Toledo during this period will be evident. American culture during the 19th and early 20th centuries dictated that a woman's place was strictly within the home and outside of the public eye. Those who dared to step beyond these boundaries were often held up for ridicule. In fact, local history books from the period that featured biographical sketches rarely included female contributors to the economy or cultural fabric of the community. As such, their efforts are all but forgotten to history. Those who excelled in writing or taught in public schools, while not included in the histories of the period, were often exempt from the public's scorn. During the later years of this period, women who were able to apply their natural, nurturing instincts to groups of needy and deserving individuals began to be recognized and publicly honored for their efforts.

While women were seldom recognized for their public achievements, members of lower-income groups earned even less attention. Prejudices of the time often prevented their successes, and even their names, from inclusion in the public records. Additionally, even though Woodlawn Cemetery was open to anyone who could afford a plot, many people did not have the resources or the inclination to purchase a family burial site during their lifetime. Therefore, most individuals included here are men of the upper and emerging middle classes, which consisted mainly of people of northern European descent. As a result, this book about the first 50 years of Woodlawn Cemetery indirectly reflects the practices and prejudices of the time.

The passages within this book are accompanied by photographs specially selected to complement and strengthen the story of each Woodlawn resident. Whenever possible, a photograph of the described person and their grave marker is included. In cases when a photograph of the person was not available, only their grave marker is shown. Additional images, such as those illustrating interesting funerary architecture and those expressing lifestyles of the period, have also been included.

Over the years, Woodlawn has remained dedicated to the rural cemetery plan. As a result, the cemetery is also used by a variety of groups and individuals, including nature lovers, genealogists, and artists. Meanwhile, Woodlawn's board members have made every attempt to adhere to the mission statement developed so long ago: to provide the resources, support, and education necessary to preserve, enhance, and share the heritage, natural beauty, and architectural significance of the Historic Woodlawn Cemetery. Because of these characteristics and historical traditions, Toledo's Historic Woodlawn Cemetery plays an important role in the quality of life in Northwest Ohio and is one of Ohio's most treasured cemeteries.

One

Woodlawn's Beginnings

Woodlawn Cemetery is one of the largest cemeteries in Northwest Ohio and the final resting place for thousands of the area's former residents. Established in 1876, Woodlawn became the cemetery of choice for many prominent citizens, who erected extravagant mausoleums and artistically engraved monuments to commemorate their lives. As the cemetery was open to anyone who could afford a lot, most families honored their loved ones with more modest headstones. Today, Woodlawn Cemetery not only serves as a final resting place for over 70,000 individuals, but also as an outdoor museum, an arboretum, a bird sanctuary, a historical archive, and an important social and cultural landmark for Toledo.

Toledo's Woodlawn Cemetery is the story of the first 50 years of the development of one of Toledo's greatest treasures. In this chapter, Toledo's beginnings, the community's changing efforts to care for the deceased, and the development of Woodlawn Cemetery are explored. It is believed that Toledo's first cemetery was on two acres of land near Madison Avenue and 17th Street. This little burial site was used for about 10 years before it was abandoned around 1840. Other cemeteries were organized over the years, but when Forest Cemetery was established in 1839, Toledo had a permanent burial ground. As this new cemetery was filling up quickly, and new traditions in cemetery development were evolving, Toledo's need for a modern cemetery became evident.

Carefully planned by its founders, Woodlawn Cemetery reflects the changing trends that occurred in the 1800s. A study of the cemetery also reveals a history of Toledo's development beginning in that period. Rapid industrialization in the late 1800s attracted many people to Toledo, brought great wealth to a select few, and offered steady employment to many. Behind the gates of this historic cemetery are citizens who contributed to the cultural, historical, and architectural heritage of the Toledo area.

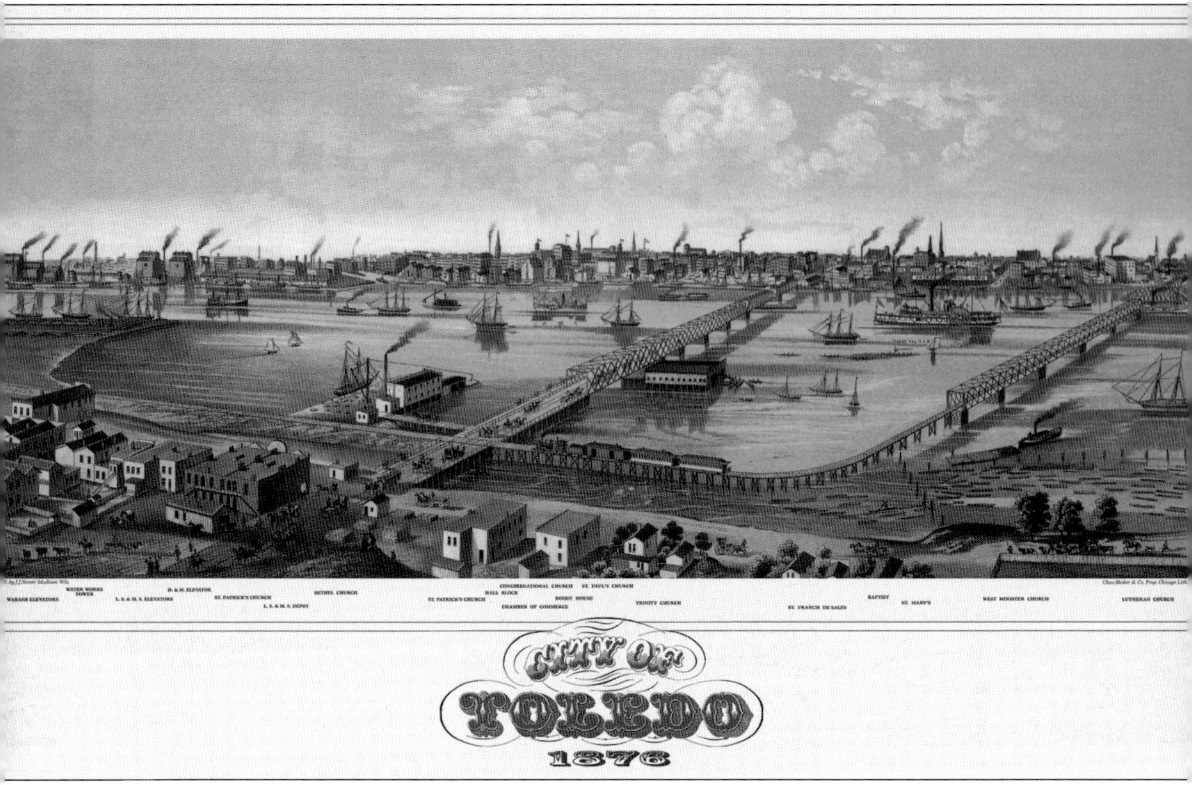

Toledo, Ohio, was formed when two small river towns, Port Lawrence and Vistula, combined in 1833, but it showed little promise of a future great city. With a population of just over 1,200, growth was slow for several years due to its location on the edge of the Great Black Swamp. At first, locals used family plots and churchyards as burial sites. In 1839, Forest Cemetery was established and became Toledo's first permanent cemetery. By 1880, Toledo had changed a great deal from its pioneer days. The census records for this year indicated that Toledo was one of the largest cities in the state, with a population of more than 50,000. Large tracts of land were needed as the city's developing industries, including carriage makers, breweries, and glass factories, became established. Additionally, housing needs and related services increased proportionately for employees who filled jobs in these new industries. To this end, existing structures, including some burial sites, were removed or relocated if they impeded plans for growth and expansion. (TPL.)

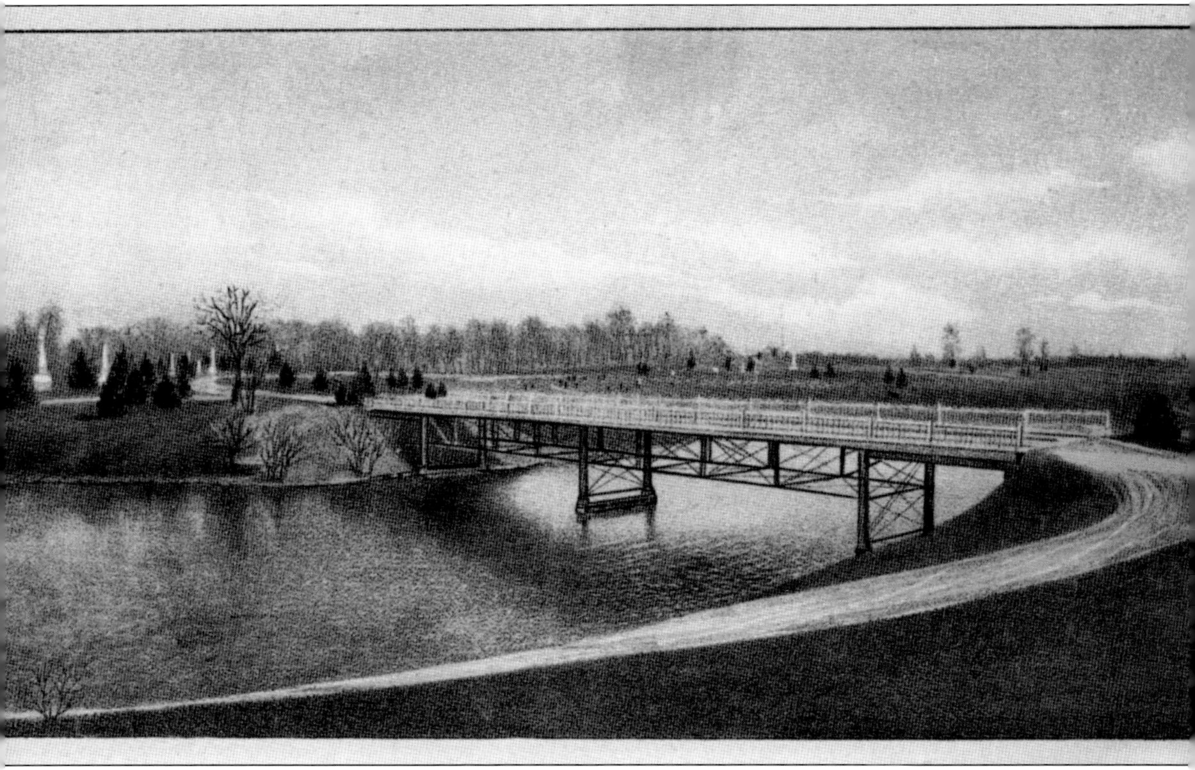

New trends relating to burial customs emerged as the 19th century advanced. These ideas are best encompassed in what became known as the "rural cemetery movement," which called for a site outside the city limits that would serve the entire population of a community. In contrast to earlier burial grounds, the new cemeteries covered vast tracts of land; through careful planning, a park-like setting emerged. Designers emphasized nature and art through the use of infinite combinations of wood, water, rock, and soil. Large granite grave markers carved with great attention to detail and imposing mausoleums were incorporated into the landscape, creating the effect of an outdoor museum. These lush landscapes promoted inspirational healing as the living paid their respects to the deceased while contemplating life in serene natural surroundings complemented by Neoclassical architecture. In this photograph, the cemetery's old bridge passes over Silver Lake, connecting different sections of the grounds. (WC.)

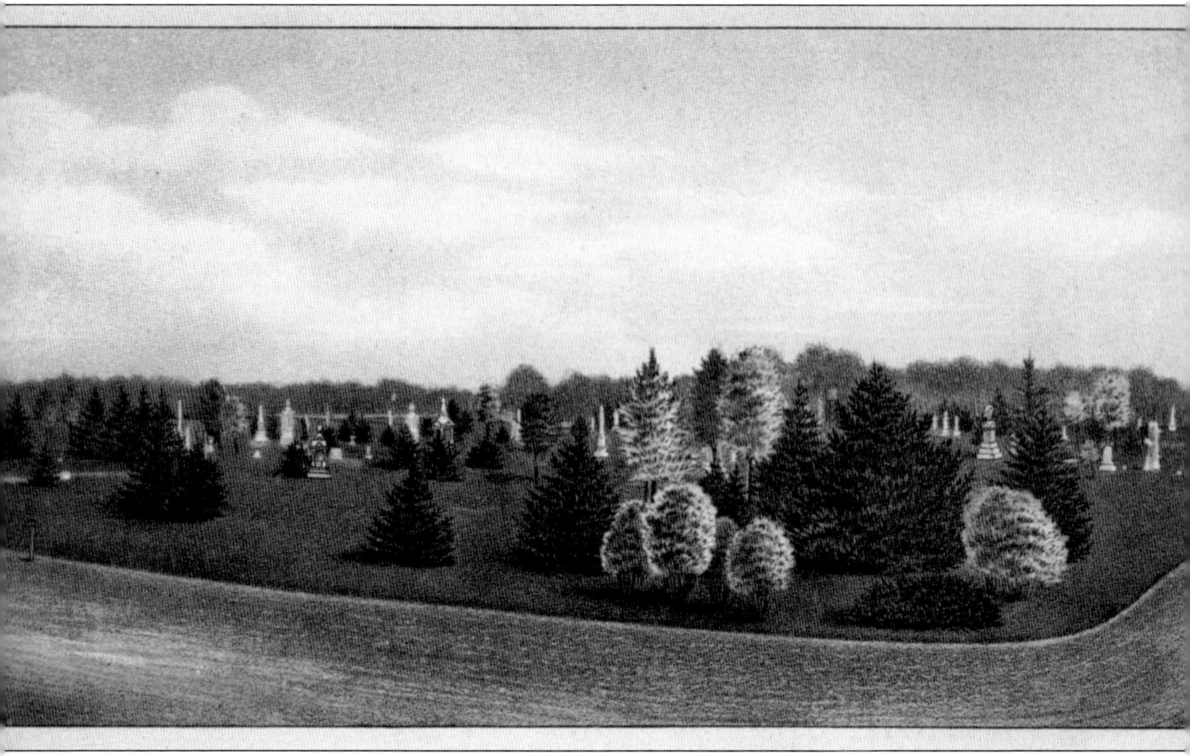

With Toledo's growing status as one of the most important cities in Ohio and a major manufacturing hub on the Great Lakes, talk of a new cemetery reflecting the latest trends and providing a more significant manner in which to honor the deceased had begun. This came to fruition when the Woodlawn Cemetery Association was incorporated and Woodlawn Cemetery was founded. A modified version of the rural cemetery movement, based on the landscape lawn plan featuring many of the same ideas but emphasizing simplicity, was adopted. Objects that ornamented individual lots in other cemeteries, including tin cans, vases, pitchers, pots, iron gates, fences, and benches were highly discouraged at Woodlawn Cemetery. In addition to a final resting place for citizens, Woodlawn Cemetery was Toledo's first effort to provide the city with a large and magnificent park. (WC.)

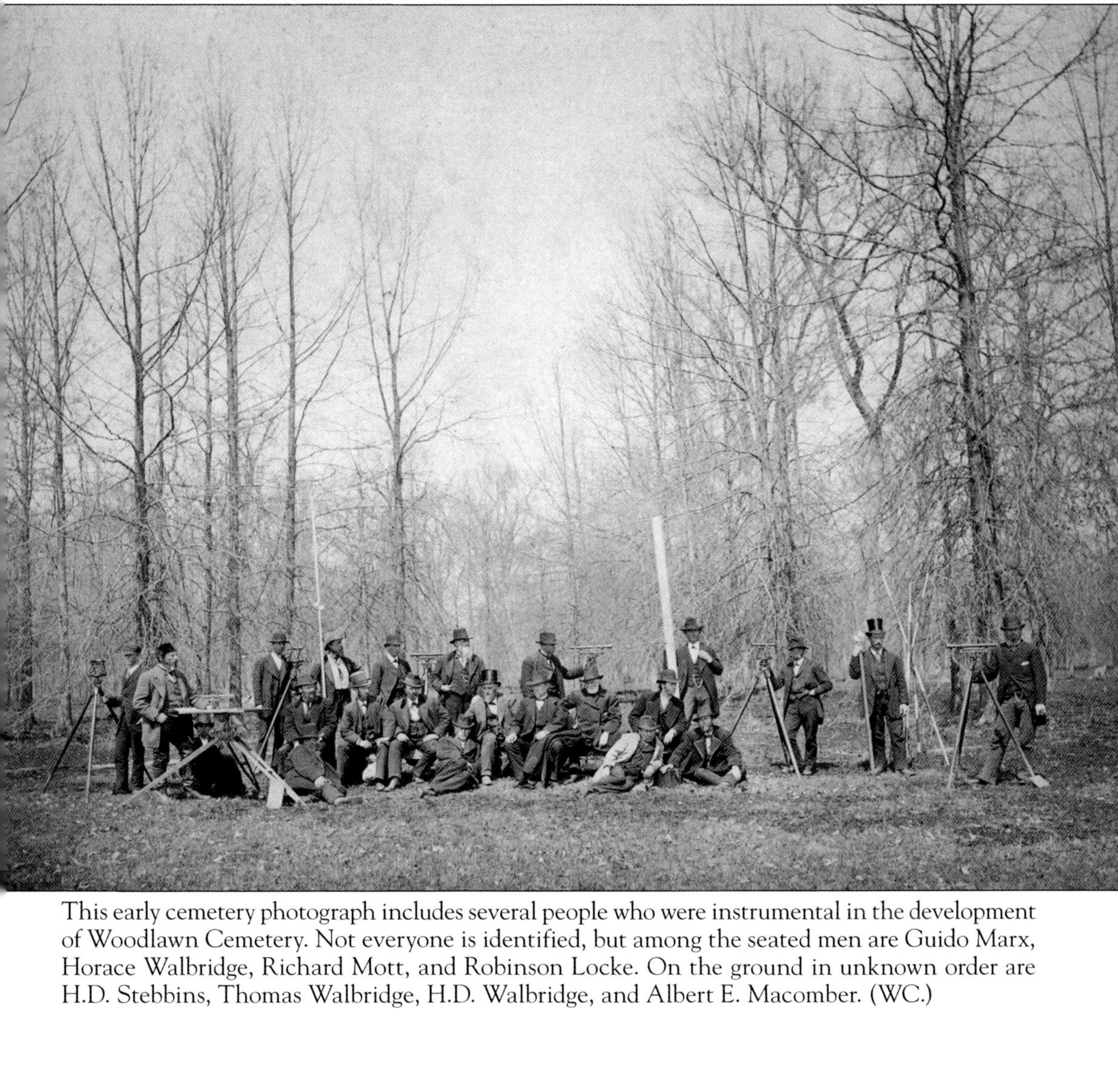

This early cemetery photograph includes several people who were instrumental in the development of Woodlawn Cemetery. Not everyone is identified, but among the seated men are Guido Marx, Horace Walbridge, Richard Mott, and Robinson Locke. On the ground in unknown order are H.D. Stebbins, Thomas Walbridge, H.D. Walbridge, and Albert E. Macomber. (WC.)

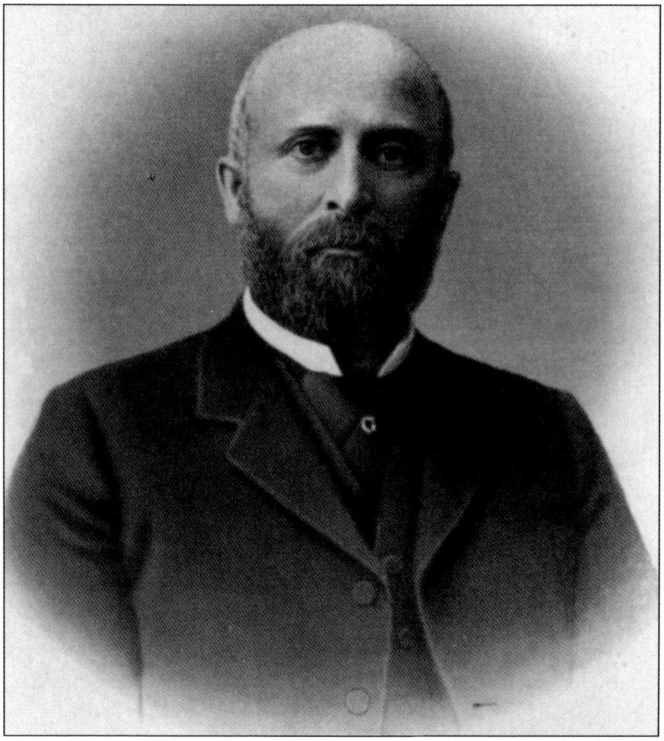

Prior to development, land had to be secured for the location of Toledo's newest and grandest cemetery. A decade earlier, the Richards Farm in Washington Township had been proposed, and then rejected, as the idea of organizing a new cemetery fizzled at that time. Later, however, with renewed interest in the development of a cemetery, this property, owned by Ransom Richards (pictured), was put forward again and purchased as the site for Woodlawn Cemetery. (TPL.)

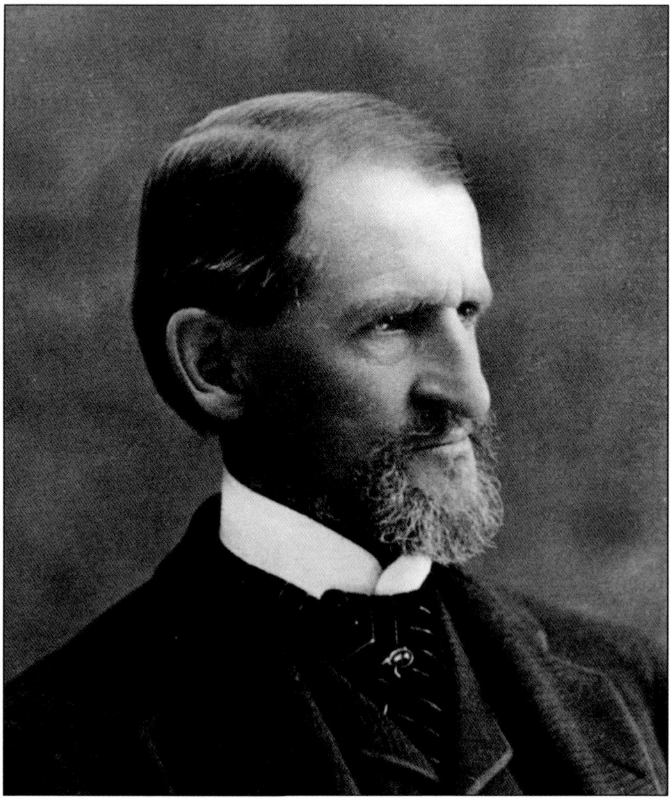

One of the original cemetery planners, Frank J. Scott, an early Toledo architect, also helped develop Toledo's Old West End, a nearby neighborhood where some of the city's elite citizens once lived in stately mansions. Many of those who lived there now rest at Woodlawn, their monuments and mausoleums as grand as their homes. At the inception of Woodlawn Cemetery, Scott was already well known due to the success of his book *Victorian Gardens: The Art of Beautifying Suburban Home Grounds,* which had an impact on the look of America's early suburbs. He is often credited with instilling in Americans an appreciation for the lawn as a symbol of community, connecting the homes within a neighborhood. (TPL.)

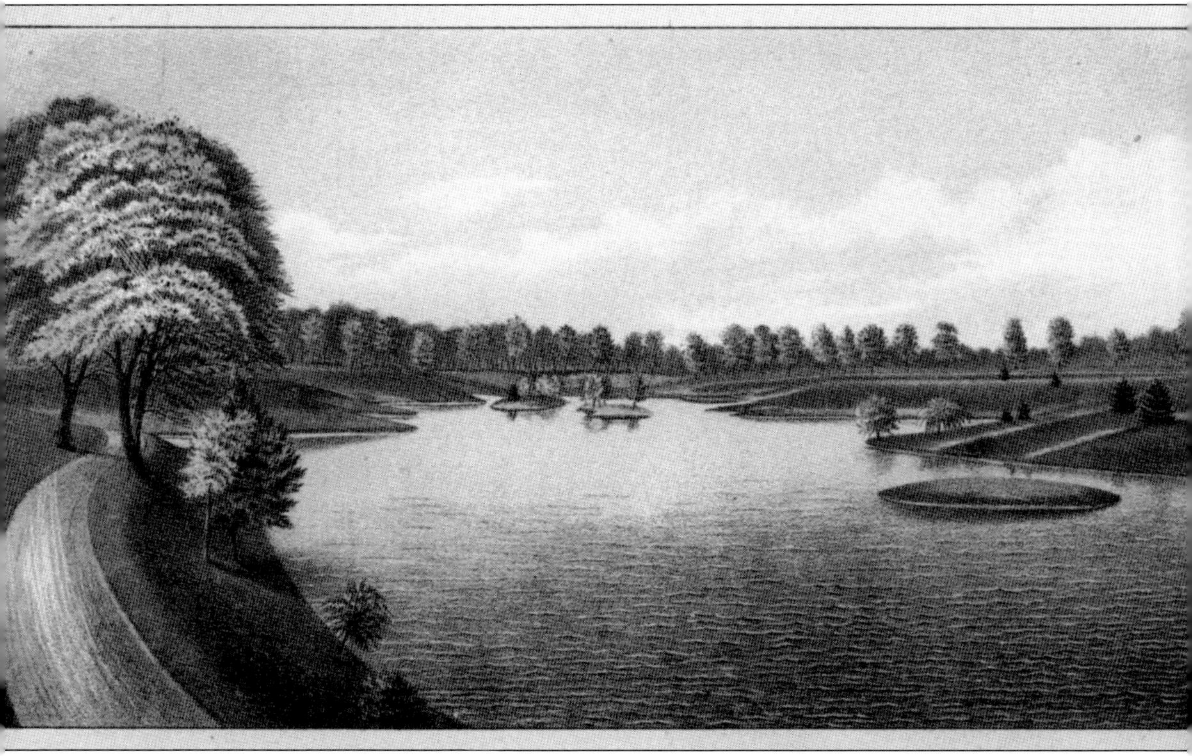

Woodlawn's first superintendent, horticulturist Frank Eurich, had a distinguished career in cemetery management. Having assisted in the creation of 25 cemeteries based on the lawn plan, Eurich translated his ideas to Woodlawn, where he banned boxes, shells, toys, chairs, and any other item "considered injurious to the beauty of the cemetery." This scenic view of Woodlawn features the tranquil charm of Silver Lake, dotted with islands and surrounded by the original dirt roadway. (WC.)

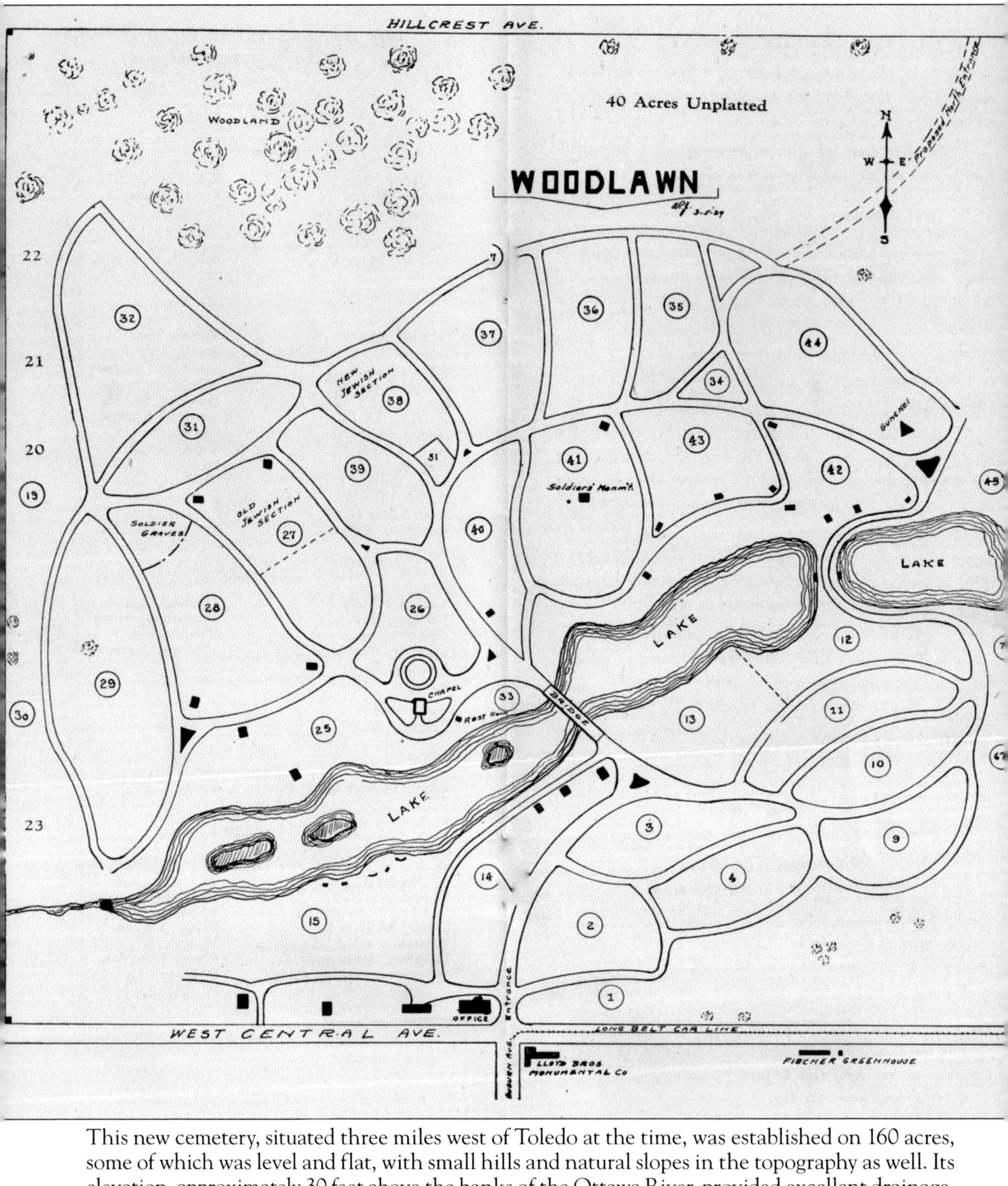

This new cemetery, situated three miles west of Toledo at the time, was established on 160 acres, some of which was level and flat, with small hills and natural slopes in the topography as well. Its elevation, approximately 30 feet above the banks of the Ottawa River, provided excellent drainage. The cemetery was laid out with more than two miles of winding roadways that sectioned off the grounds. Undeveloped land around the site was available for future expansion. (WC.)

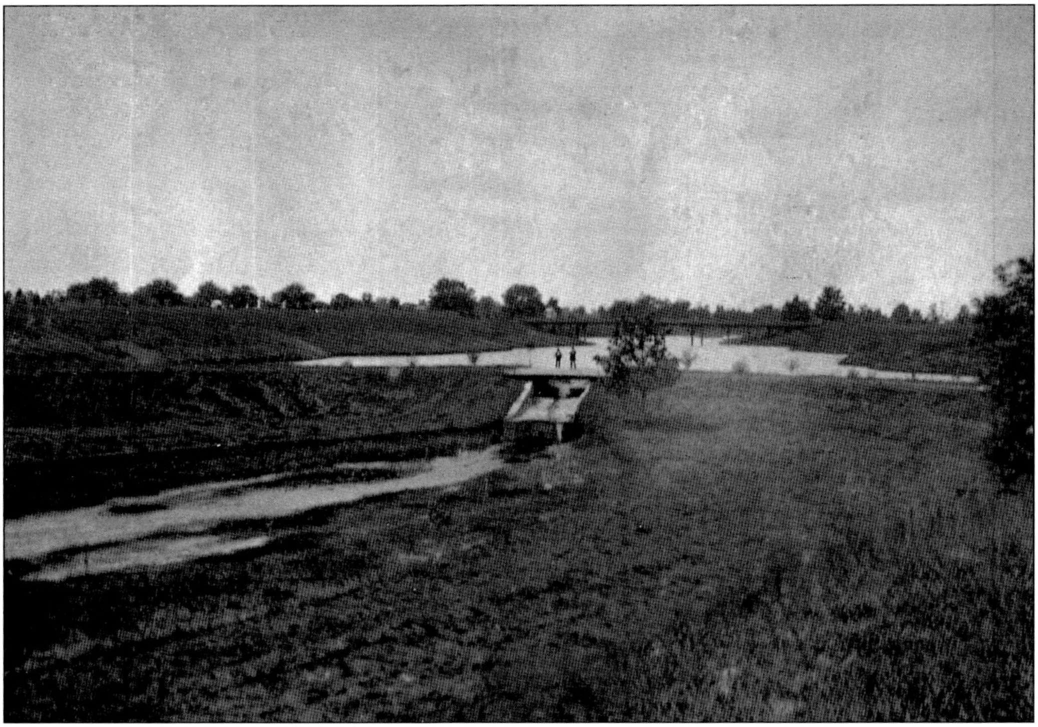

The cemetery had originally been farmland. A deep ravine cut through a section of the property. Developers decided early on to dam this narrow waterway, creating beautiful Silver Lake to enhance the landscape. (WC.)

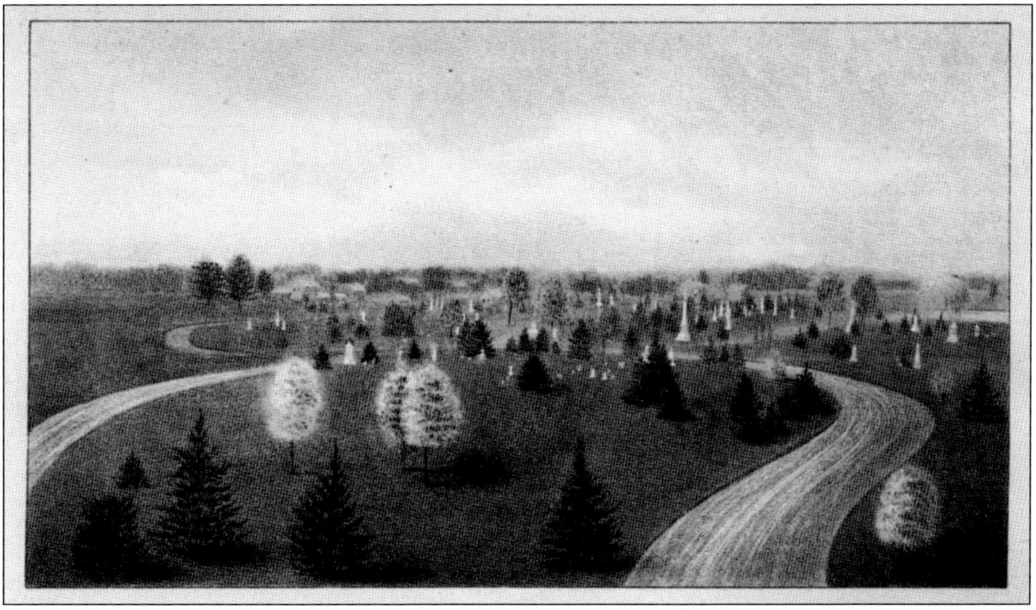

Within a few years, the scenic beauty of the cemetery began to emerge from the original farmland, as recently planted trees transformed the landscape. Following the trends of the rural cemetery movement, special attention was given to the placement of winding roadways. Trees and shrubbery of various colors and shapes were strategically planted across the green carpet of grassland. (WC.)

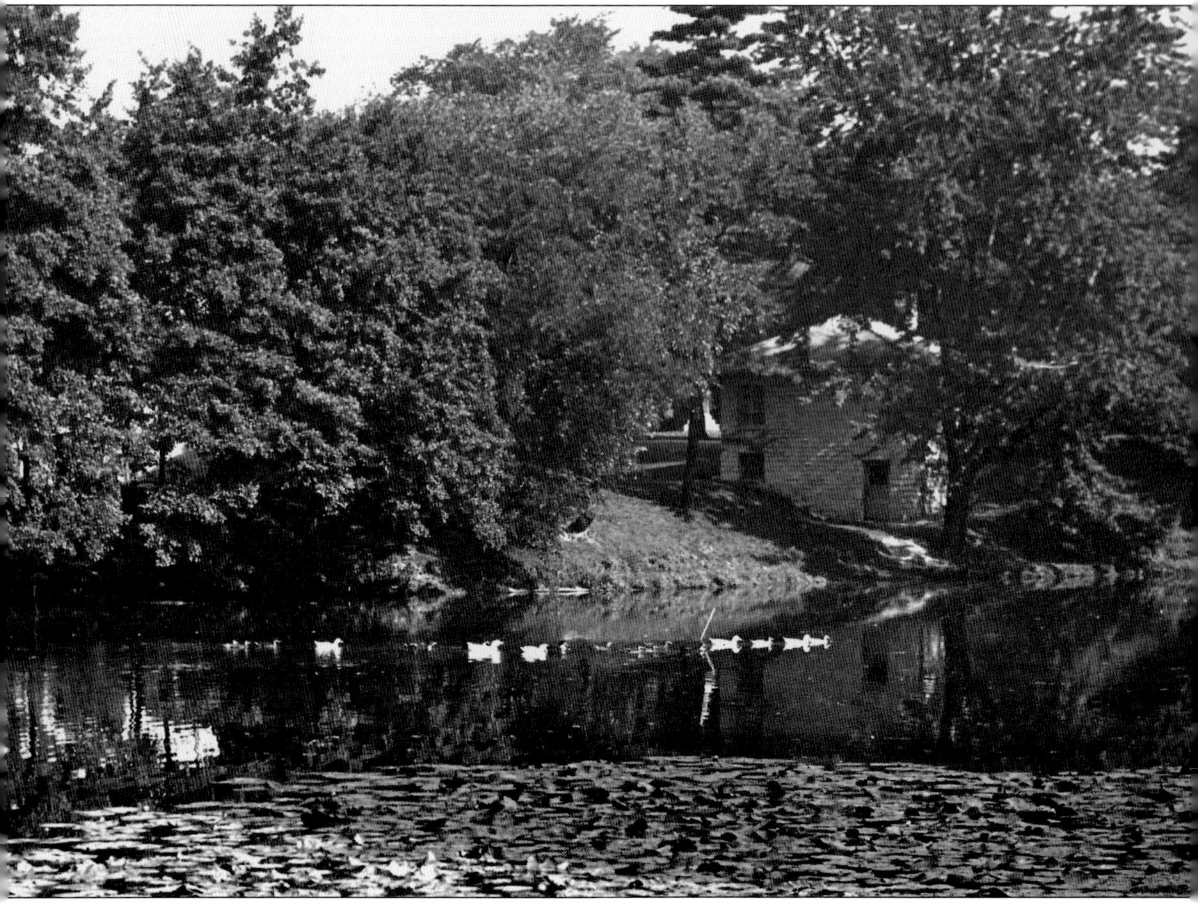

Much of the original landscaping on the site, the result of Eurich's hard work and vision, gained Woodlawn national recognition as an arboretum. Eurich planted a mixture of domestic and international flora, both rare and common. The 150 species of trees at the cemetery include tulip, ironwood, American elm, purple beech, chanticleer pear, Siberian pea, and pecan. Throughout the years, board members have made a concerted effort to protect the environment as well as the birds at Woodlawn. Today, the cemetery features 200 different migratory and resident birds that continue to attract botanists, birdwatchers, and schoolchildren. The National Audubon Society recognizes the exceptional richness of the cemetery and has, for more than 100 years, conducted its annual Northwest Ohio "Christmas Count," a census of every bird seen at that time, at Woodlawn Cemetery. Visible in the background of this photograph is the cemetery's old comfort station. (WC.)

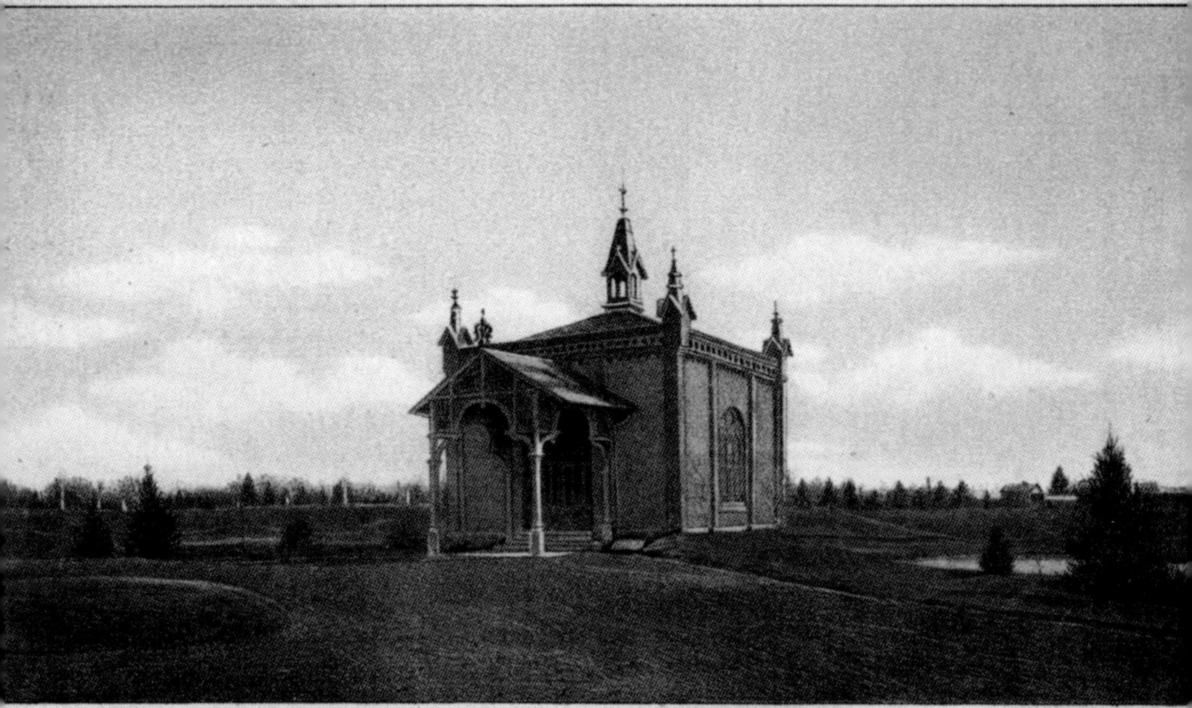

The cemetery association constructed several buildings necessary to maintain the grounds and to provide storage of equipment for excavation of burial sites. The Conservatory Chapel, dedicated in 1883, was the first building on Woodlawn's grounds. Originally, the chapel's lower level (called the vault) was designed to shelter bodies over the winter months when, before mechanized equipment was available, graves could not be opened in frozen ground. In 1923, when this vault was no longer needed, one of Ohio's first crematories was installed in the lower level of the chapel. (WC.)

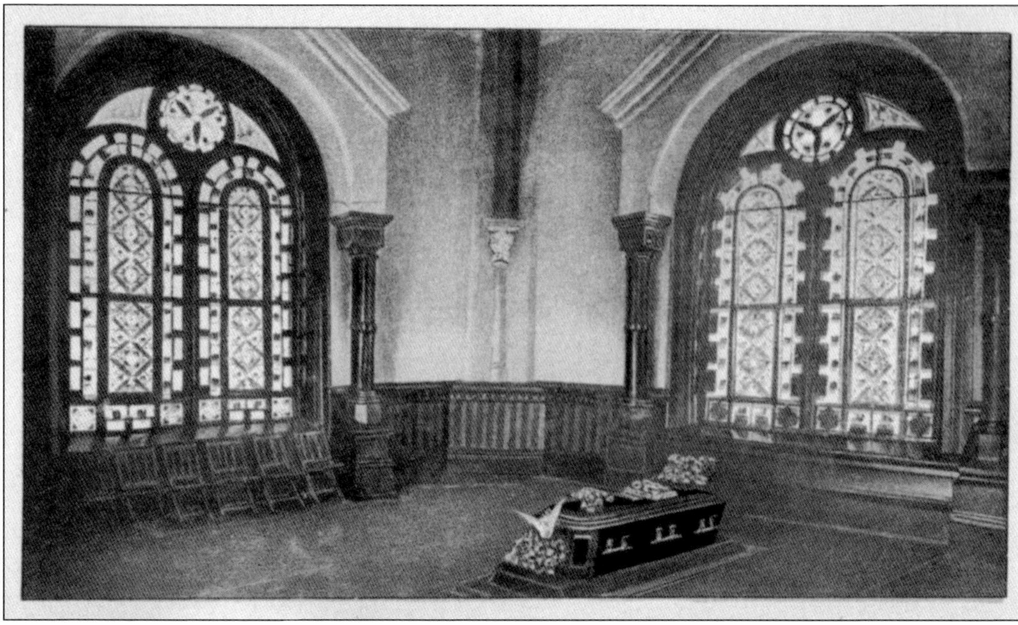

An inside view of the chapel from an 1883 marketing brochure displays the large stained-glass windows. In the center of the room is a pedestal for placement of the coffin of the deceased. Ivy and other creeping vines twist around the pillars and arches supporting the roof. (WC.)

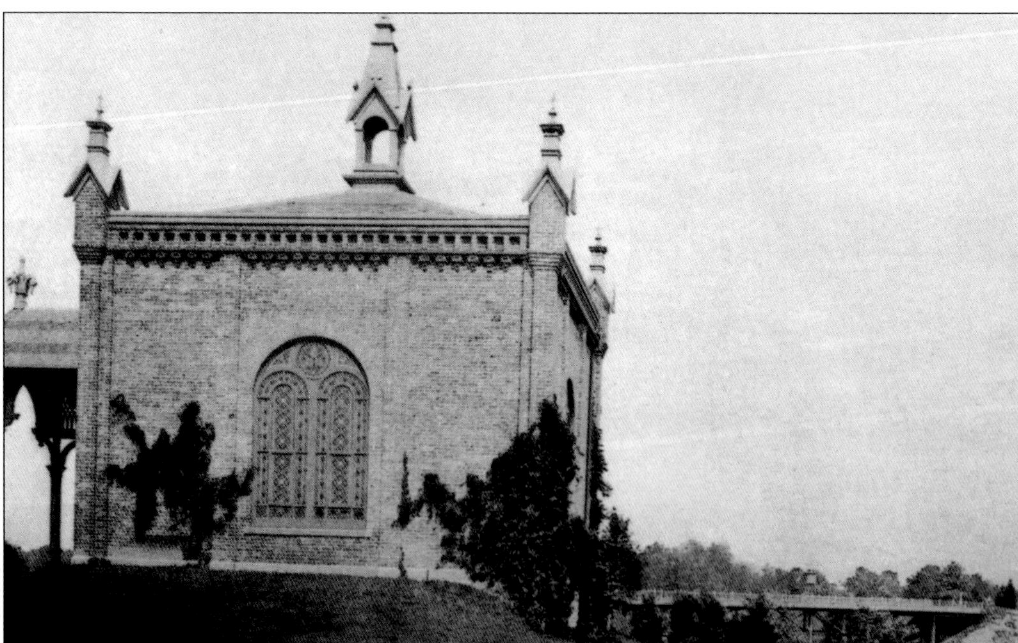

Over the decades, accidental fires, smoke damage, repairs, and midcentury remodeling work altered the facade of the chapel. Today, it is no longer used for services or cremation. (WC.)

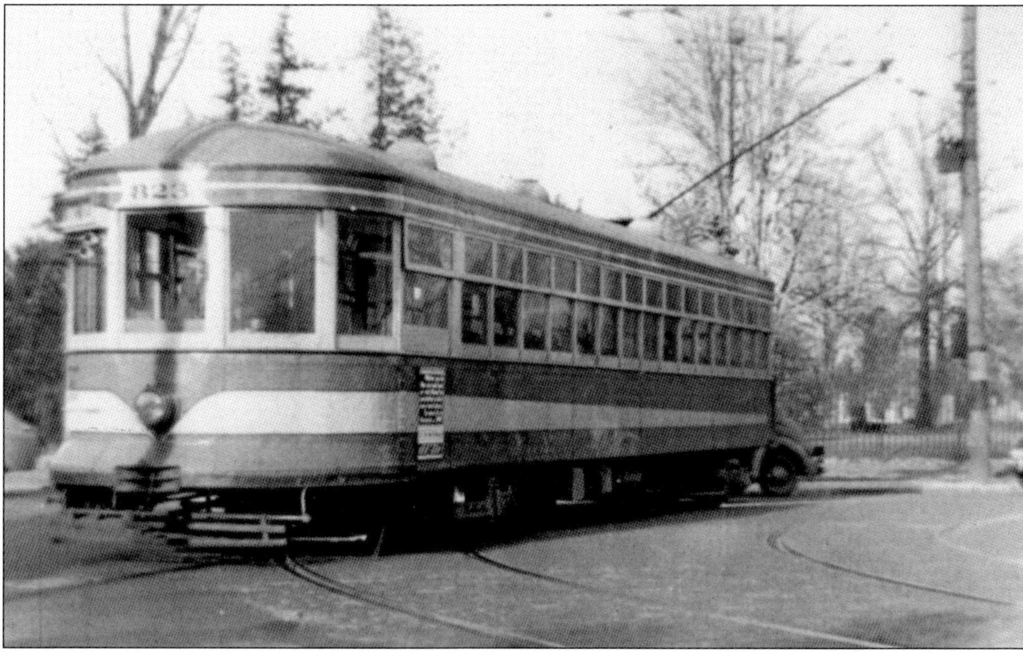

In 1892, the Metropolitan Street Car Railway Company developed a single car track along Central Avenue. This extension was an effort to make the grounds more accessible to those living in the city. By 1908, the city limits reached the Central Avenue boundary of the cemetery. Increased use of the park-like setting permitted by the streetcars, the close proximity of the city, and the advent of the automobile raised new challenges for cemetery management. Woodlawn proved so popular that the majority of the visitors were sightseers and people seeking recreational space. The crowds and holiday mood became so excessive at times that cemetery management had to pass rules forbidding activities such as smoking, use of obscene language, and drinking liquor on the cemetery grounds. (Above, FF; below, TLP.)

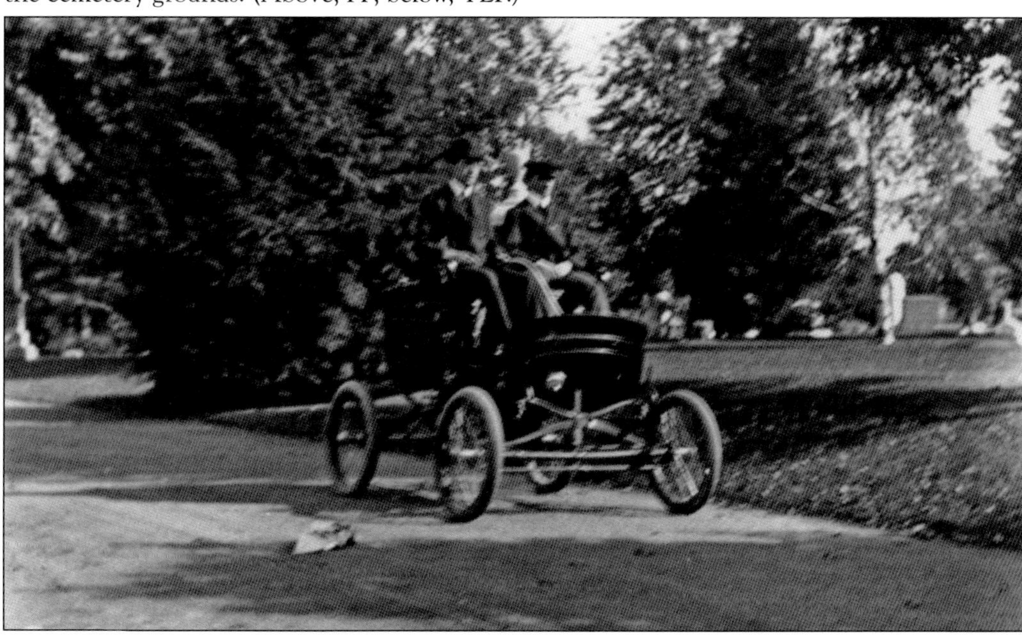

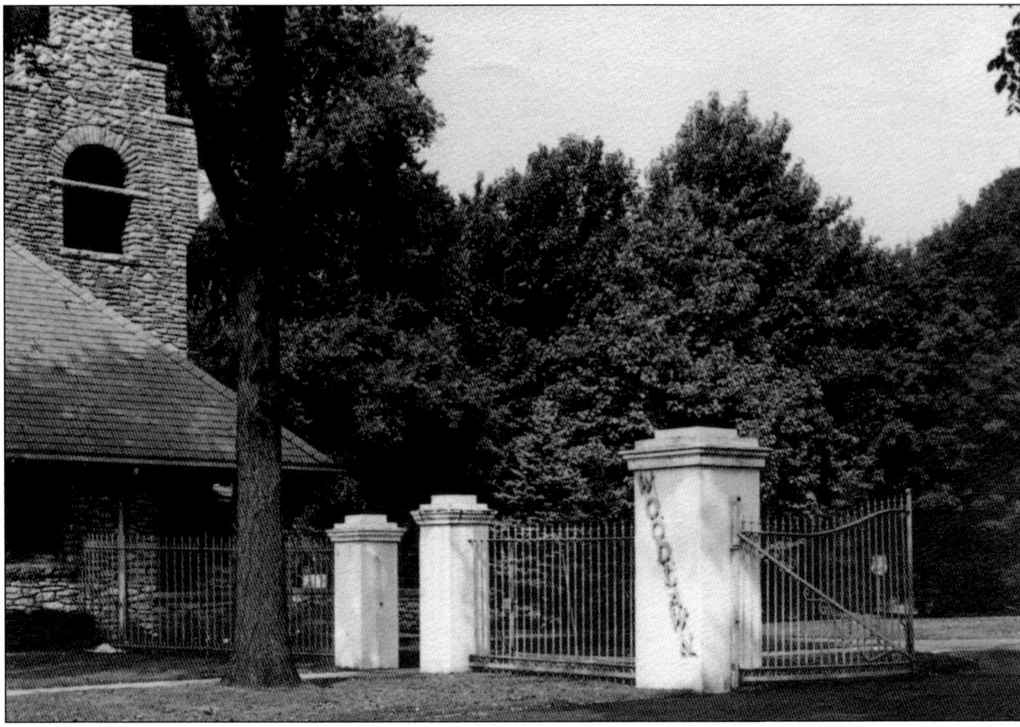

This stone building, located just inside the main gates, serves as the cemetery's administrative offices. Built in 1903 in the Romanesque style, its walls are made of Ohio limestone, and a slate roof tops the structure. The building is dominated by an impressive bell tower, which is believed to have been a section of a 19th-century windmill located on this site. Until recently, office personnel tolled the bells upon the arrival of each funeral procession. In 1996, the cemetery installed an electronic carillon that can be heard throughout the property. (TPL.)

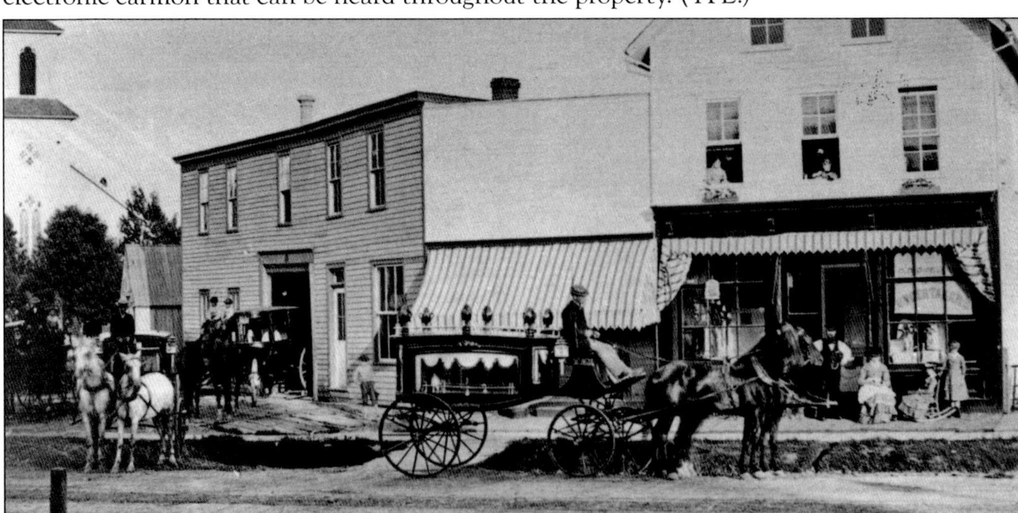

By the latter part of the 19th century, undertakers more frequently provided services for the deceased that had previously been handled by friends and family members. For instance, the use of elegant glass-paneled carriages, such as the ones shown here in front of a Toledo livery, were often employed to transport the deceased to their final resting place. (TPL.)

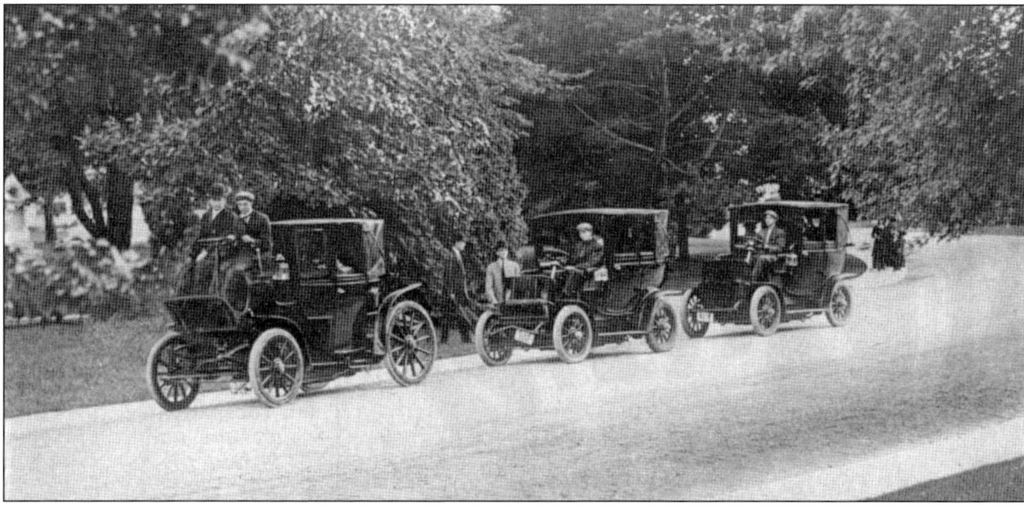

As the cemetery matured, additional roads were built to provide access to newly opened sections. Paving methods evolved from dirt to gravel to concrete, as modes of transportation changed from horse-drawn vehicles to automobiles. In 1911, Toledo's first motorized funeral procession (pictured) took place at Woodlawn Cemetery. (WC.)

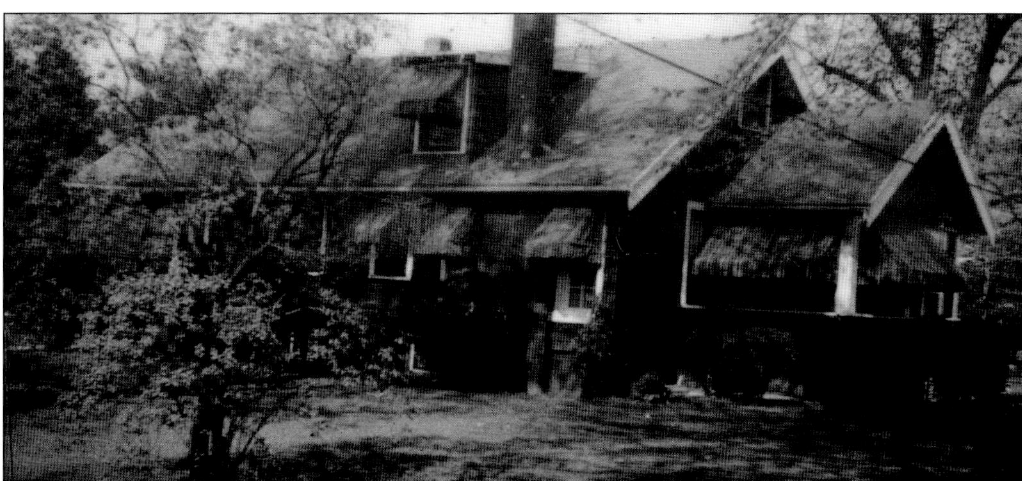

Several other structures were erected on the grounds in the early 1900s. A concrete bridge was built in 1913 to traverse the lake. In 1915, the Stewart Iron Works Company of Cincinnati erected the two-mile-long iron fence surrounding the cemetery. About two years later, the one-and-a-half-story caretaker's house (pictured) was built. In 1923, a comfort station, constructed of Ohio limestone and featuring a hipped roof and an interior chimney, was added near the edge of the lake. (TPL.)

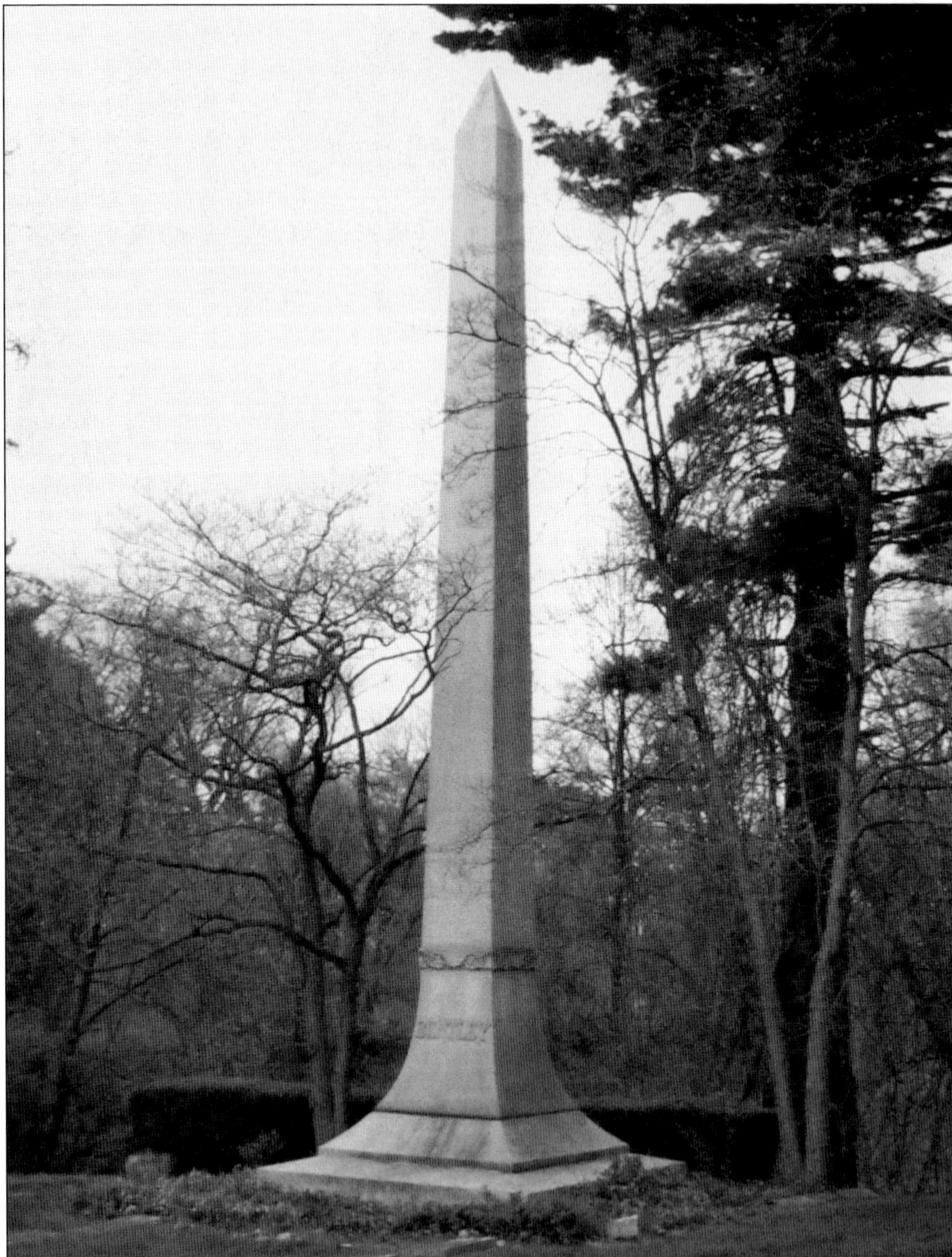

Lloyd Brothers work can be seen throughout the cemetery, and several of their monuments are identified within each chapter. The final chapter discusses their work in greater depth. This stately, beautifully proportioned obelisk commemorating the Bentley family is a splendid example of their craftsmanship. Note the perfect symmetry, from the concave base to the apex of the spire. (WC.)

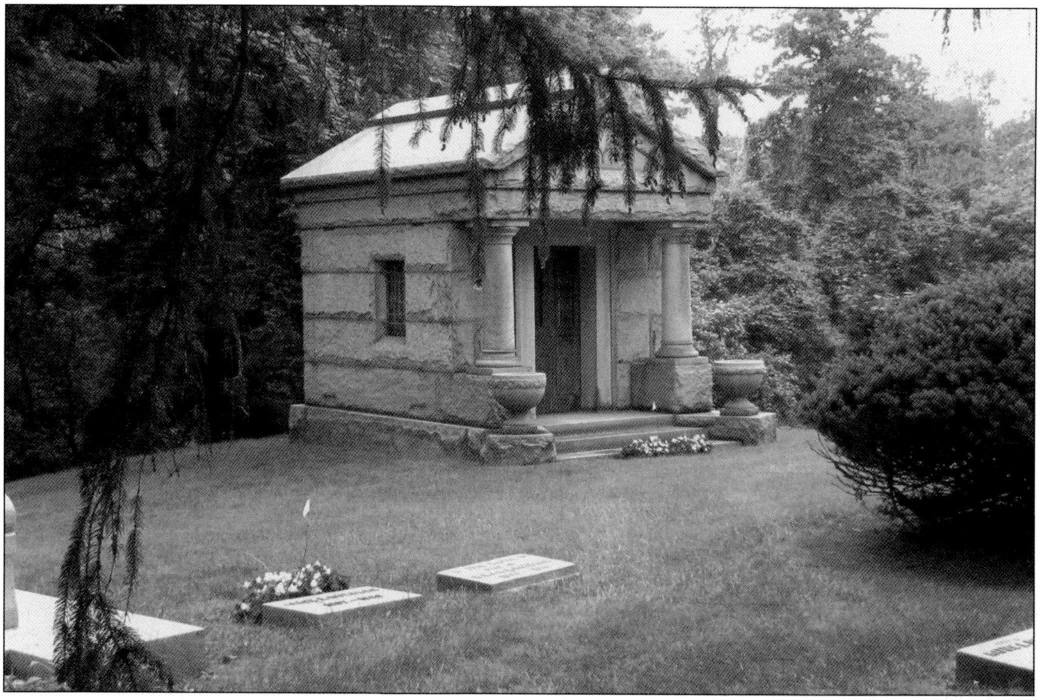

The Layng mausoleum is just one of the 42 private mausoleums dating from the late 1800s found at Woodlawn Cemetery. Many of the mausoleums provide eloquent examples of funereal architecture incorporating Greek, Roman, and Egyptian elements. When they were originally constructed, some of the mausoleums contained impressive examples of Tiffany stained-glass windows, which have since been removed to the Toledo Museum of Art.

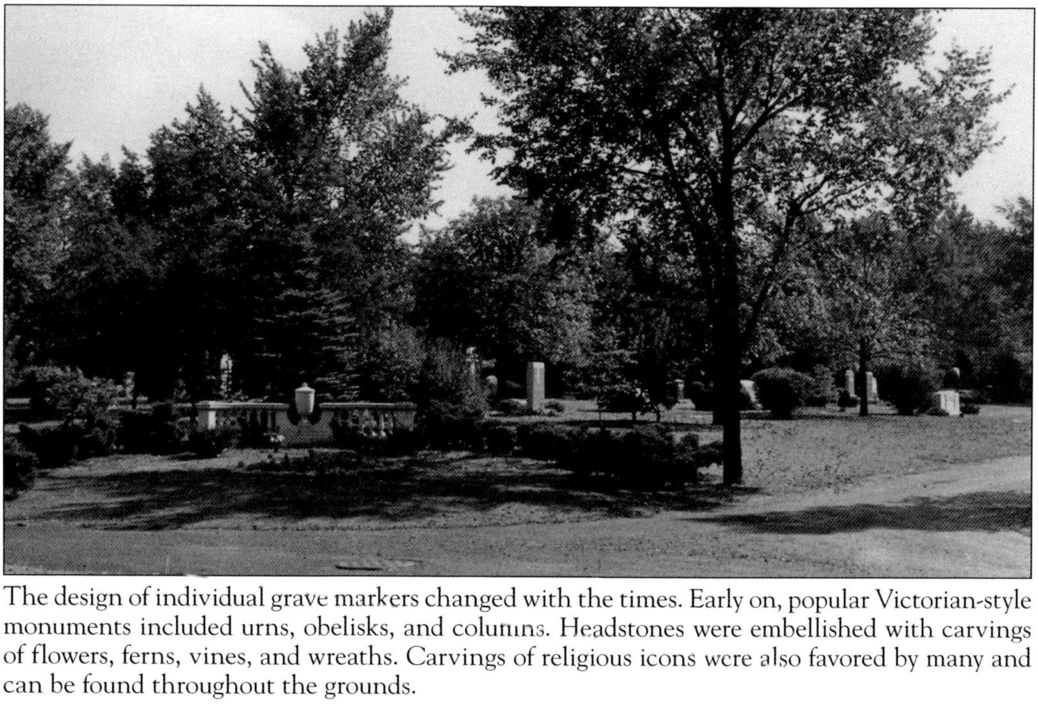

The design of individual grave markers changed with the times. Early on, popular Victorian-style monuments included urns, obelisks, and columns. Headstones were embellished with carvings of flowers, ferns, vines, and wreaths. Carvings of religious icons were also favored by many and can be found throughout the grounds.

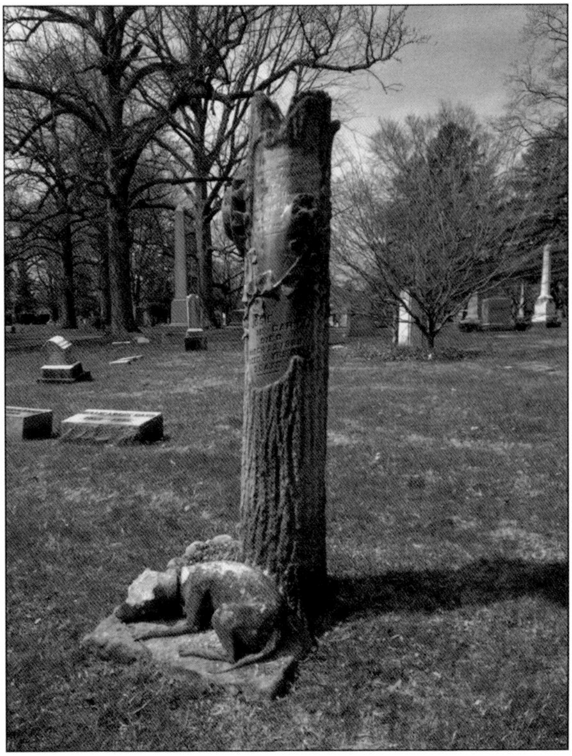

One of the more fascinating monument styles found in the cemetery is that of a tree trunk, symbolizing a life cut short. There are several examples of this type of monument on the cemetery grounds. This one commemorates a five-year-old child named Josie McCarty who died in 1880. This Lloyd Brothers monument includes several interesting and sentimental items, including ivy, symbolizing both memory and immortality; a wide-brimmed hat, possibly a representation of one worn by little Josie in life; and her devoted dog resting at the base. Much of the epitaph on her memorial has been worn away, but a close look reveals the following message: "Thou were so loving and so bright, But God thought He's to call her hence, Even yet the world had cast light on thy innocence."

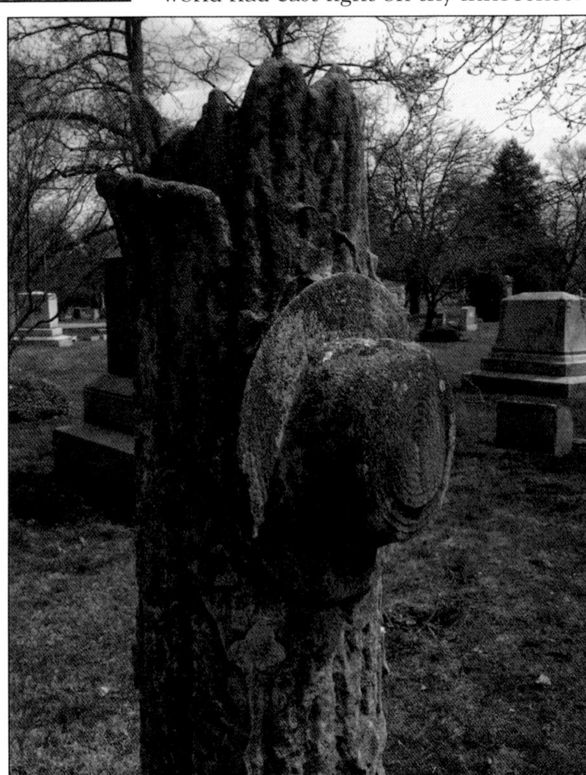

Two

THE BUSINESSMEN

Business in Toledo centered on Lake Erie and the Maumee River in the early years, as inland transportation and agricultural activities were difficult due to the swampy terrain. Pioneer merchants received and shipped goods with the use of canoes and pirogues along the river, trading venison, fish, and furs with local Indians as well as with trappers and traders. In those early days in the 1800s, most businessmen relied on a bartering system of commerce, as hard cash was scarce. With the development of schooners and steamships, business ties between Toledo and other ports along the lake strengthened. Local businessmen could provide customers with household goods and fulfill the needs of small farms and businesses as the century progressed.

Talk of a canal connecting the Ohio River to Lake Erie began in the 1820s and generated much local interest, as a terminus for the Miami and Erie Canal would be located in this area. With great effort, local businessmen were able to secure the location for Toledo. Meanwhile, the number of newcomers steadily increased. They arrived from New England and northern European countries to start businesses, provide professional services, or simply seek more gainful employment. While the Miami and Erie Canal cut transportation costs of goods considerably, this method of moving merchandise was quickly outdated by a new industry, the railroad. This more efficient mode of transportation contributed to the development of Toledo's first factories by midcentury.

The transportation industry has always been a vital component of Toledo businesses. It was no surprise, then, that a number of Toledo businessmen diversified by becoming involved in that industry. As the entrepreneurial spirit increased, larger business ventures were undertaken. The need for cash to secure these projects resulted in the establishment of Toledo's earliest financial institutions. This in turn generated the funds needed to launch much of the large-scale industrialization of Toledo by the end of the 19th century.

Many of the people responsible for Toledo's business development chose Woodlawn Cemetery as their final resting place. Their importance to the community, financial status, and personal tastes are reflected in several of the monuments erected in their honor.

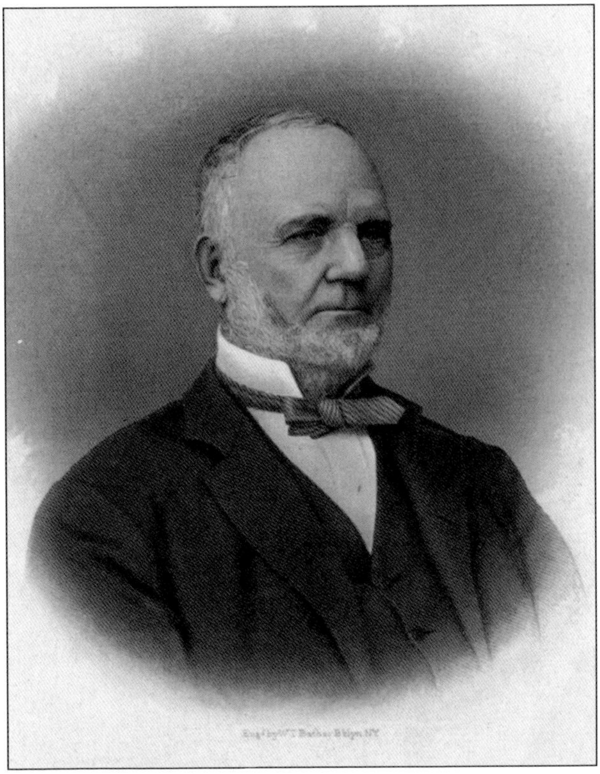

Valentine H. Ketcham (1815–1887) was successful in the businesses of wholesale merchandising, real estate, and banking, which led to his noteworthy position as Toledo's first millionaire. With his brother-in-law, John Berdan II, he established the banking concern of Ketcham, Berdan & Company. Ketcham's sarcophagus was inspired by Scipio Barbatus's sarcophagus, the earliest known Roman sarcophagus in existence, now housed in the Vatican Museum. (Left, TPL.)

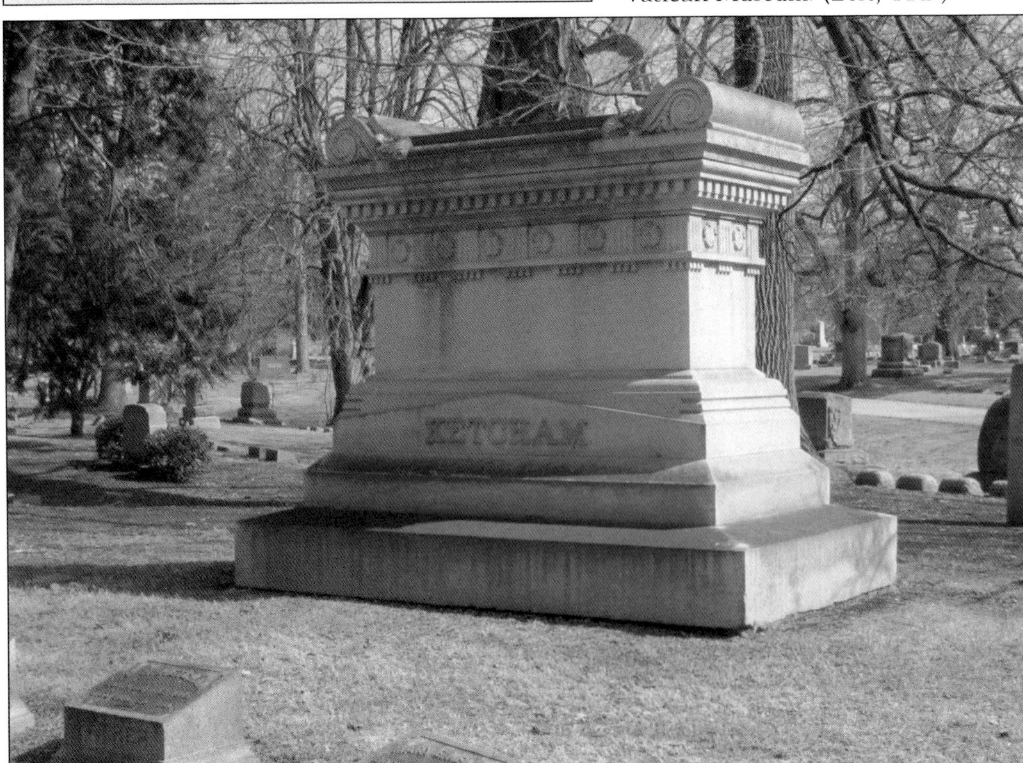

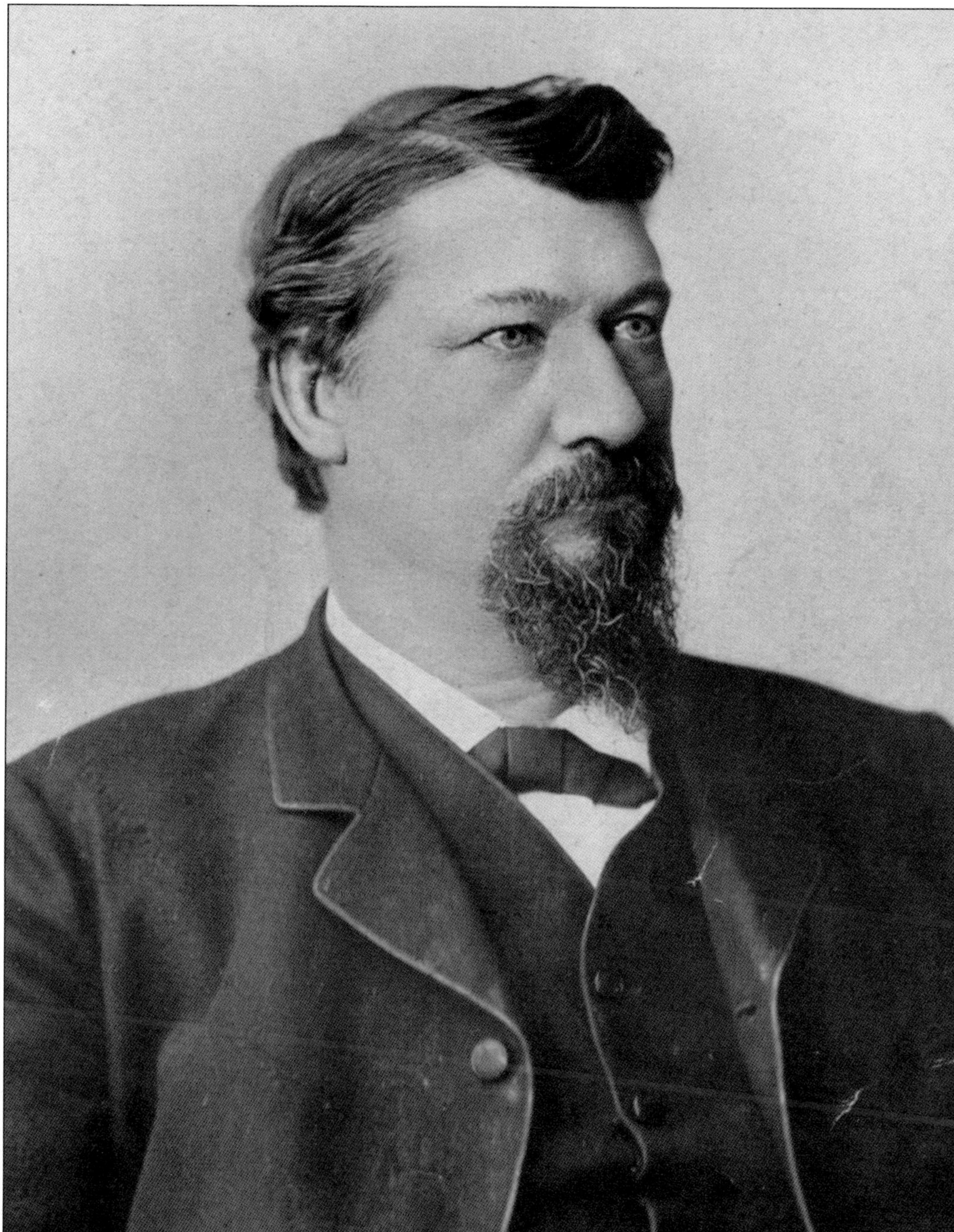

As a journalist, David R. Locke (1833–1888) used satire to support Pres. Abraham Lincoln's policies by writing the "Nasby Letters" under the pseudonym Petroleum Vesuvius Nasby. These letters propelled Locke into the national spotlight during the Civil War, eventually making him the most influential humorist of his era. Lincoln enjoyed his humor and frequently quoted the Nasby Letters. In fact, Locke and Lincoln became friends. At one point, Lincoln jokingly offered to "swap places" with Locke. After the war, Locke continued to write the Nasby Letters, seeking social justice and reform. (WC.)

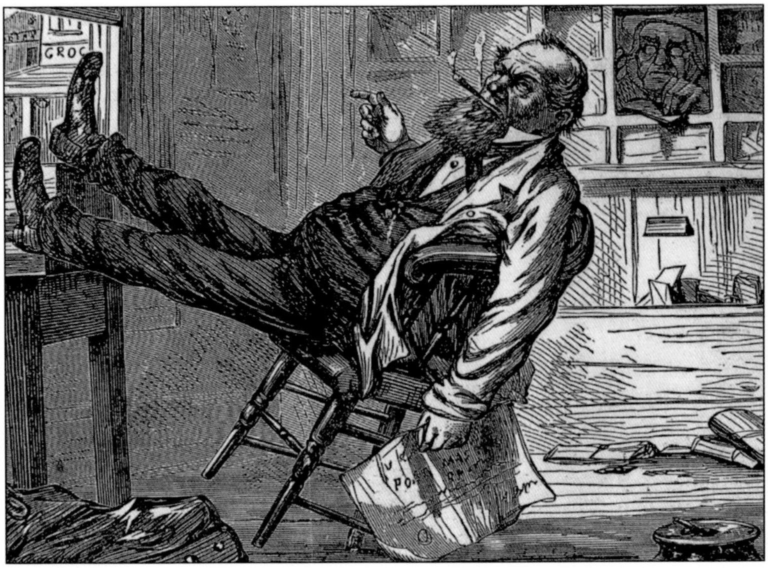

The *Toledo Blade* prospered under David R. Locke's management as editor, writer, and publisher during the last 20 years of his life. Locke developed a reputation as a leading newsman. He was a nationally recognized and popular public lecturer. This cartoon pokes fun at Locke's usual disheveled appearance. (WC.)

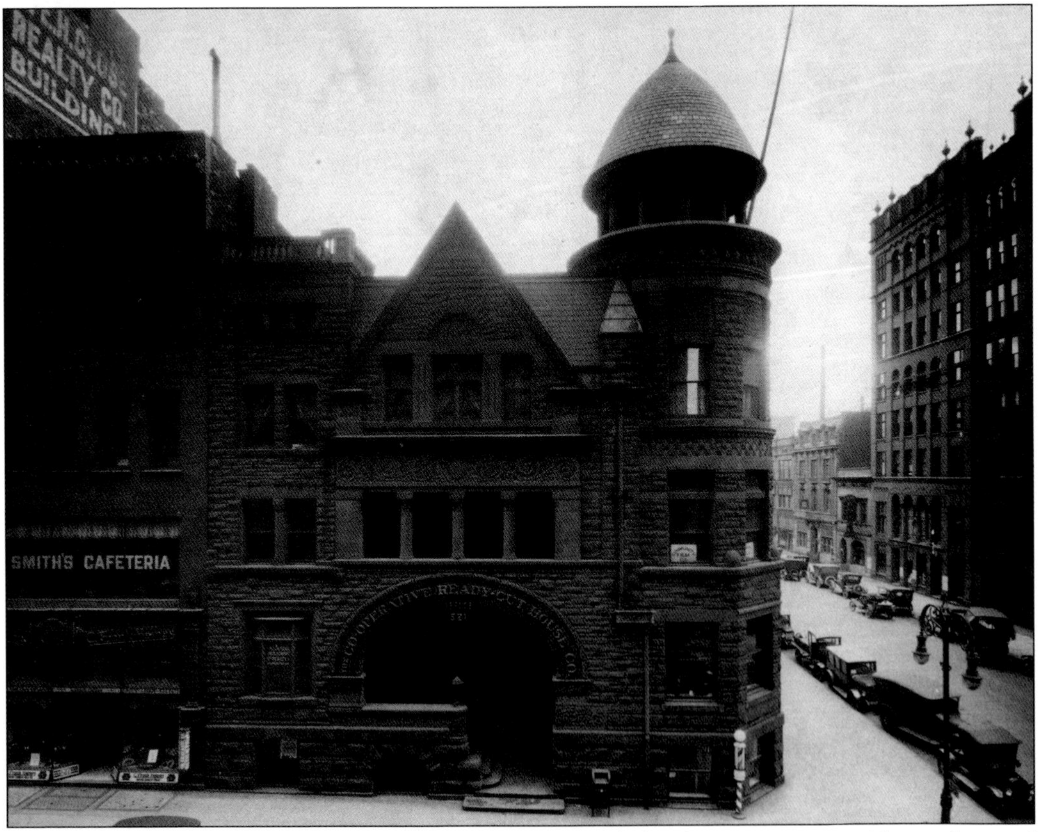

David Locke proposed the formation of a club where Toledo's businessmen could socialize and discuss trade. The result was the formation of the Draconian Club in 1882, with Locke serving as the first president. The club name was changed a few years later to the Toledo Club (original building pictured), which to this day continues to serve its members in the same tradition Locke proposed over 130 years ago. (TPL.)

Tucked into a hillside at Woodlawn Cemetery, the Chesbrough mausoleum provides the final resting place of a Toledo lumber baron, Alonzo Chesbrough (1817–1887). His business supplied lumber to the government during the Civil War, including wood used on the United States' first ironclad warship, the *Monitor.* After his death, his four sons continued his business under the name Chesbrough Brothers. (WC.)

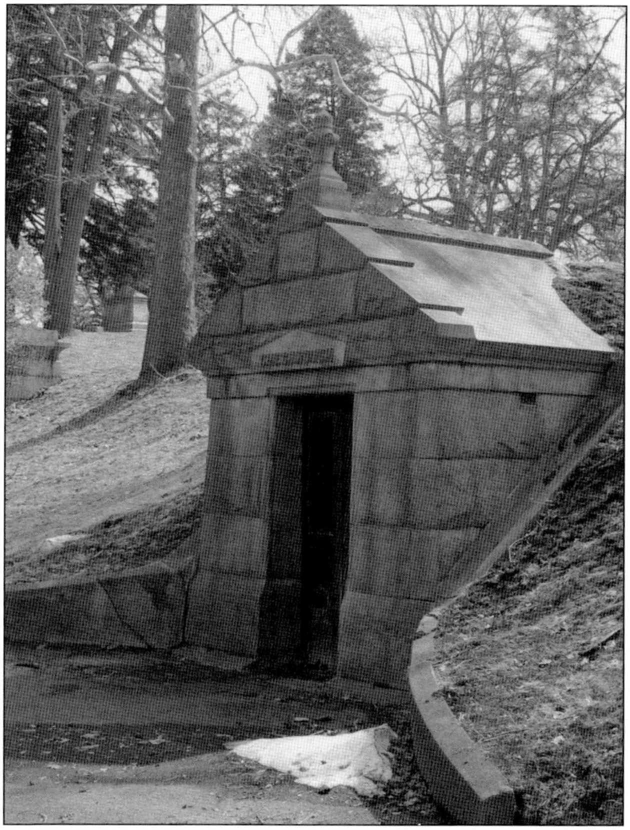

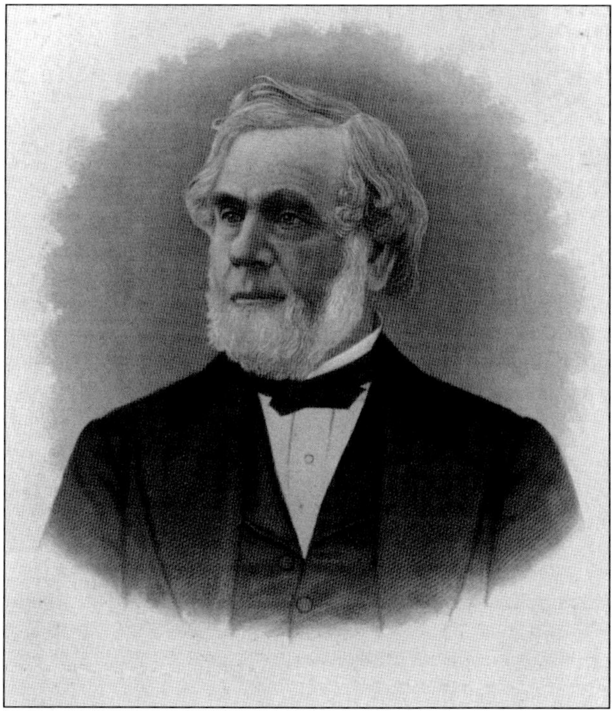

Samuel Young (1806–1897) is remembered as one of Toledo's most prominent and honored businessmen and citizens. As a young man, he shared a legal firm with Morrison Waite, who would become chief justice of the Supreme Court. Young's interests outside the legal profession led to several business opportunities, including the construction of grain elevators on the Maumee River. He was also a toll bridge operator and president of the Toledo Hotel Company. (TPL.)

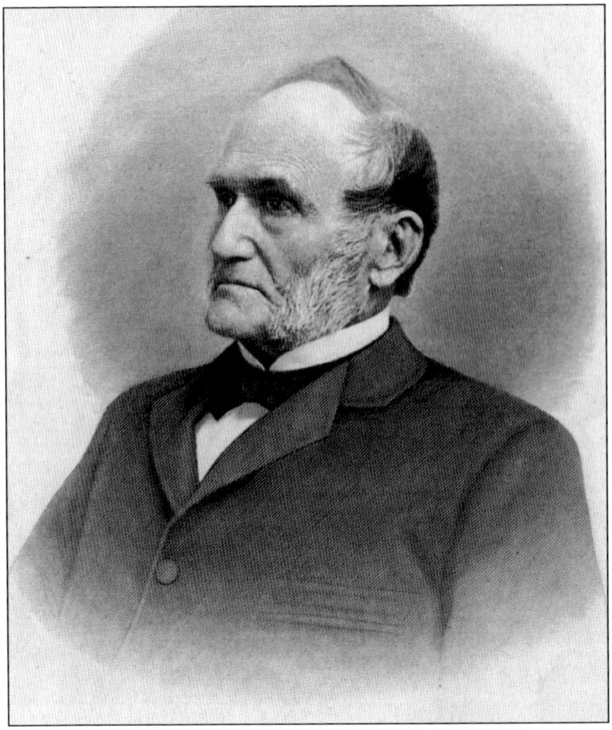

A pioneer businessman in Toledo, Sanford L. Collins (1806–1889) made his home here before Toledo became a city. He operated a general store and traded wares with the local Indians. Collins eventually gave up his business and became a successful grain dealer. He served the community as a justice of the peace and was the first treasurer of Lucas County. The Collins family monument is situated near the front of the grounds and features a single column crowned by a decorative finial. (Left, TPL.)

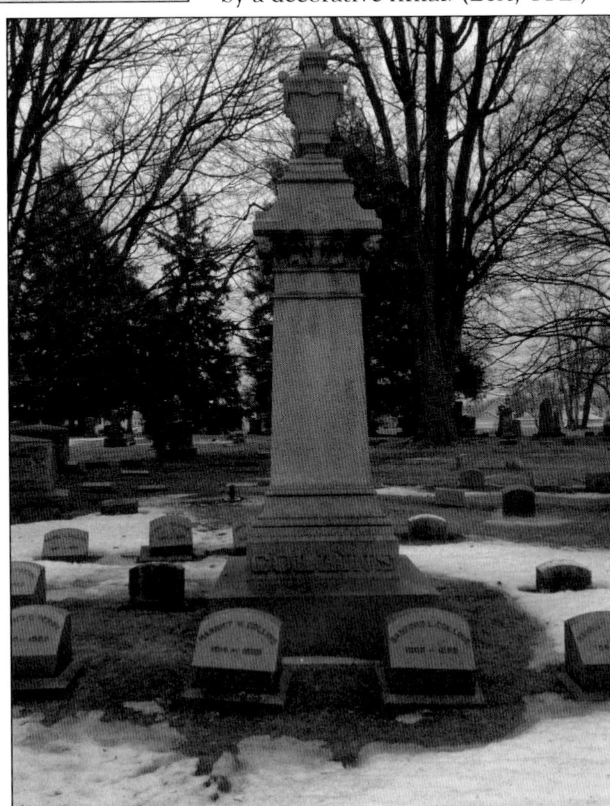

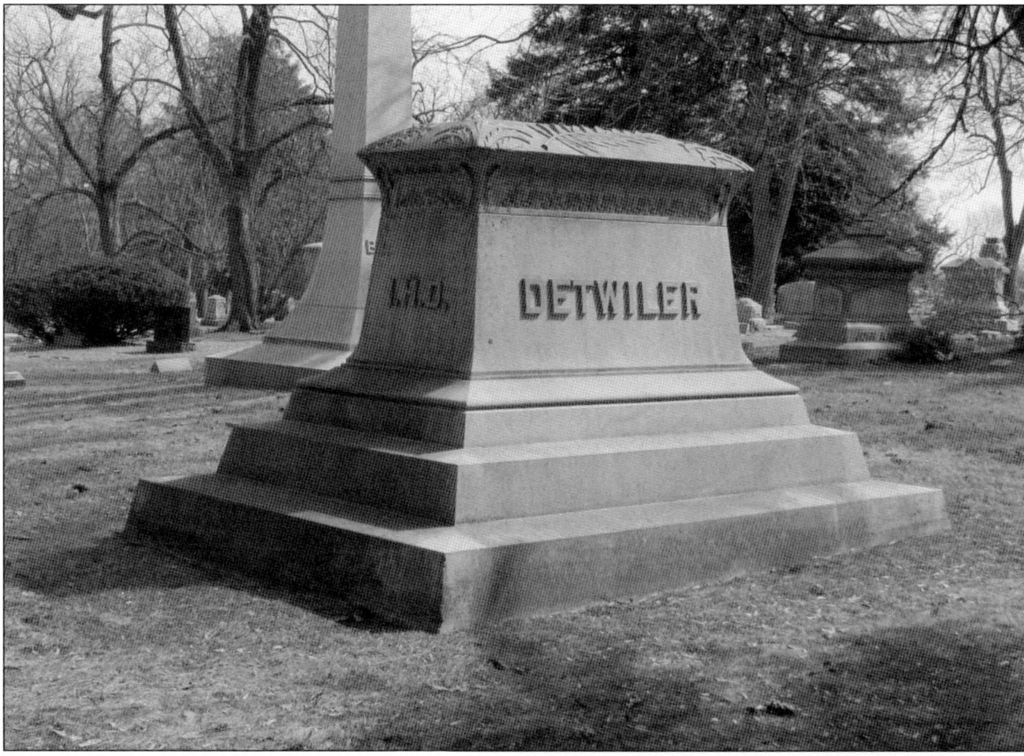

Isaac H. Detwiler (1820–1889), one of 10 children, left home early in life to begin working at farming and flour milling. Later, he started the grain-commissioning business of Detwiler and Bashere. In 1872 he started a new firm, I.H. Detwiler and Company, which quickly assumed a leading position among real-estate firms in Toledo. Detwiler Park in Toledo is named for his family. A close inspection of Isaac Detwiler's memorial reveals that his initials are carved into the left side of the stone.

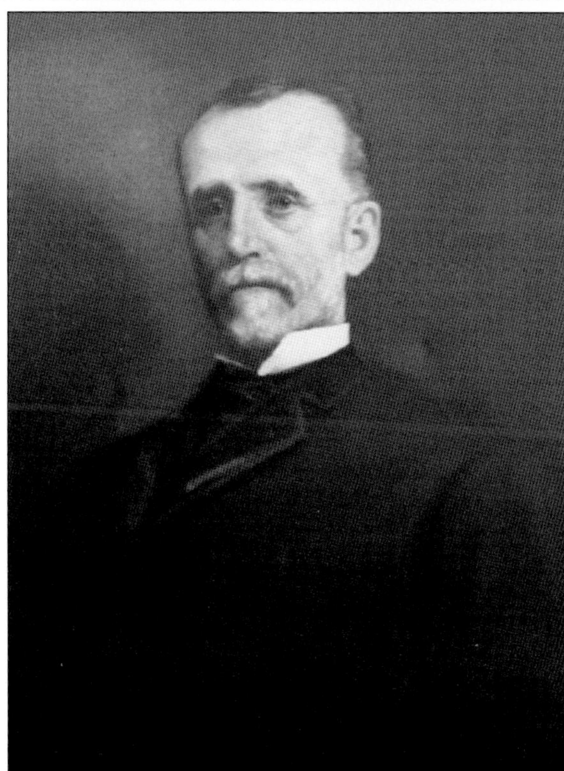

Early in his career, Joseph K. Secor (1822–1892) became partners with Valentine H. Ketcham in a wholesale grocery business. This company also operated as a private bank for several years. When Ketcham retired, Secor, along with his new partner, Peter F. Berdan, established Secor, Berdan & Company, dealing with wholesale groceries. Later, he helped organize Toledo's First National Bank and served as a director and vice president. (SF.)

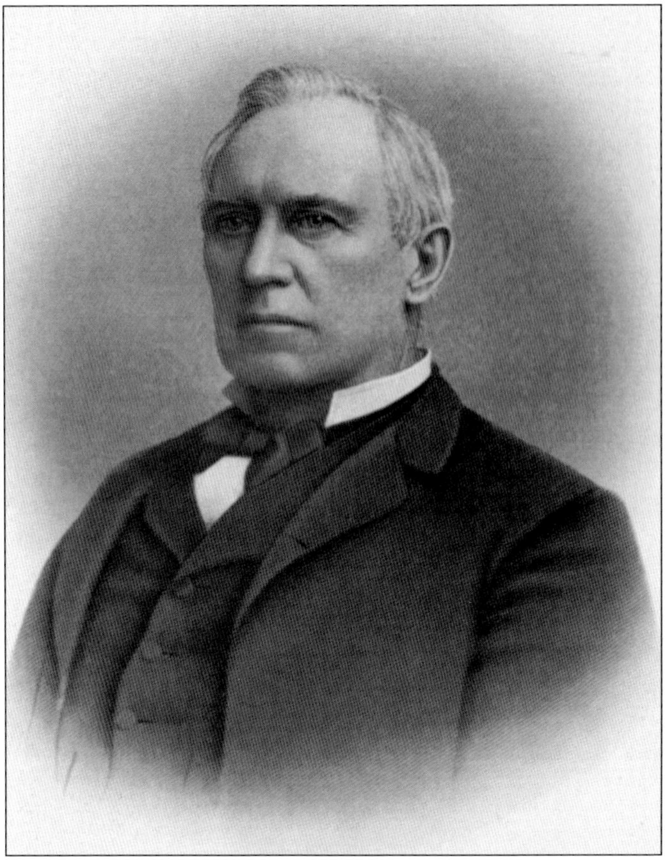

Horace S. Walbridge (1828–1893) was a prominent Toledo businessman involved in many successful enterprises, including banking, real-estate development, and railroads. Walbridge served as president of the Board of Trade and built the landmark Toledo skyscraper the Nasby Building in 1895. This tower was named for the fictional character Petroleum V. Nasby, created by the *Toledo Blade's* publisher, David Ross Locke. Walbridge was also a founder and the first president of Woodlawn Cemetery. Walbridge Park (below), on the Maumee River, a favorite place to spend a Saturday or Sunday afternoon, was named in his honor. Visitors could rent a canoe, stroll along the midway, enjoy rides, and even see exotic animals such as polar bears and zebras. (Both, TPL.)

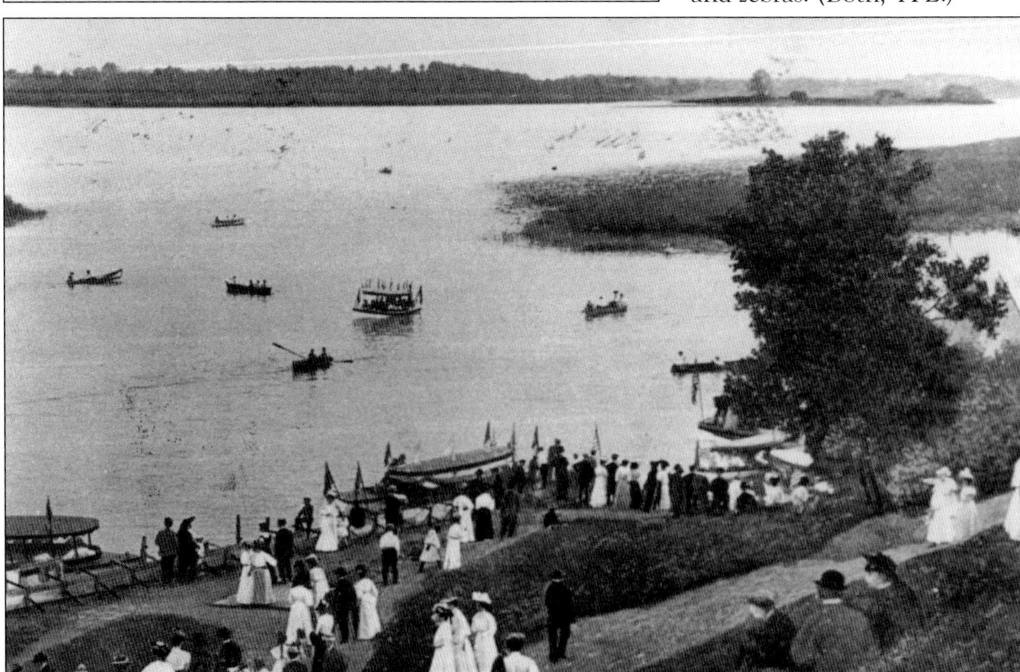

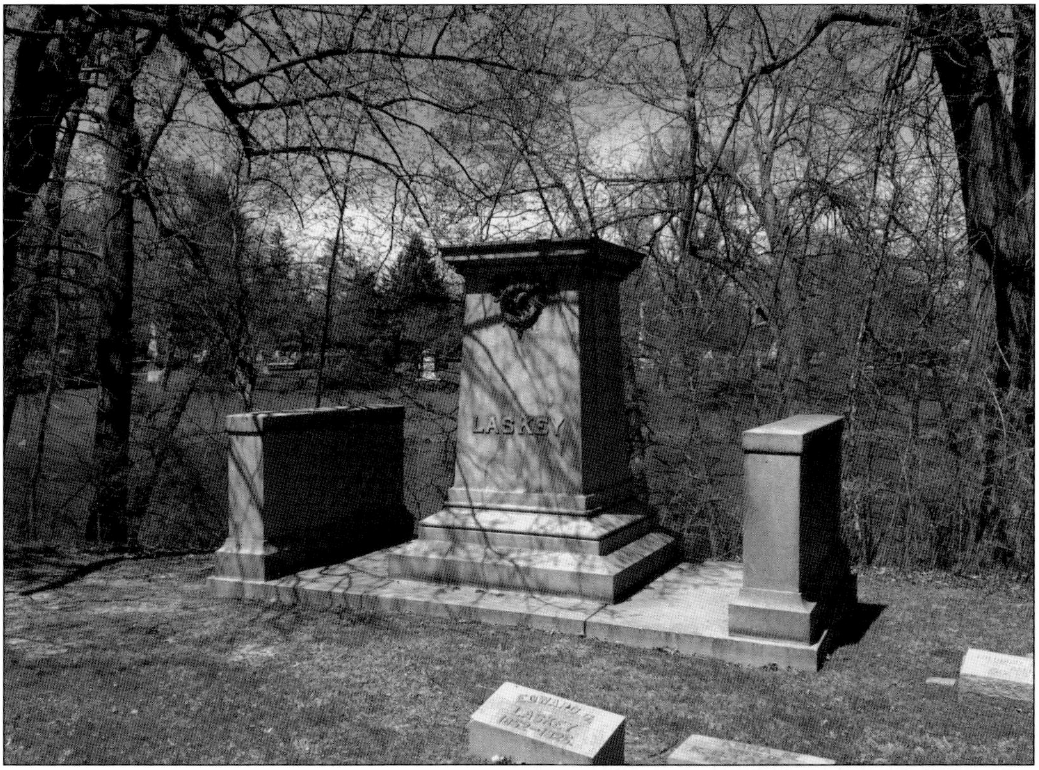

George Laskey (1824–1899) began his professional career at the age of 13, working as a clerk. For many years, he was in the mercantile business in Grand Rapids, Ohio. Elected to the Ohio Senate in 1859, Laskey worked on legislation to develop a drainage system for Northwest Ohio's Great Black Swamp. Later in life, he moved to Collingwood Avenue in Toledo and focused on his real-estate interests. Longtime business partner to George P. Hinsdale, he sealed their friendship for eternity by choosing a nearby plot within the cemetery.

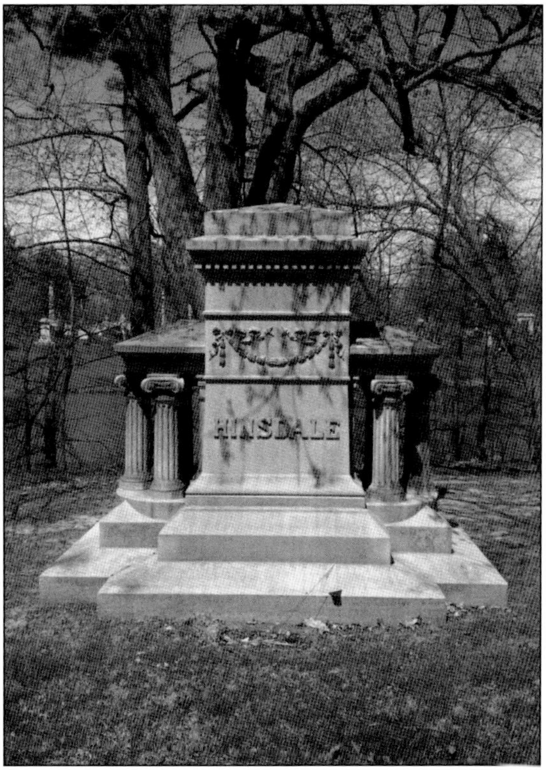

For many years, George P. Hinsdale (1824–1899) ran one of the largest and most successful general stores in Northwest Ohio. Living in Grand Rapids, Ohio, Hinsdale also served as mayor and school director of that village. Meanwhile, he and his business partner, George Laskey, bought several farms and other properties in the area. He eventually sold his shop and moved to Toledo, where he continued his real-estate ventures.

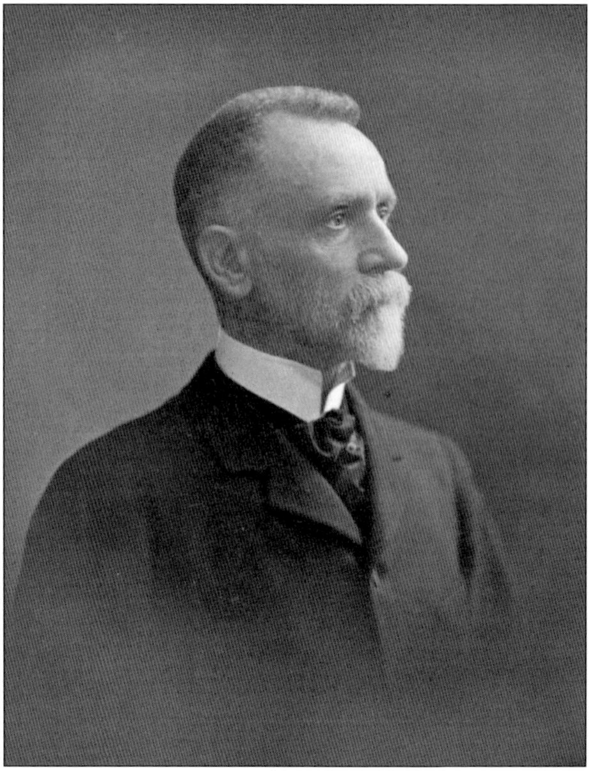

James Secor (1834–1901) joined his older brother, Joseph, in the wholesale grocery firm Secor, Berdan and Company, a pioneer Toledo business. He was also involved in banking interests and helped organize such institutions as the Union Safe Deposit & Trust Company, the Union Savings Bank, and the Woolson Spice Company. He served as president of all three companies. (TPL.)

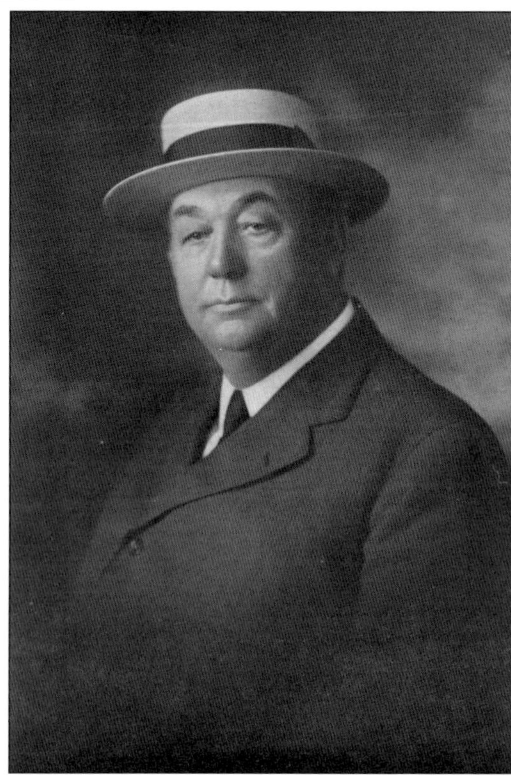

With his cousin Adelbert as a partner, Ceilan Milo "C.M." Spitzer (1849–1919) developed the first firm west of New York City to engage in the buying and selling of bonds. He traveled abroad extensively. Spitzer's beautiful home, Innisfail, on Collingwood Avenue in Toledo, contained many rare and wonderful examples of art and trinkets collected from all parts of the Old World. (TPL.)

Son of the first mayor of Toledo, John Berdan II (1832–1902) worked at several jobs as a young man. He was in charge of the construction of a section of the Wabash and Erie Canal. After that, he drove an ox team from Indiana to California, where he tried his hand at mining. While there, Berdan became superintendent of the Sacramento City Water Works. He returned to Toledo in 1855 and joined his brother-in-law, Valentine Ketcham, in a successful banking partnership, Ketcham, Berdan and Company. Later, he joined the firm of Secor, Berdan and Company. Berdan also held high management positions in several other notable Toledo firms. The Berdan mausoleum stands under the shade of two trees, presenting an eloquent example of Neoclassical architecture within the natural setting of the cemetery.

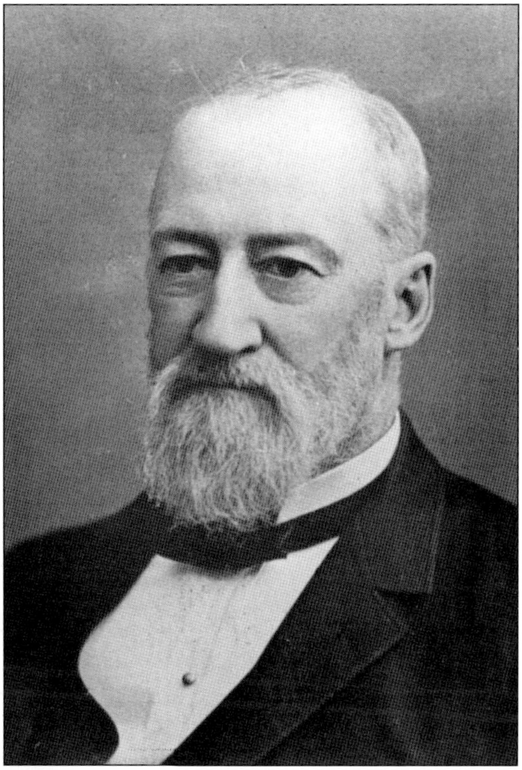

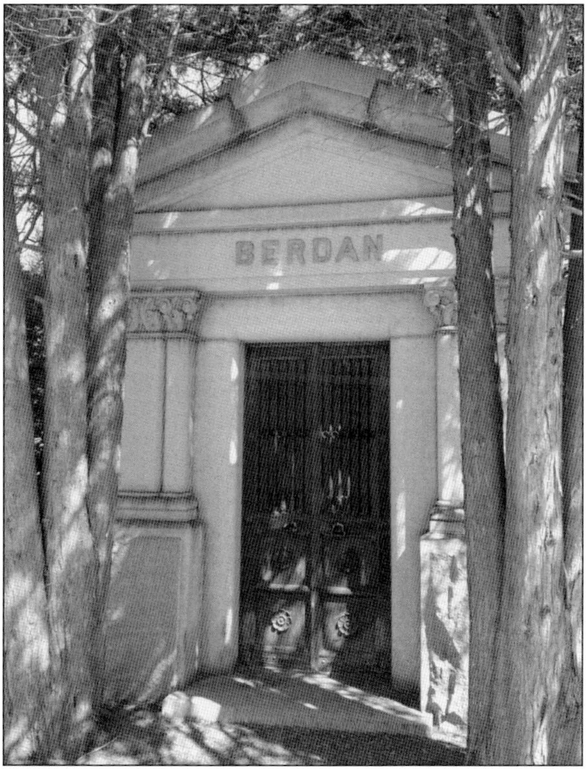

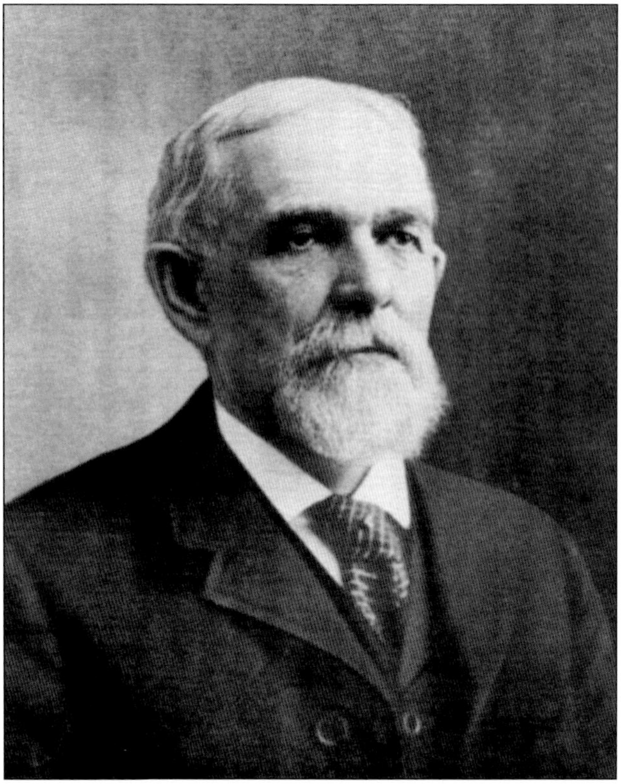

Earlier in his life, Stevens Warren Flower (1832–1908) served in a New York artillery unit during the Civil War and saw much combat, including at Cold Harbor, Petersburg, and Richmond. Later, Flower moved to Toledo and bought an interest in the Reynolds Flour Mill in Maumee. Eventually, he established S.W. Flower and Company, a successful grain and seed business in Toledo's Warehouse District. (FH.)

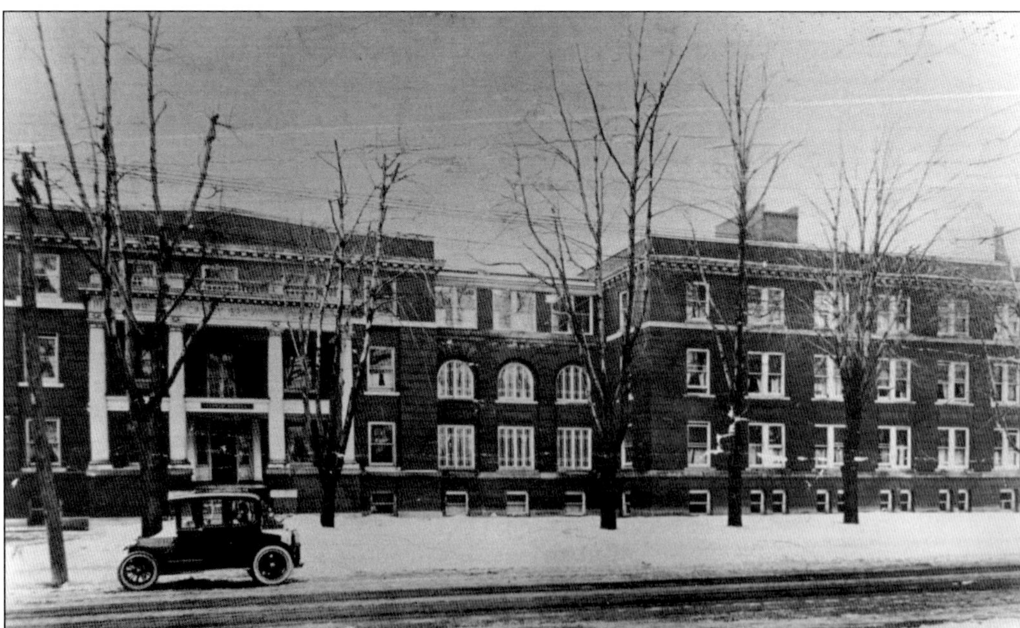

In memory of his late wife, Ellen, Stevens W. Flower left his fortune to the establishment of Flower Hospital, an institution that still serves Northwest Ohio over 100 years later. It was originally built near his home in Toledo at Cherry Street and Collingwood Avenue, but in 1975, it was relocated to Sylvania, Ohio. (TPL.)

David Robison Jr. (1830–1914) is credited with the development of the Toledo Electric Street Railroad System, once the chief mode of public transportation in Toledo. He is also responsible for the construction of the old Steam Plant on Toledo's waterfront. Robison also built the Ohio Savings Bank & Trust Company and its office building on Madison Avenue. The Robison obelisk was created with attention to detail and architectural accuracy. (Right, TPL.)

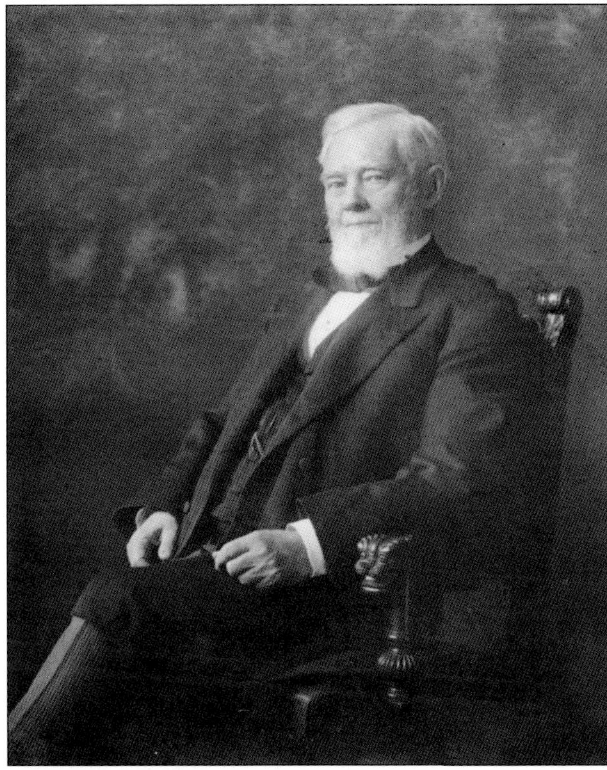

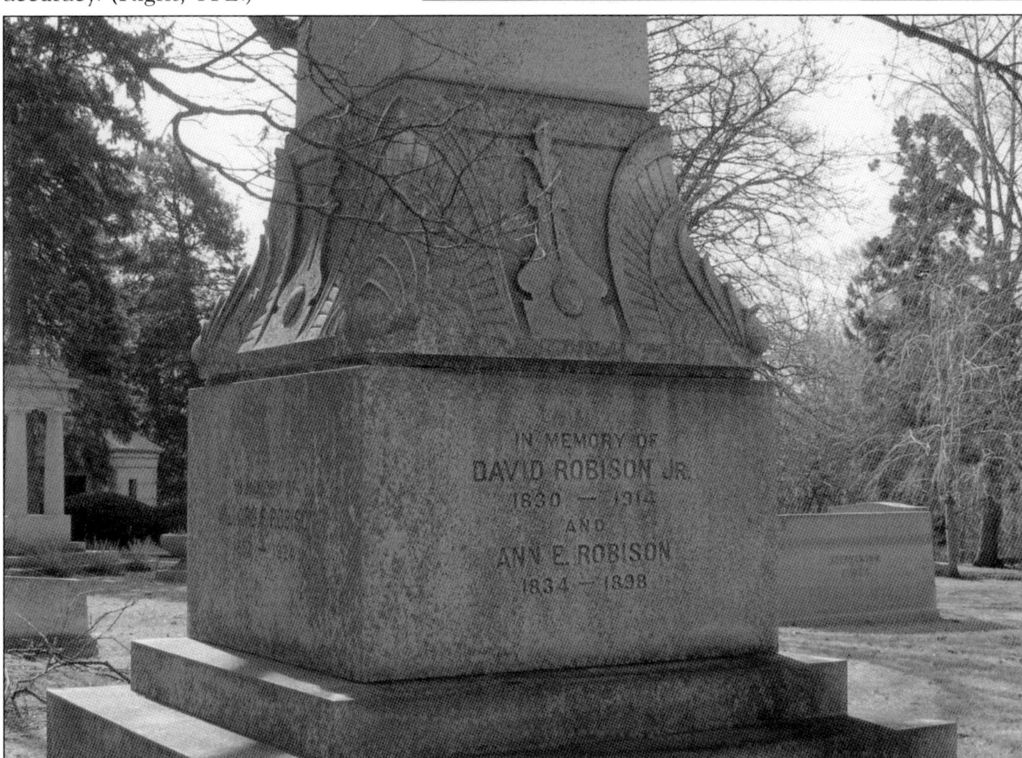

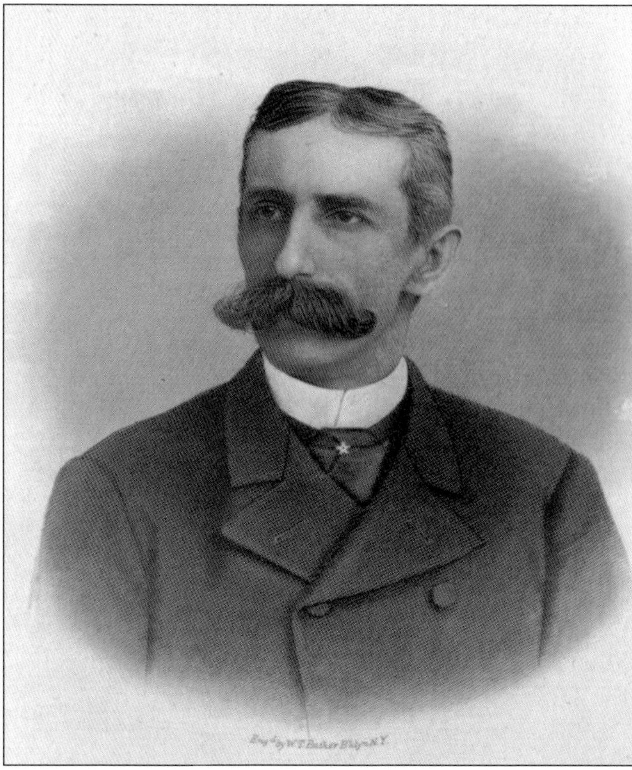

Sheldon C. Reynolds (1835–1912) worked in partnership with his brothers. Their grain-commission business became the largest in the country. Later in life, Reynolds's business interests expanded, as he held the position of president of the First National Bank and was director of several railroads. (TPL.)

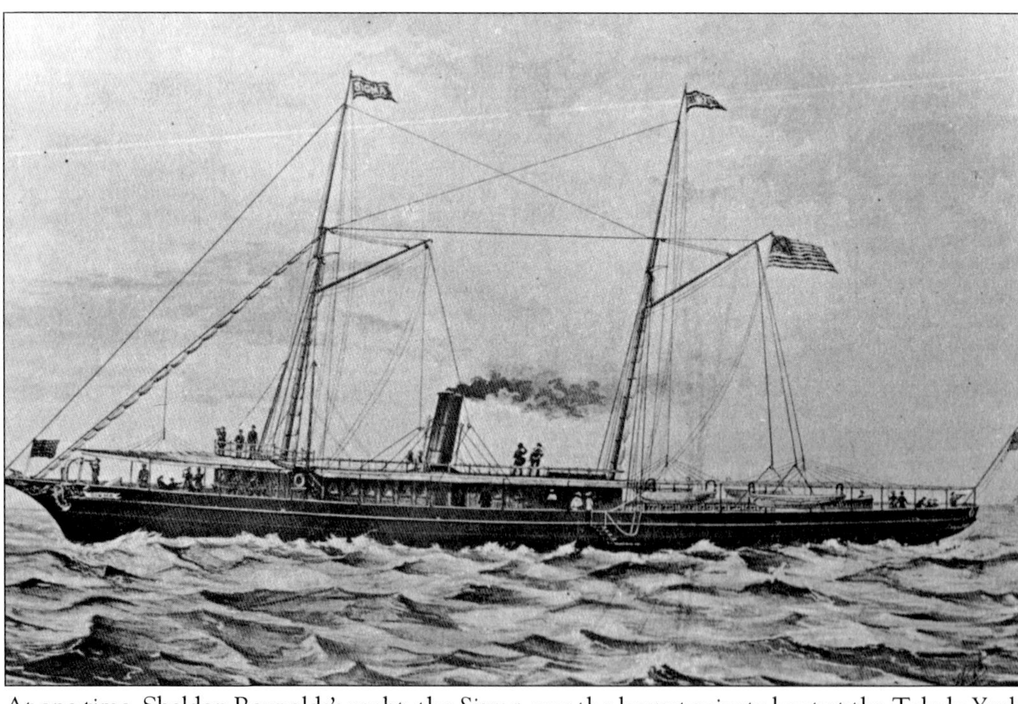

At one time, Sheldon Reynolds's yacht, the *Sigma*, was the largest private boat at the Toledo Yacht Club. Built in 1882, she had an iron hull with a length of 154 feet. Reynolds, a prominent member of the New York Yacht Club, purchased the yacht from the original owner in 1898. (TPL.)

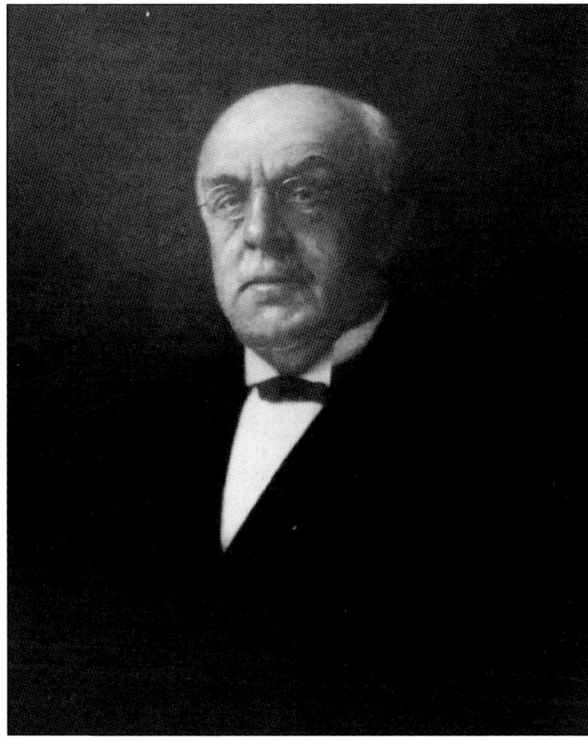

Anderton Lewis Bentley (1845–1916) founded a construction company shortly after his immigration to the United States from England. His company constructed several of Toledo's largest buildings, including the Toledo Museum of Art and Toledo Hospital. The Gardner Building (below), built in 1893 by the Bentley Company, displays an early Renaissance style. Because the Gardner building was an experiment in the use of reinforced concrete, it was overbuilt and is thus one of the heaviest and strongest buildings in Ohio. Additionally, the building is one of the earliest, if not the first, reinforced concrete office building in the nation. (Right, BC; below, TPL.)

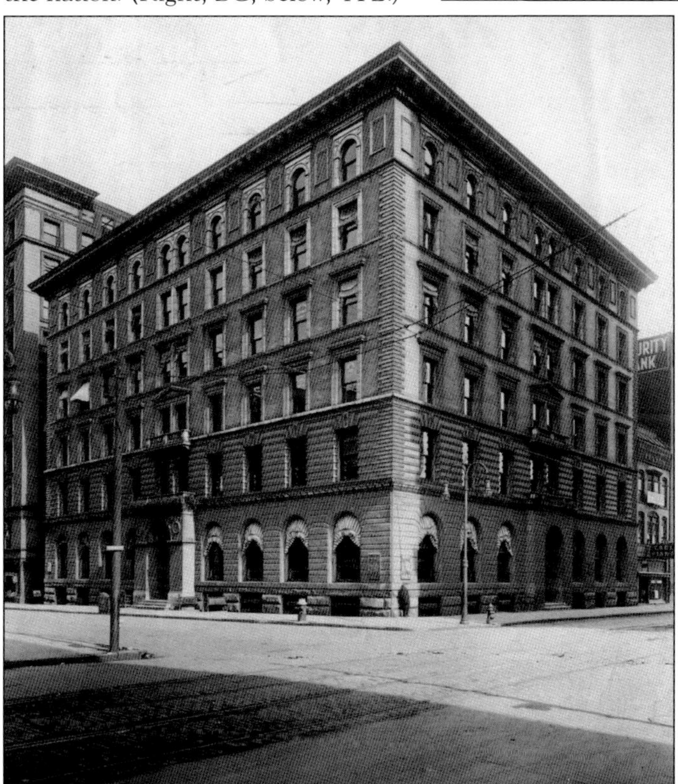

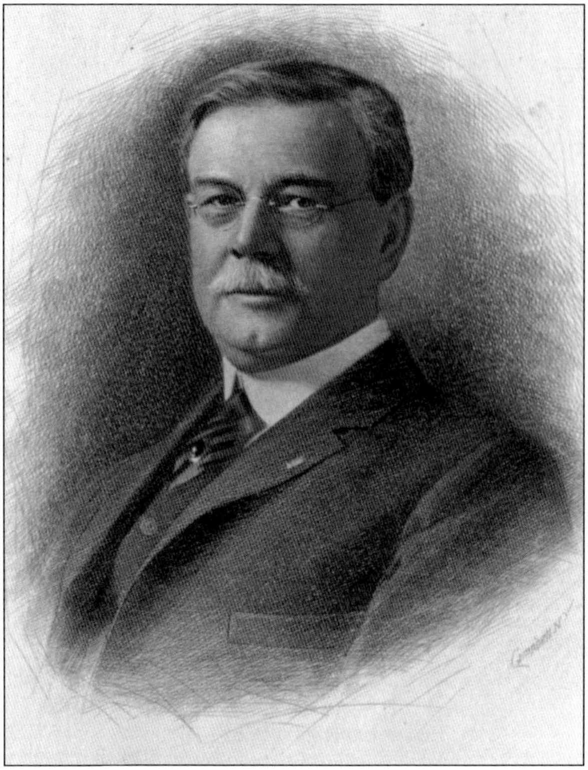

Robinson Locke (1856–1920) took over management of the *Toledo Blade* upon the death of his famous father, David Ross Locke. He eventually became president of the company and editor of the paper. During his tenure, the *Toledo Blade* prospered and its influence increased. During his adult life, Locke was involved in many civic activities, including his position as the first vice president of the Toledo Museum of Art. In his spare time, Locke collected theater memorabilia and owned a biographical library of early-20th-century American actors and actresses. In fact, his walls in the old Blade Building on Jefferson Avenue at Superior Street (below) were covered with autographed portraits of these celebrities. (Left, HM; below, TPL.)

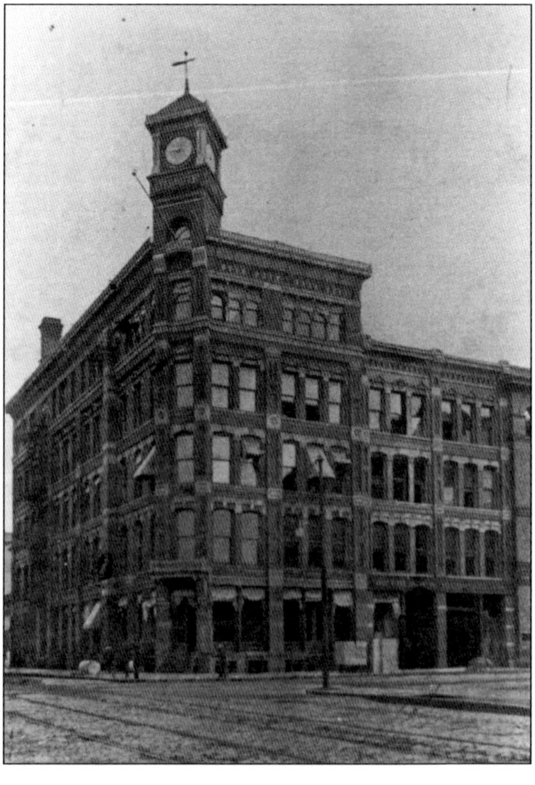

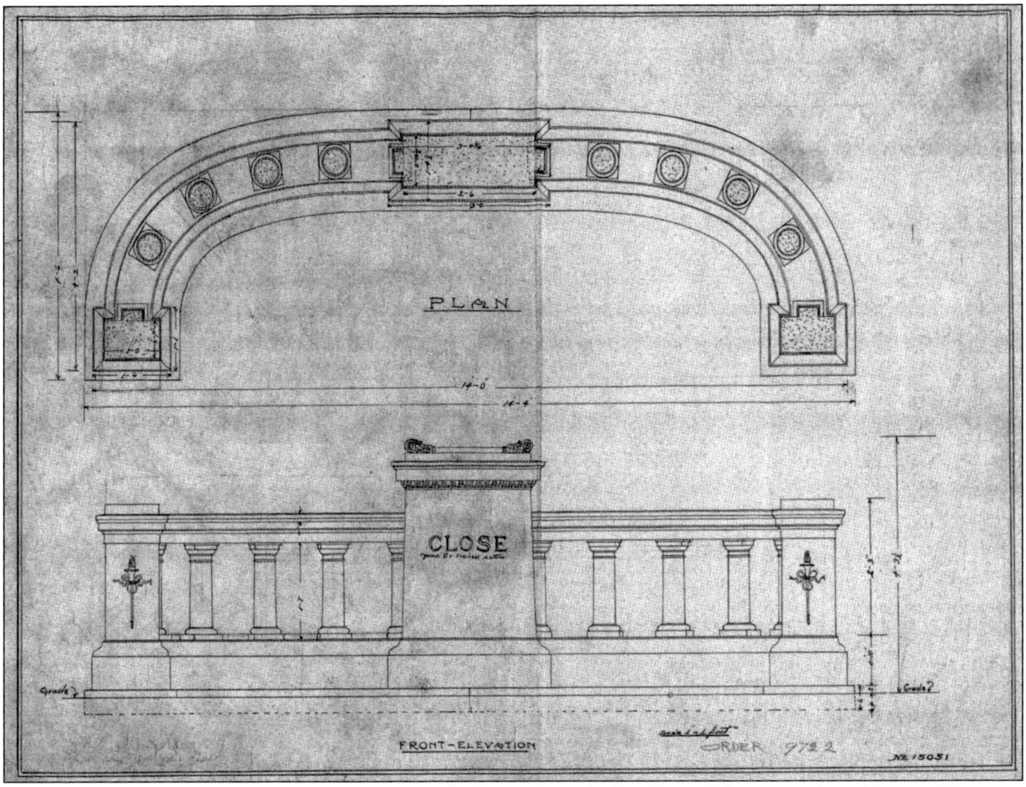

A prominent Toledo realtor, Elmer H. Close (1872–1924) developed the upscale village of Ottawa Hills. He was also instrumental in the development of other outstanding neighborhoods, including Harvard Place and several West Toledo areas. Close Park in West Toledo was named in his honor. His monument is shown below. The blueprint (above) reveals the specific placement of the balustrade, reaching out from the central tablet to the beautifully detailed newel posts. (Above, MW.)

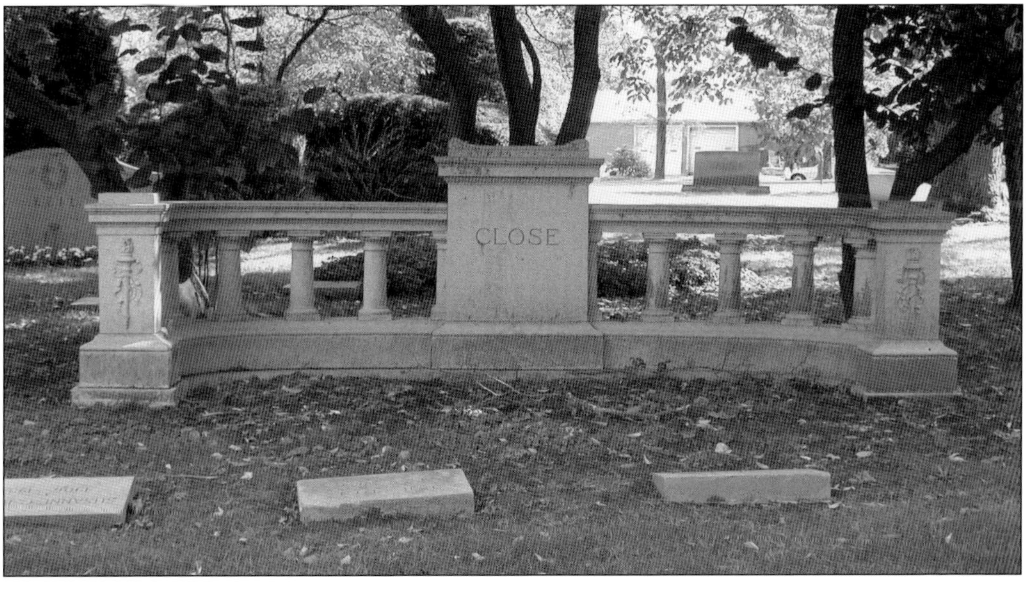

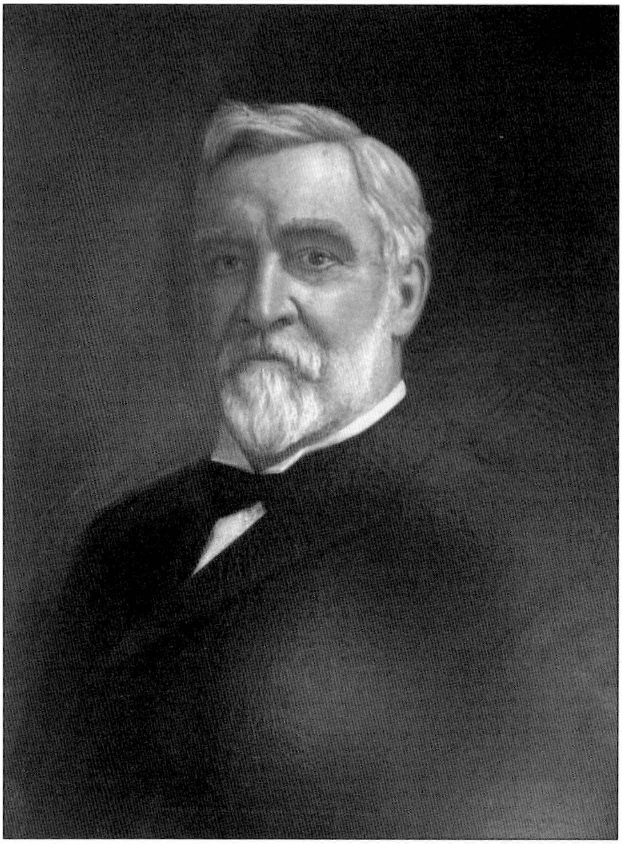

Otis Avery Browning (1841–1923), a prominent Toledo businessman for over 55 years, was reputed to be one of the city's richest men. He built his fortune in the crude-oil business and became known for his activities in real estate and in the oil land business. His firm, Otis A. Browning and Company, set up over 150 wells in Wood County. (BNH.)

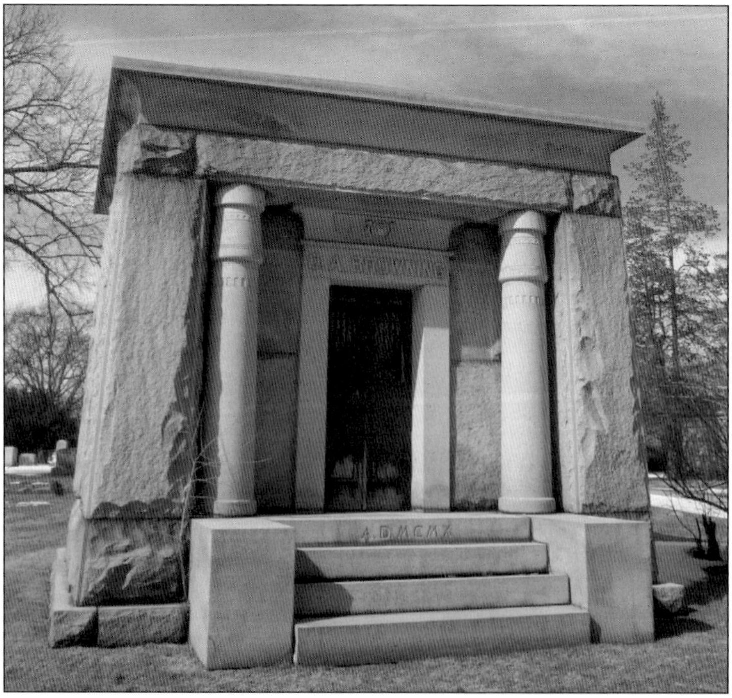

Browning's will provided for the establishment of a Home for Aged Masons, now the Browning Masonic Community. His mausoleum is an example of Egyptian Revival architecture, reflecting his Masonic affiliation. This style was popular in the early 20th century. Inscribed on the top step is "A.D. MCMX," indicating the year of construction (1910).

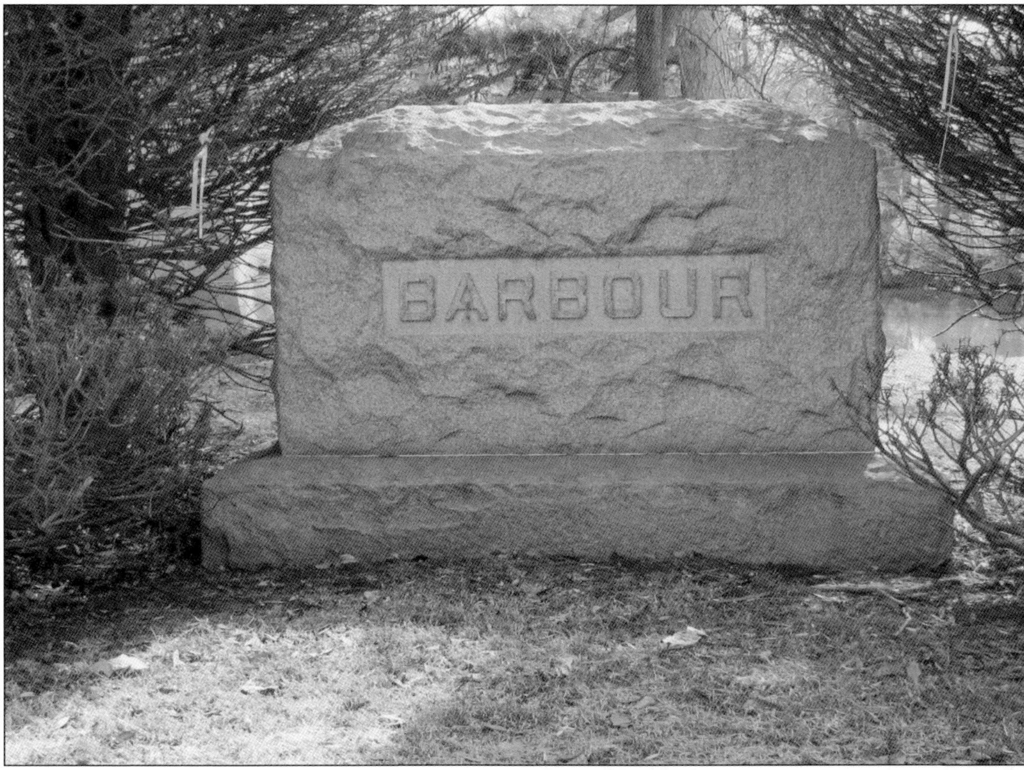

Marcus Victor Barbour, a former president of the Woodlawn Cemetery Association, was a native of Vermont. Barbour (1847–1921) moved to Toledo in 1872 with William Gosline Sr. to establish the coal firm Gosline and Barbour. The company owned two large mines in Ohio, the Shawnee Company in Perry County and the Jackson Company in Jackson County, which yielded the two leading grades of coal in the state. His handsome gravestone reflects classic simplicity.

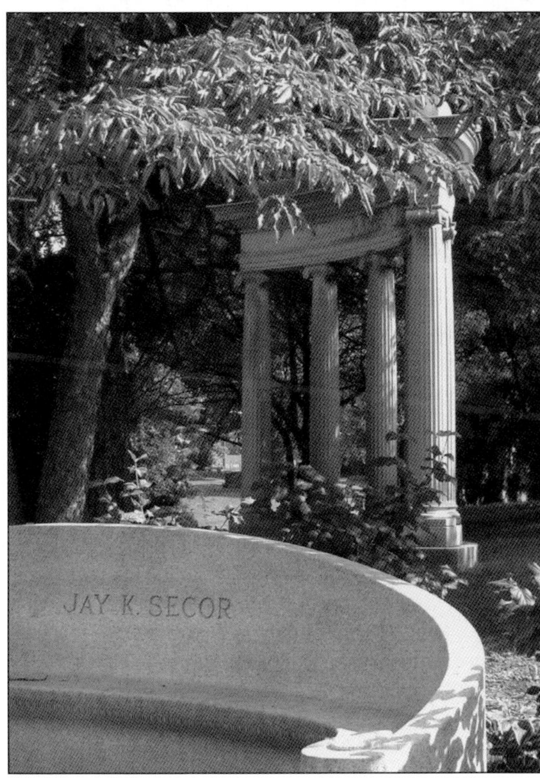

Jay K. Secor (1873–1921) was the son of James Secor and a prominent businessman who established the brokerage house Secor and Bell. He had a major interest in building the Secor Hotel in downtown Toledo in 1908. Secor and his family were the third family to occupy the home now known as Mansion View Inn, a well-known landmark on Collingwood Avenue. Secor's gravesite is marked by this welcoming bench. The colonnade in the background marks the plot of another Woodlawn resident. (JK.)

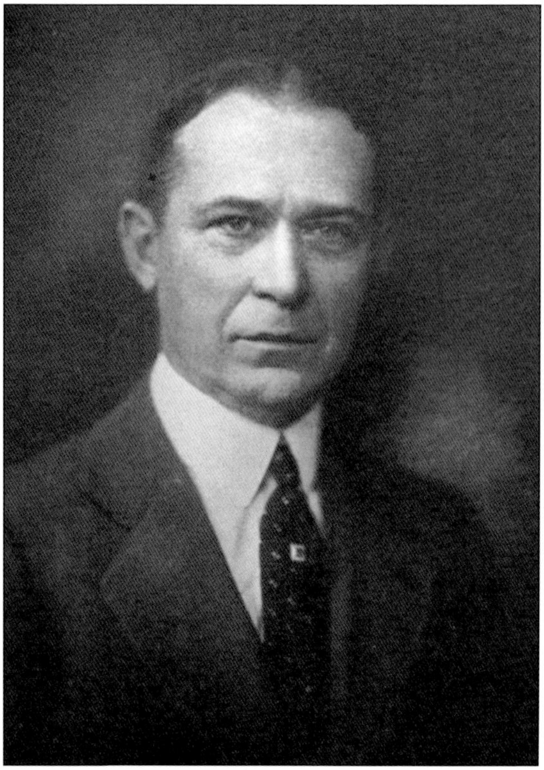

James B. Bell established the respected brokerage firm Secor and Bell. Upon his partner's death, the firm reorganized as Bell and Beckwith. During World War I, Bell (1871–1924) devoted much time to the support drives of various organizations, including the Liberty Loans, Red Cross, and YMCA. Upon his monument is written: "Life is a span—a fleeting hour." (Left, TPL; below, JK.)

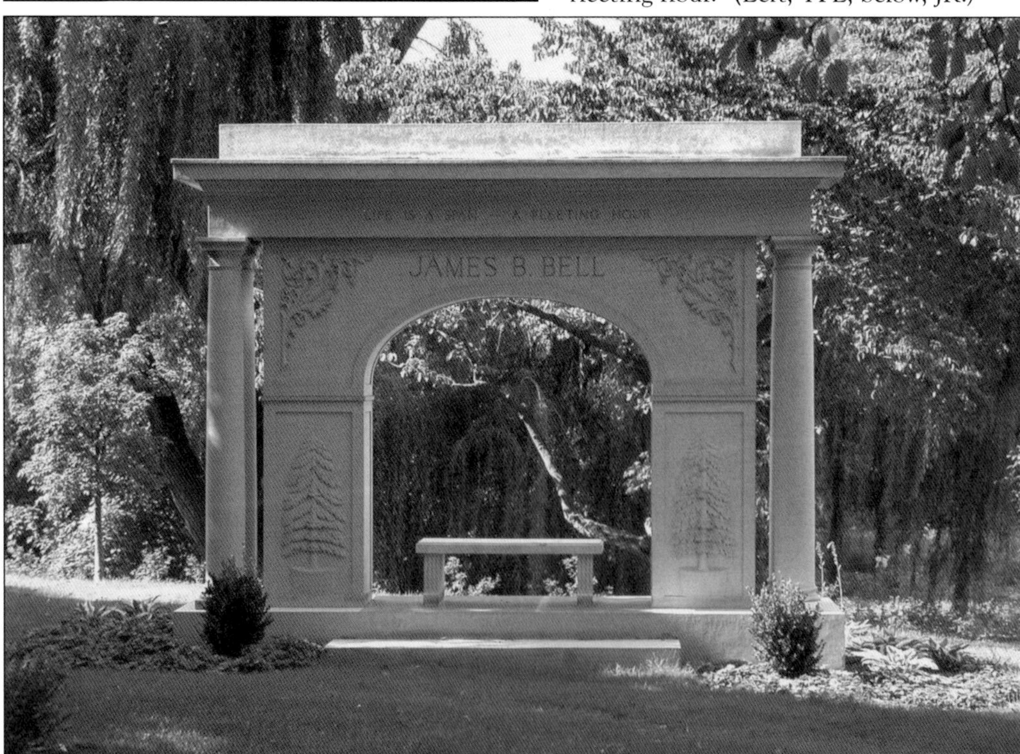

As a young man, Alvin M. Woolson, a Civil War veteran, followed many other former soldiers out West to work on the transcontinental railroad. Later, Woolson and his brother founded the Woolson Spice Company in Toledo. Its best-selling product was Lion Coffee. He virtually revolutionized coffee merchandising by roasting and grinding the beans. This resulted in a nationwide customer base and allowed Woolson Spice to become the second-largest coffee company in the world. Woolson (1841–1925) was also an active supporter of many civic causes, including the GAR, the Toledo Newsboys Association, and the Toledo Museum of Art. Woolson's mausoleum, constructed of granite blocks, sits at the edge of scenic Silver Lake. (Right, TPL.)

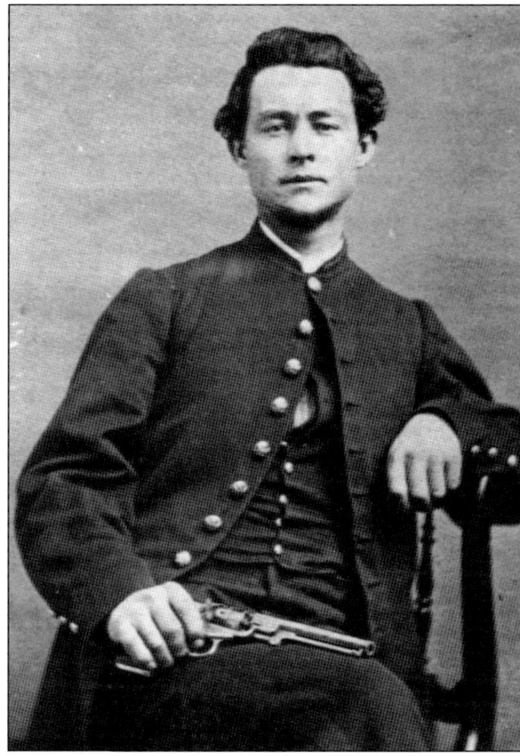

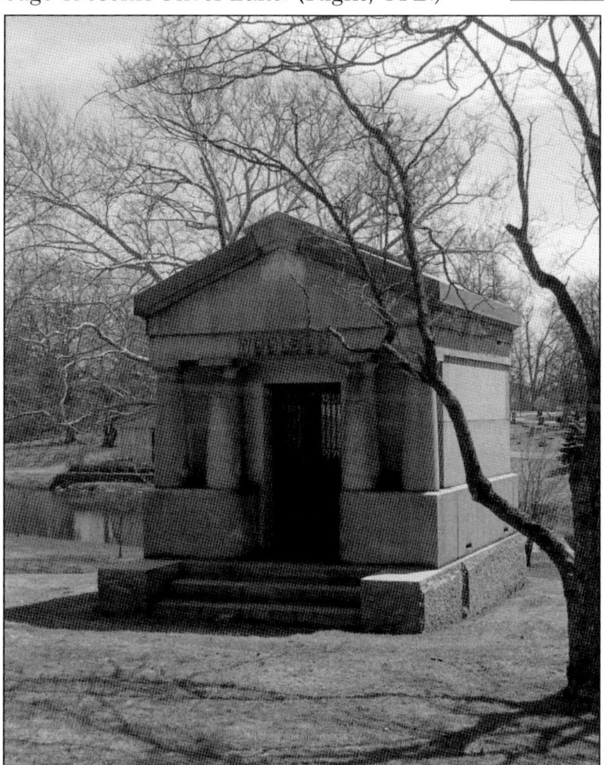

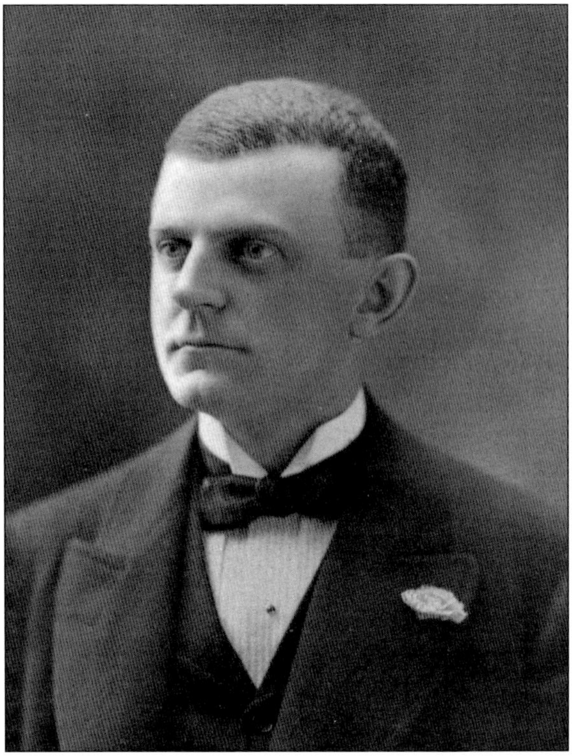

George H. Ketcham (1862–1925) was a prominent Toledo businessman who built the Valentine Office Building in 1892. This structure served as City Hall and as the Valentine Theater in 1895. To this day, the theater remains one of Toledo's most illustrious centers dedicated to the arts. The Valentine Theater poster shown below is a delightful mixture of illustration, advertising, and typography typical of the period. Besides his business ventures, Ketcham had a lifelong passion for horses, which he raised on his farm. Ketcham has the distinction of being the only man to date to have bred, owned, trained, and driven a horse to the world's trotting record. (Both, TPL.)

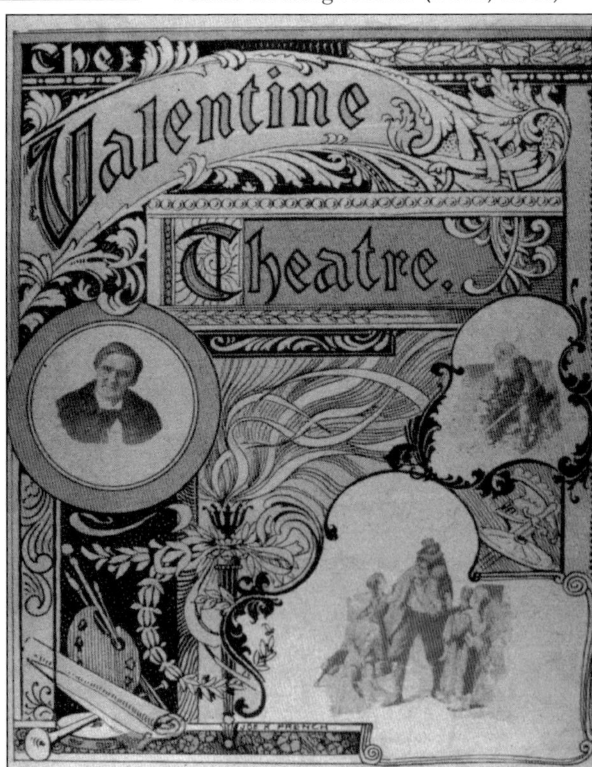

Three

The Soldiers

Upon the gentle rise of Section 41 of the cemetery grounds is the final resting place of those who fought in the nation's bloodiest conflict. The four long years of the Civil War claimed the lives of nearly two percent of the entire population of the United States, including the Confederacy. During the struggle, many Toledoans distinguished themselves by saving the lives of fellow soldiers at the risk of their own. Other local boys fought gallantly and consistently alongside members of their unit until the war ended. Many of the grave markers in this area show reminders of the war, including shields, eagles, crossed swords, and cannons.

One soldier, Henry G. Neubert, stood out for the letters he wrote home, sharing with family and friends the day-to-day events that occupied his time while serving his country. Many of Neubert's letters were published in the *Toledo Blade*. The following is an excerpt from one of his letters, dated July 12, 1864, describing the scene of Union and rebel encampments on opposite sides of the Chattahoochee River: "We are now in bivouac near the river, where we all go to bathe and swim. . . . The rebel picket force, stationed on the opposite bank, belong to the 1st Regiment of Regular Confederate Army. . . . The boys swim back and forth. . . . The Confeds swim over to our side with tobacco and papers tied to their heads, which they trade for coffee and Yankee notions."

The Spanish-American War and World War I took young Toledoans away from home once again. After each conflict, many of the soldiers returned to Toledo and used skills honed in the military to pursue successful careers in business, farming, and public service. These men helped shape Toledo by contributing to its successful evolution from an agrarian community at midcentury to an industrial port by the end of the century.

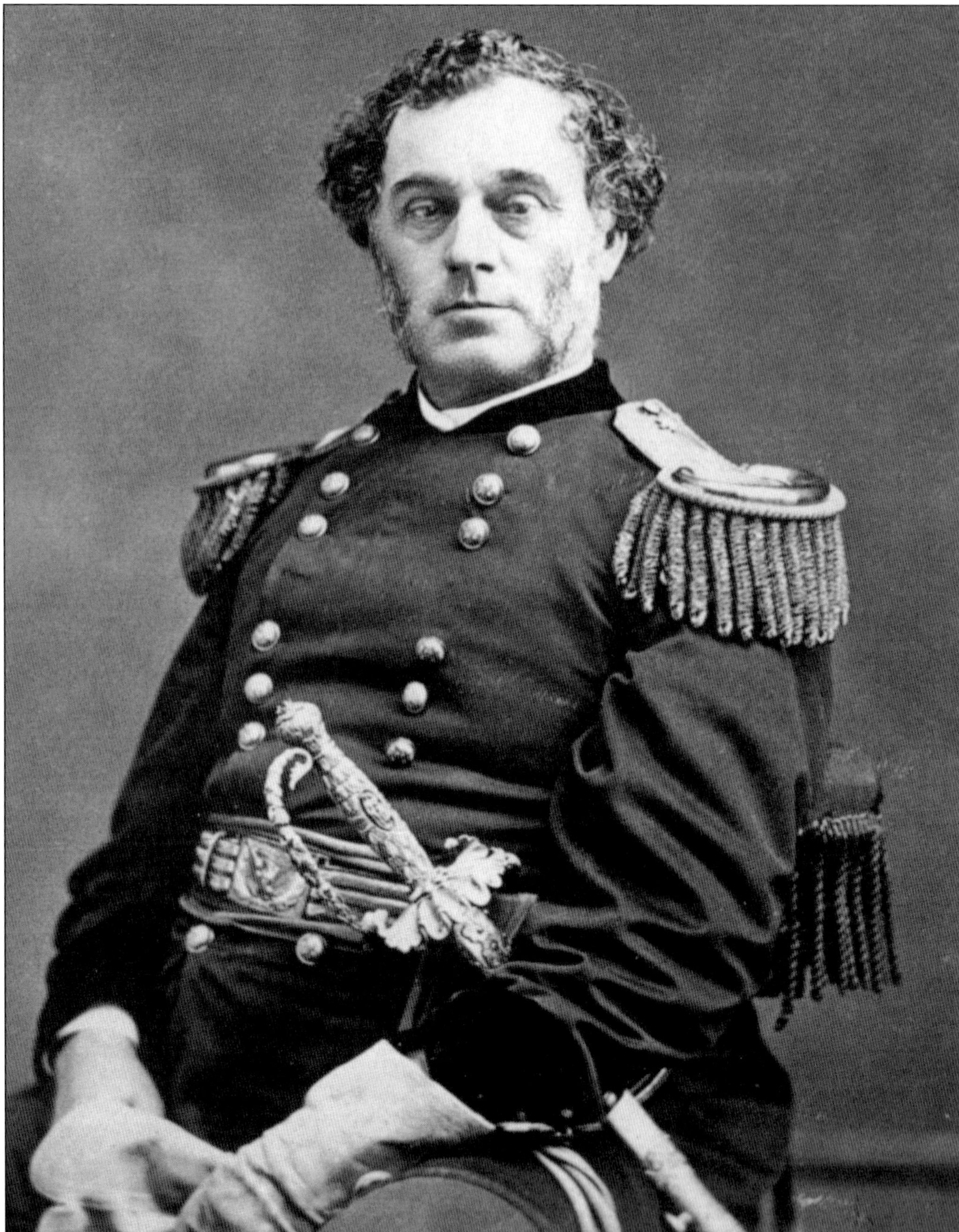

James B. Steedman (1817–1883), a newspaperman, canal builder, and soldier, is said to be Toledo's most famous Civil War veteran, heroically saving the lives of many fellow soldiers at the Battle of Chickamauga. Throughout his lifetime, Steedman was often in the forefront of historic events. For instance, he joined Sam Houston's expedition during Texas's fight for independence and traveled to California in 1849 during the Gold Rush. For two years, he served in the Ohio House of Representatives. During Reconstruction, Steedman was appointed military governor of Georgia. Upon his return to Toledo, he held the position of chief of police for several years. (TPL.)

At his burial site, a bronze bust of Gen. James Steedman sits high atop a massive stone monument.

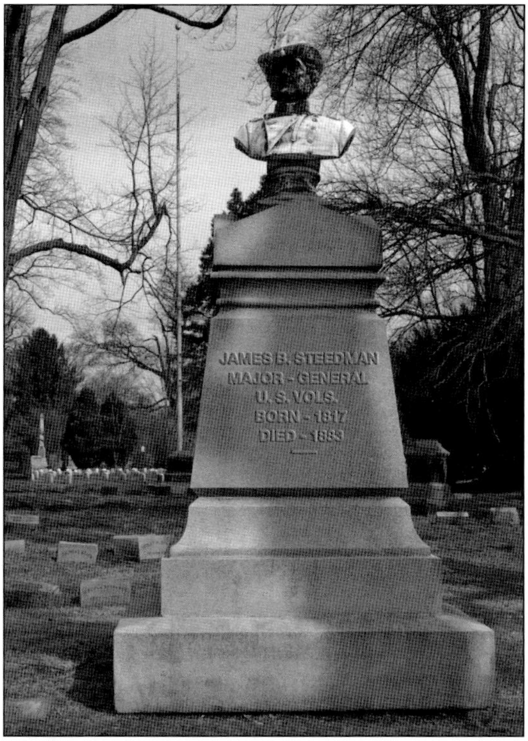

After James Steedman's death, this 26-foot-tall monument topped with a larger-than-life bronze statue of him stood guard over Toledo for many years at the corner of Summit and St. Clair Streets. It was later moved to Jamie Farr Park. It commemorates his service during the Civil War, in which he rose to the rank of major general with the 14th Ohio Volunteer Infantry. (TPL.)

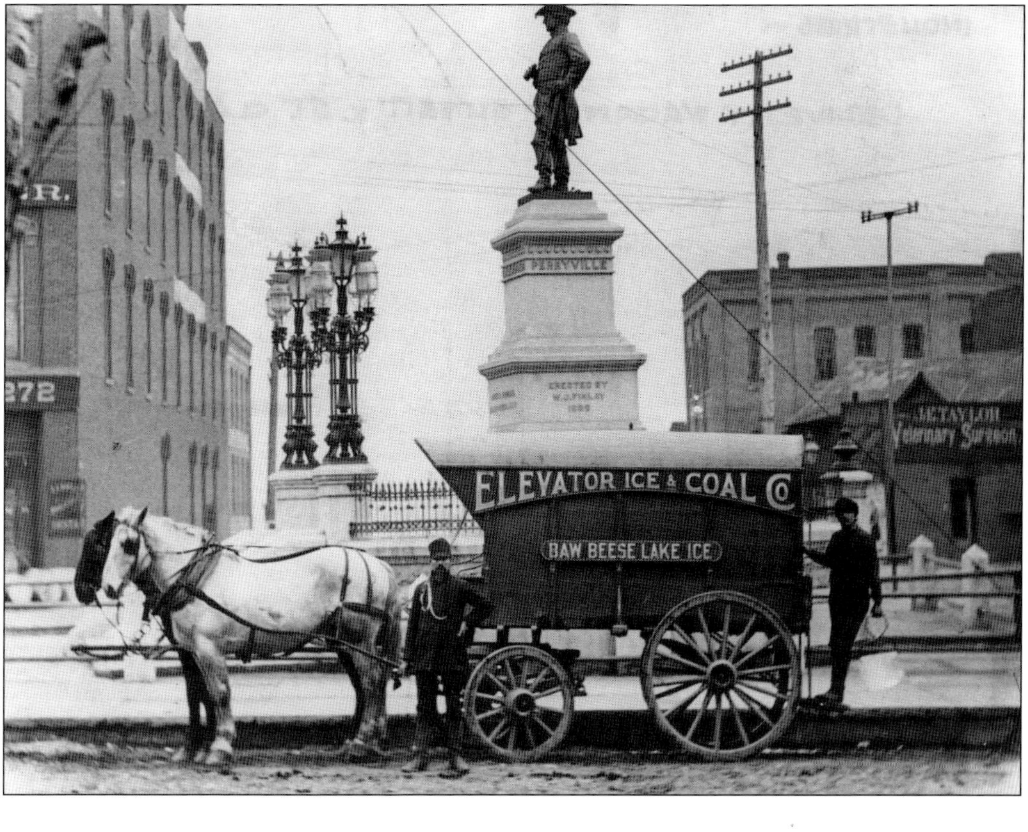

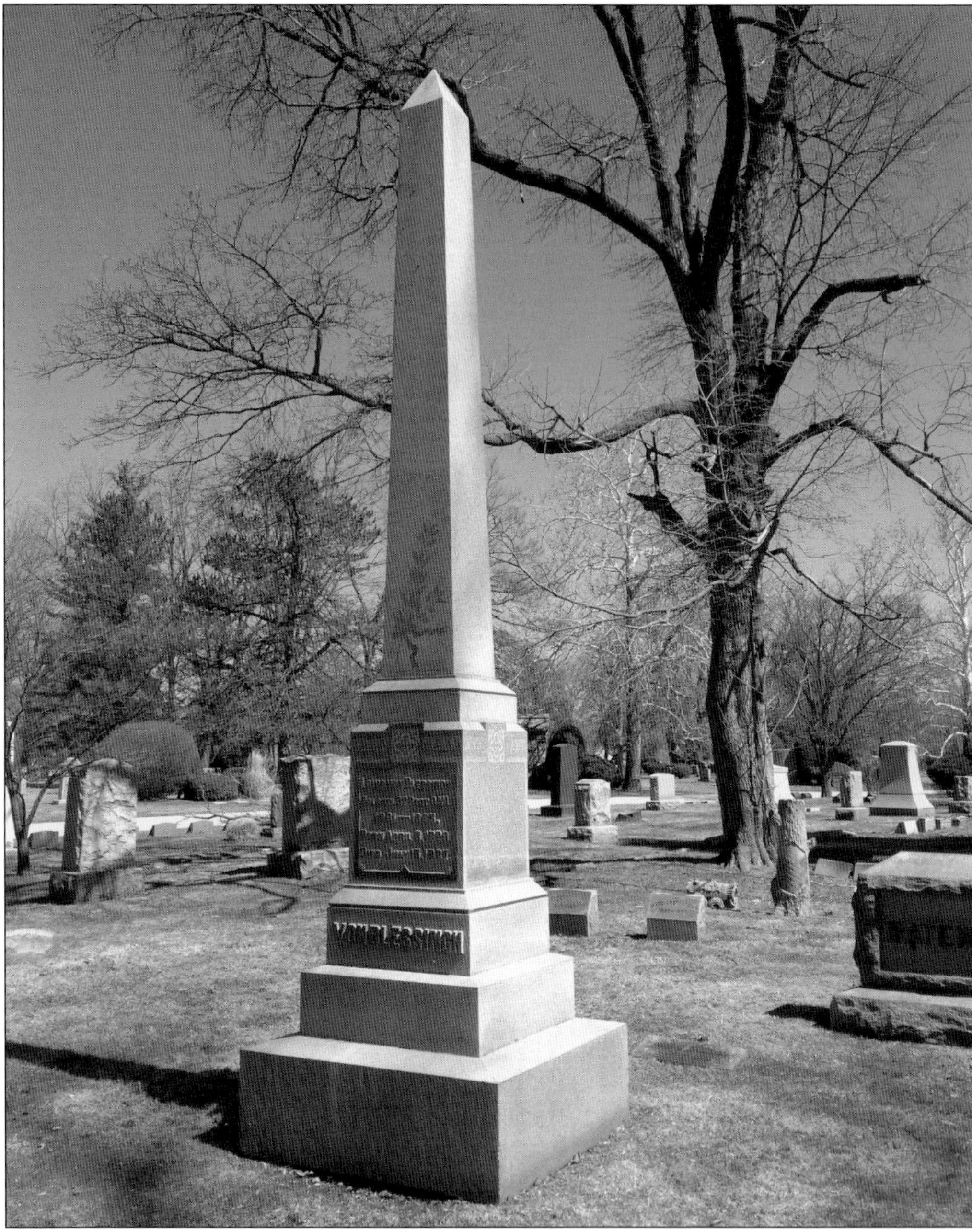

German-born Louis Von Blessingh (1829–1887) arrived in the United States in his early 20s. At the start of the Civil War, he enlisted in the 37th Ohio Volunteer Infantry, the third German regiment raised in Ohio. For his actions against Confederate forces on the Kanawha River in West Virginia, he was promoted to lieutenant colonel on October 12, 1861. In assaults at Vicksburg and Jackson, Mississippi, he was wounded, but remained with the 37th through campaigns in Tennessee, Alabama, and Georgia. On November 13, 1864, he was promoted to colonel in command of the 37th; they destroyed the tracks of the Columbia & Charleston Railroad during the campaign of the Carolinas under Gen. William Tecumseh Sherman. For merit and devotion to duty, he was brevetted brigadier general of the 37th Ohio Volunteers on March 13, 1865.

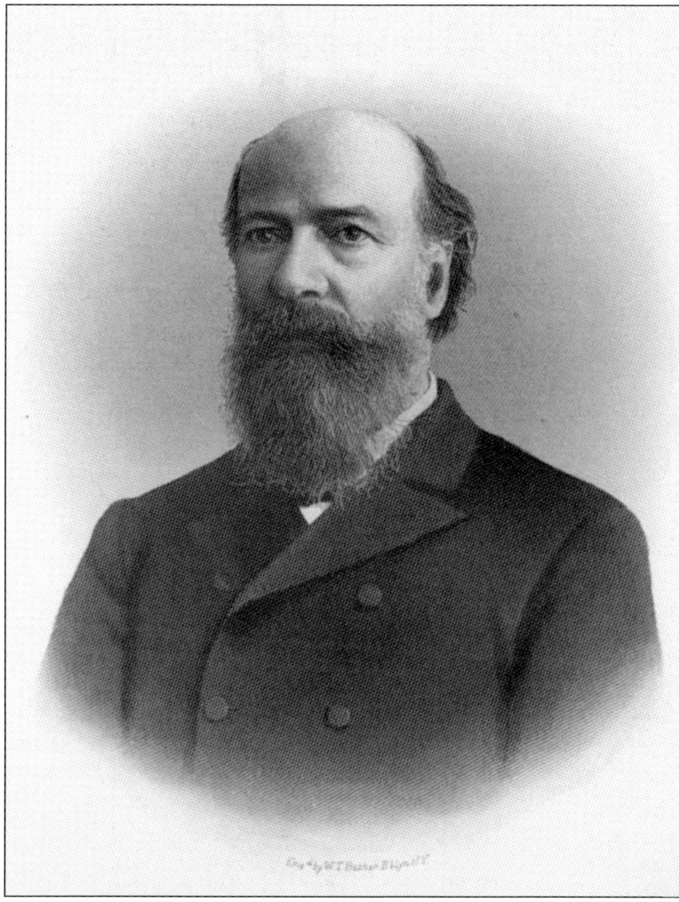

John W. Fuller (1826–1891) attained the rank of brigadier general of volunteers in the Union Army during the Civil War and participated in Sherman's March to the Sea. After the war, he became a senior partner with the firm Fuller, Childs & Company in Toledo, a wholesale boot and shoe business. Later, Pres. Ulysses Grant appointed him collector of the Port of Toledo. In the group photograph below, Civil War veterans gather on either side of Fuller's monument during the 42nd National Grand Army of the Republic Encampment, held in Toledo in 1908. Note the bust of Fuller that once stood within the niche in the monument's face. (Right, TPL; below, WC.)

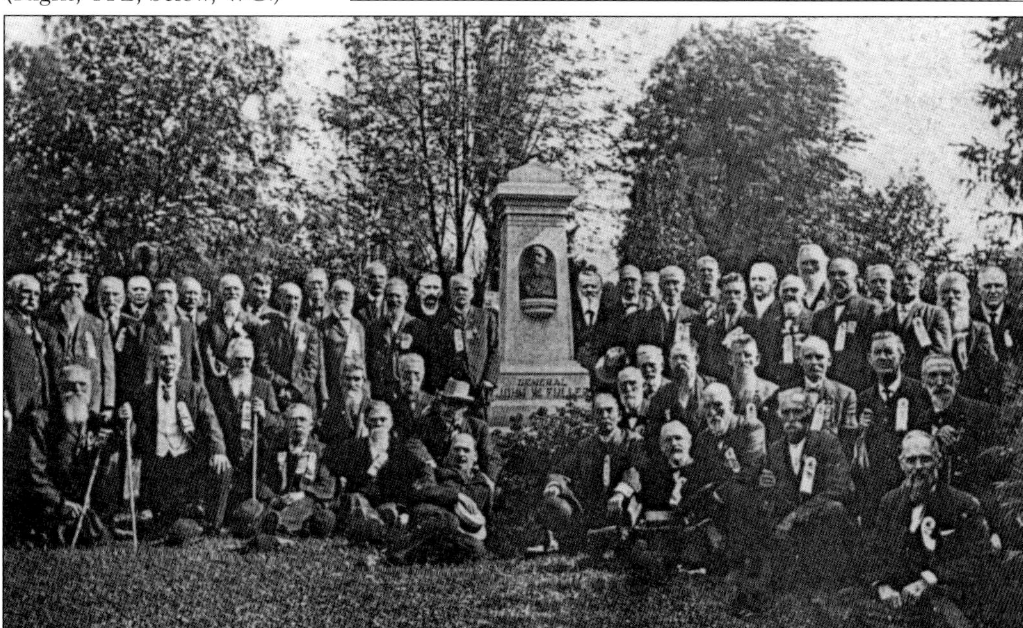

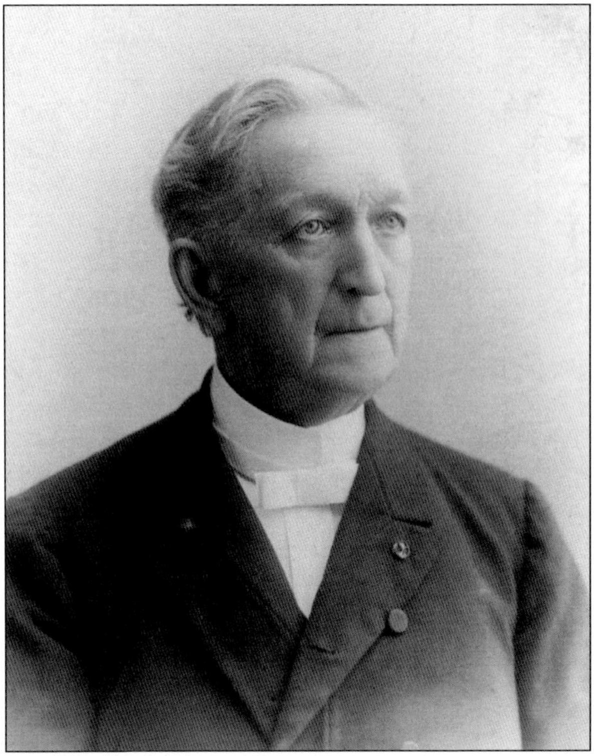

A gifted orator, Civil War general Patrick Sumerville Slevin was influential in raising troops for the war effort. After the war, Slevin (1815–1894) prospered from his legal practice as well as other business affairs. Later in life, he took on the position of city missionary at the Adams Street Mission, dedicating his final years to helping those in need. Slevin's monument is formed with an interesting combination of rough and smooth finished areas. (Both, DC.)

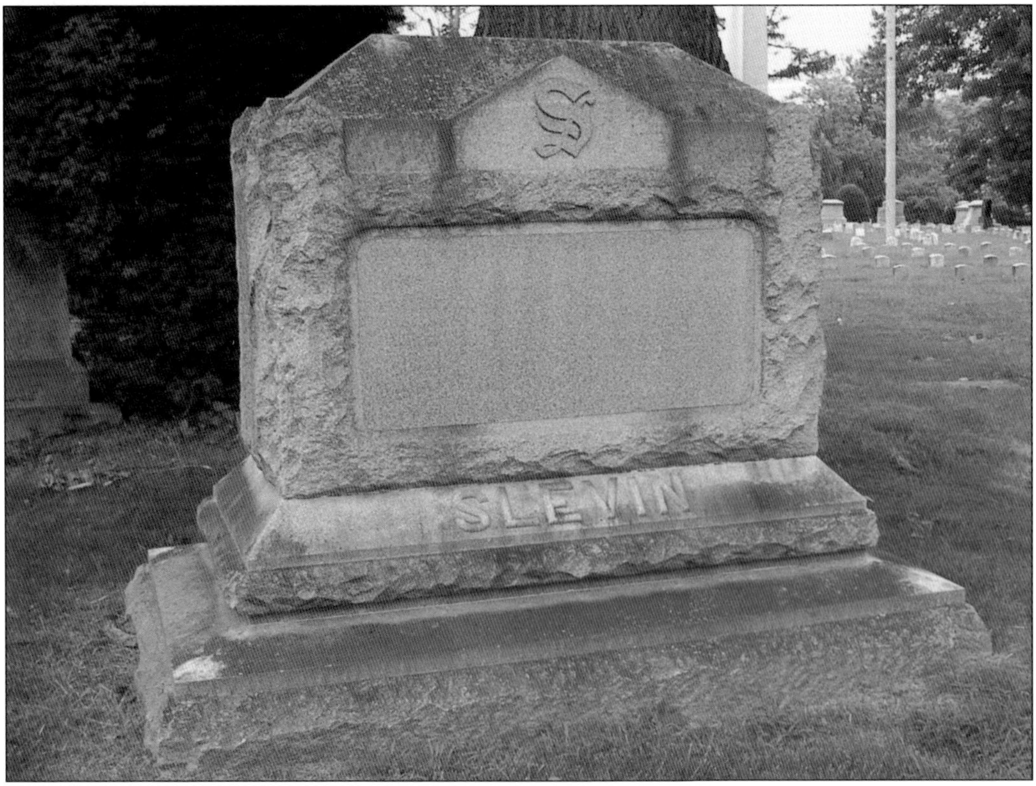

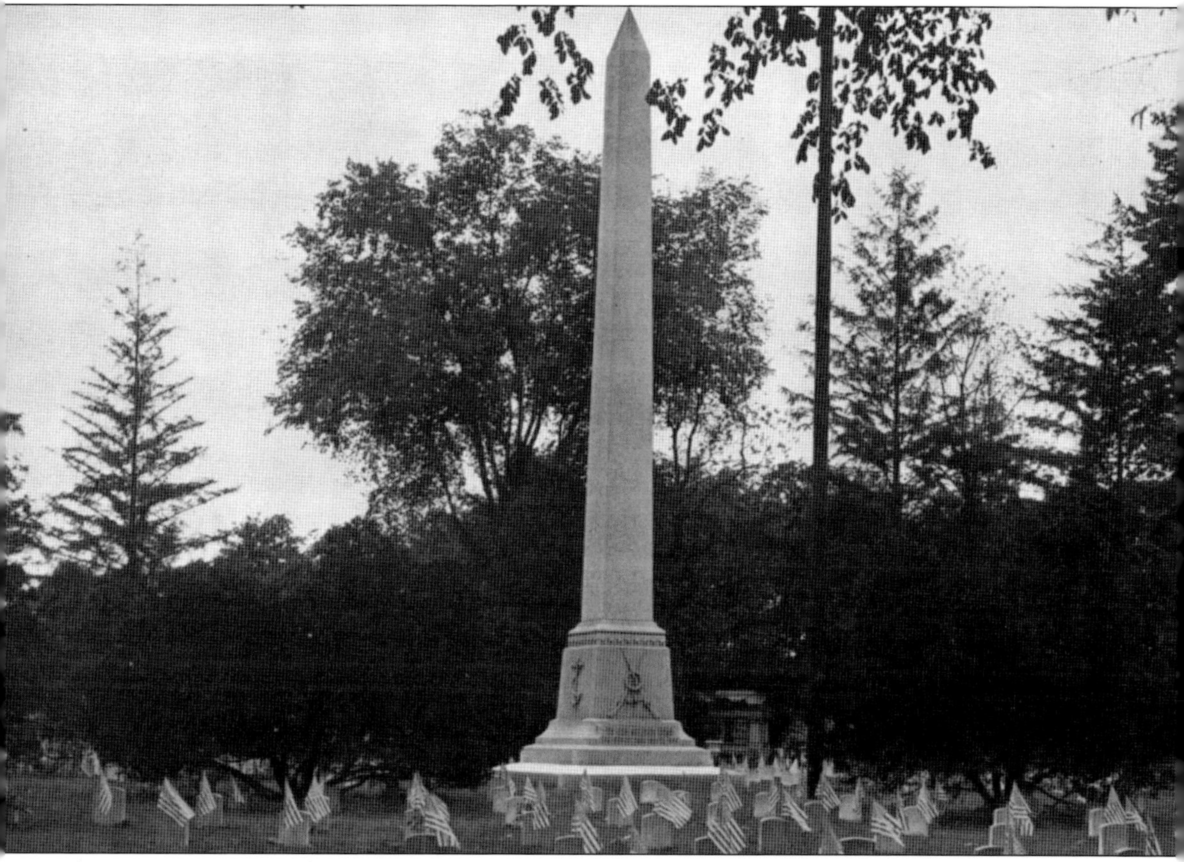

The Lucas County Civil War Monument, dedicated in 1901, stands in memory of the heroism of area veterans who fought to preserve the Union. Made of granite, the obelisk reaches a height of 65 feet. The memorial is surrounded by 295 graves that are laid out in the shape of a pentagram, the symbol of the Grand Army of the Republic. The GAR, as it became known, and its auxiliary Women's Relief Corps, provided support for veterans' organizations and used its political clout for federal and state Soldiers Homes for invalids. The groups advocated for a day set aside to remember and honor those who fought and died in military service to the country; that day is now known as Memorial Day. (WC.)

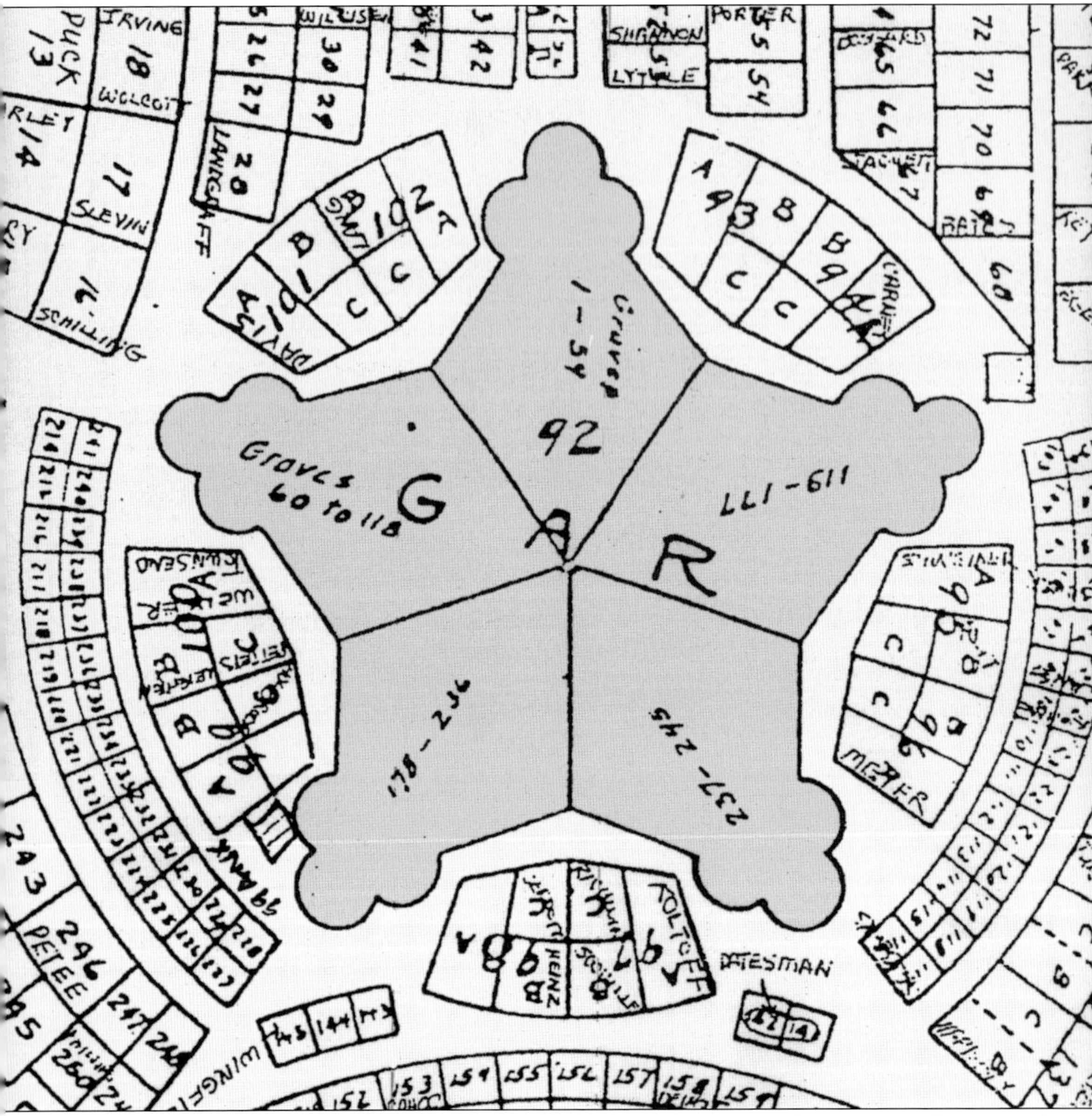

This map of Section 41 shows how the burial plots were lined up in order to create a five-pointed star, the symbol of the GAR. Larger plots were available on the outer edges of this section, allowing soldiers of higher rank to construct larger monuments.

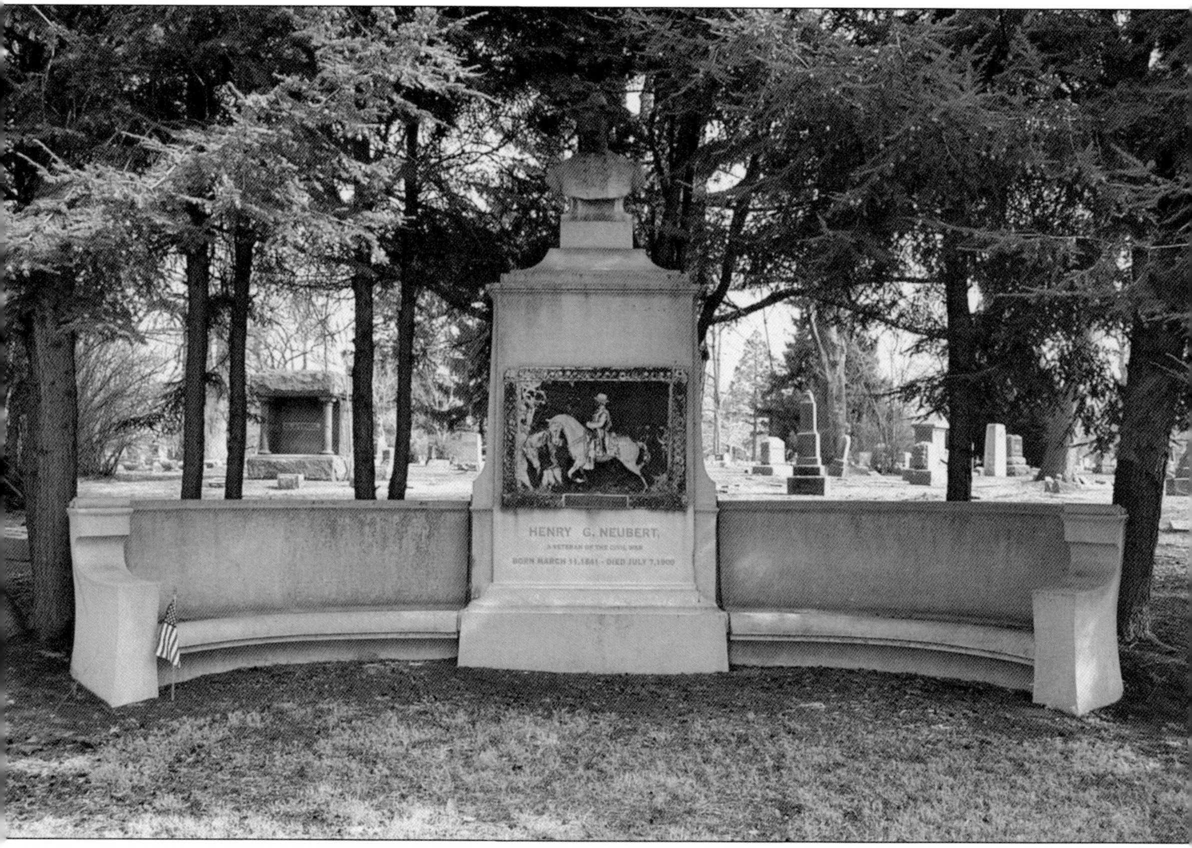

During the Civil War, Henry G. Neubert sent home several descriptive letters from the front lines, and these were printed in the *Toledo Blade*. After the war, Neubert (1842–1900) became a successful Toledo businessman, was active in veterans' affairs, and helped raise money for Toledo's Memorial Hall. Curiously, Neubert seems to have laid the plans for his own monument at Woodlawn. A *Toledo Blade* article two days after his death reported his desire to be represented by a historical tablet. Colonel Neubert received his wish, as a bronze relief sculpture on the monument's face commemorates his role in Sherman's March to the Sea. His bust sits atop the shaft of his monument, while stone benches extend on either side. (JK.)

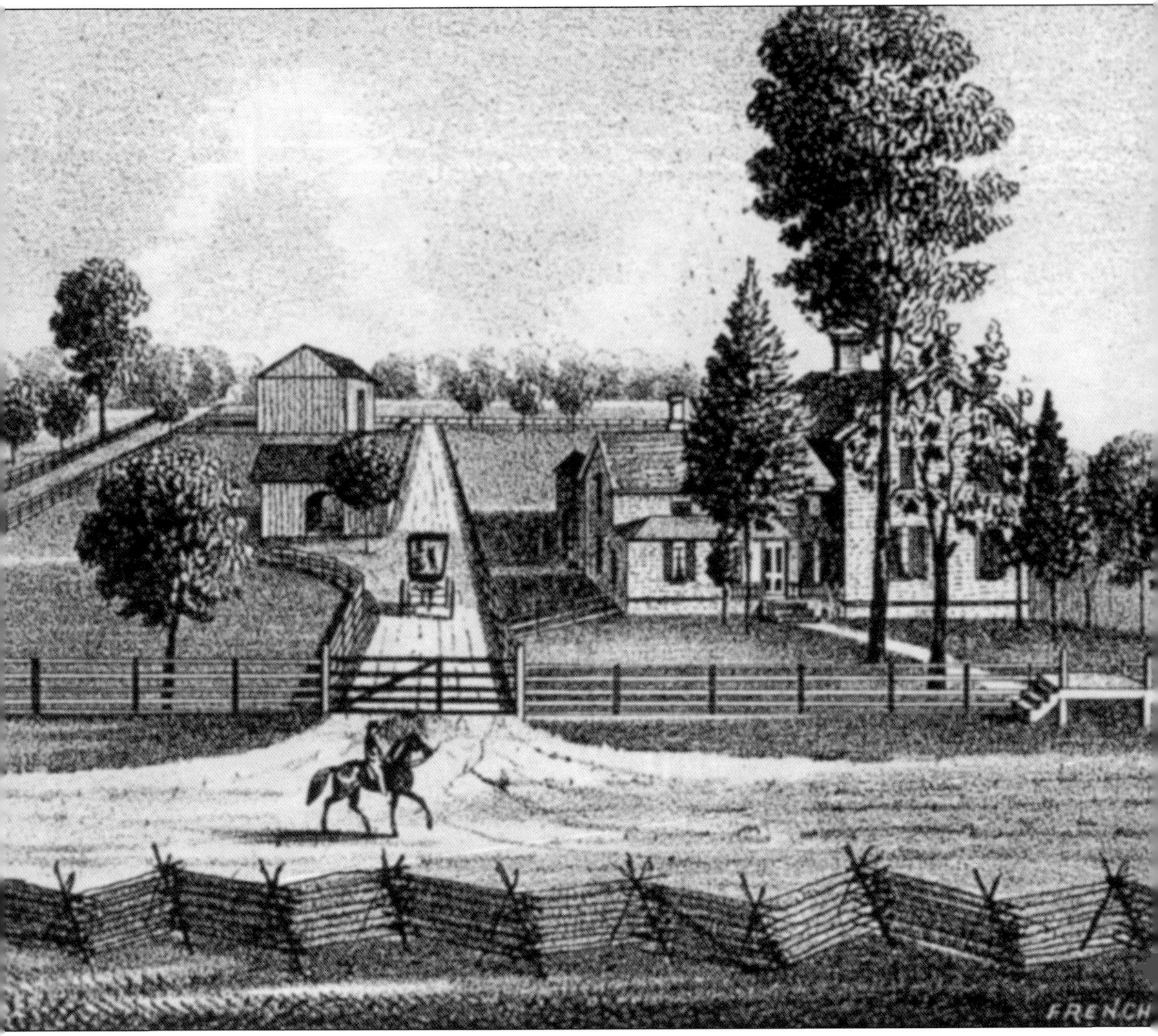

A veteran of the Civil War, Thomas W. Secor (1828–1909), brother of Toledo businessmen James and Joseph Secor, chose to live in the countryside just outside Toledo. He established an impressive farmstead, as depicted in this drawing, at the southeast corner of Central Avenue and Secor Road. Beginning in 1854 he lived and worked here for the rest of his life, with the exception of his years away from home during the Civil War. Along with a cluster of farmhouses, a general store, a schoolhouse, and a cemetery, the surrounding area became known as Secorville. (TPL.)

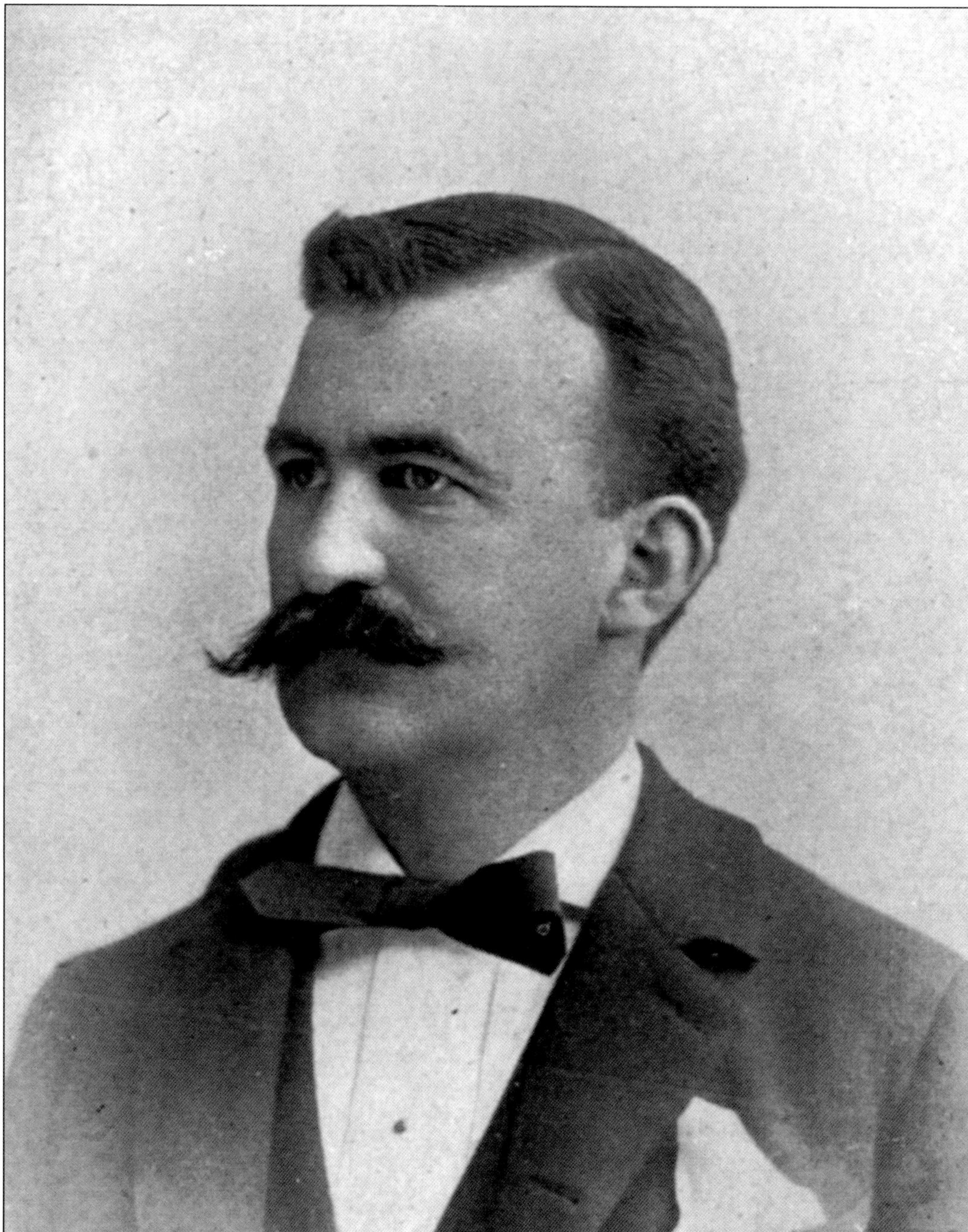

Besides his civic and business affairs in Toledo, William V. McMaken had a long and distinguished military career. Upon graduating from high school, he attended the US Military Academy at West Point. During the Spanish-American War, McMaken (1857–1923) commanded troops deployed to Cuba, and became governor general of Cienfuegos, Cuba. Upon his return to Toledo, he was appointed brigadier general of the Ohio National Guard. He held this position until 1918, when, after serving his country once again with the 37th Division in World War I, he retired from the military due to physical disabilities. (TPL.)

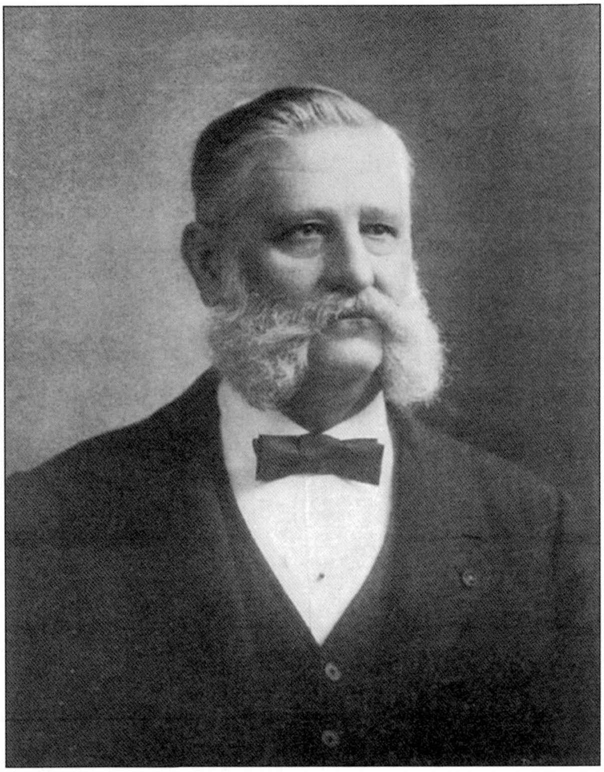

William H. Raynor (1834–1912) volunteered at the start of the Civil War and was quickly captured during the first Battle of Bull Run. Sent to the infamous Libby Prison, Raynor soon made a daring and successful escape by posing as a medic. He was discharged later in the war after he was wounded near Vicksburg, Mississippi. After the Civil War, for his "distinguished and gallant services," Raynor was promoted to brigadier general in the Grand Army of the Republic.

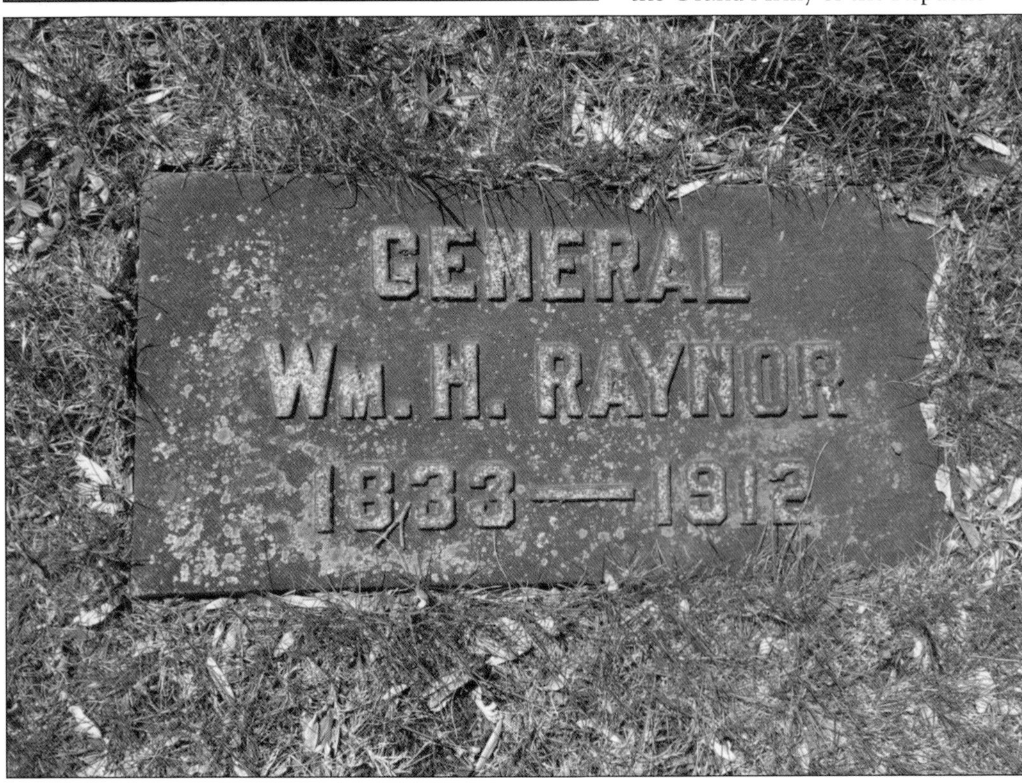

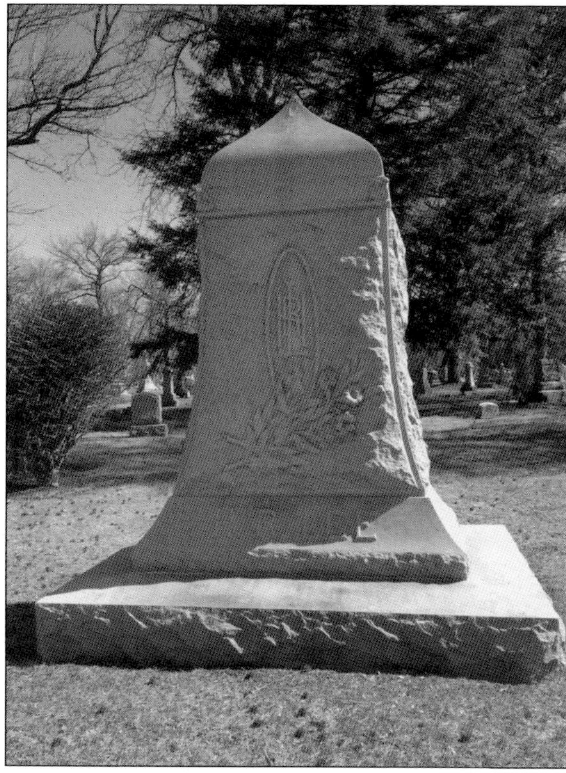

Harry R. Lee, born George Shue, enlisted in the military at the outbreak of the Civil War. He served honorably, but was discharged after three years due to a head wound. Upon his return home to Pennsylvania, it was apparent that the injury had affected his mind, and, at some point, he stole a horse and buggy. Captured and severely fined for this incident, Shue decided to move west and start over, as his reputation by now was completely ruined in his hometown. Upon his arrival in Toledo, he changed his name and appears to have regained his mental stability. Over the years, Lee (1843–1920) became a well-respected and wealthy man. He was instrumental in founding the University of Toledo and became president of the Mutual Savings Association. Lee's monument features several beautiful, hand-carved lilies along with his monogram.

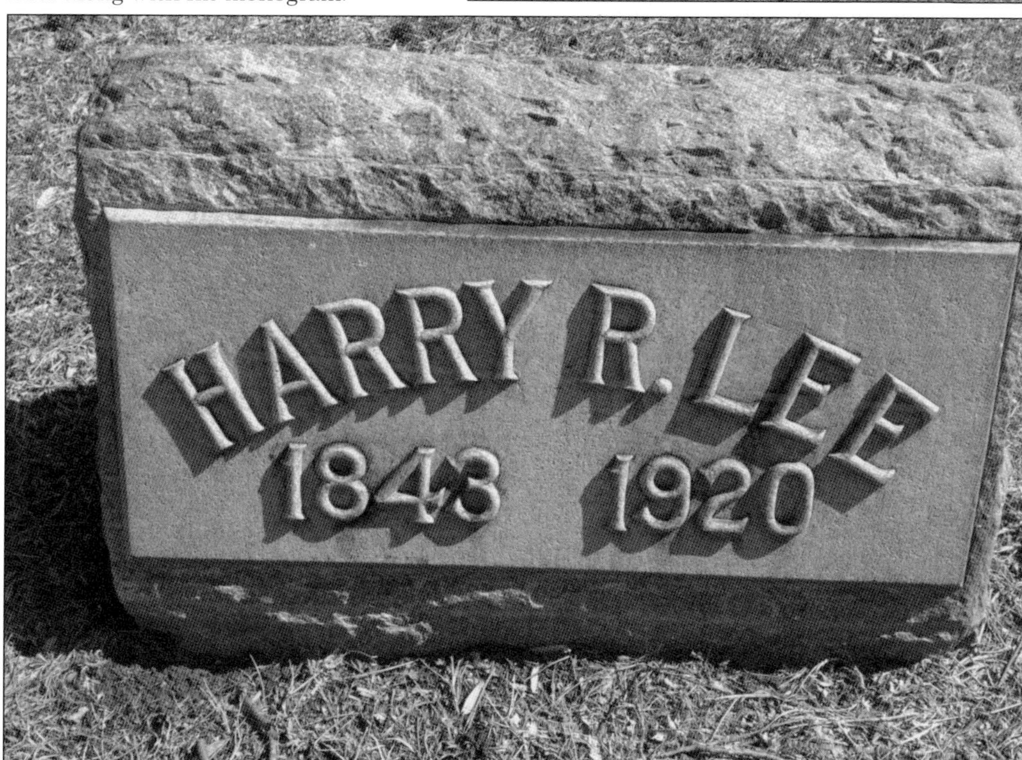

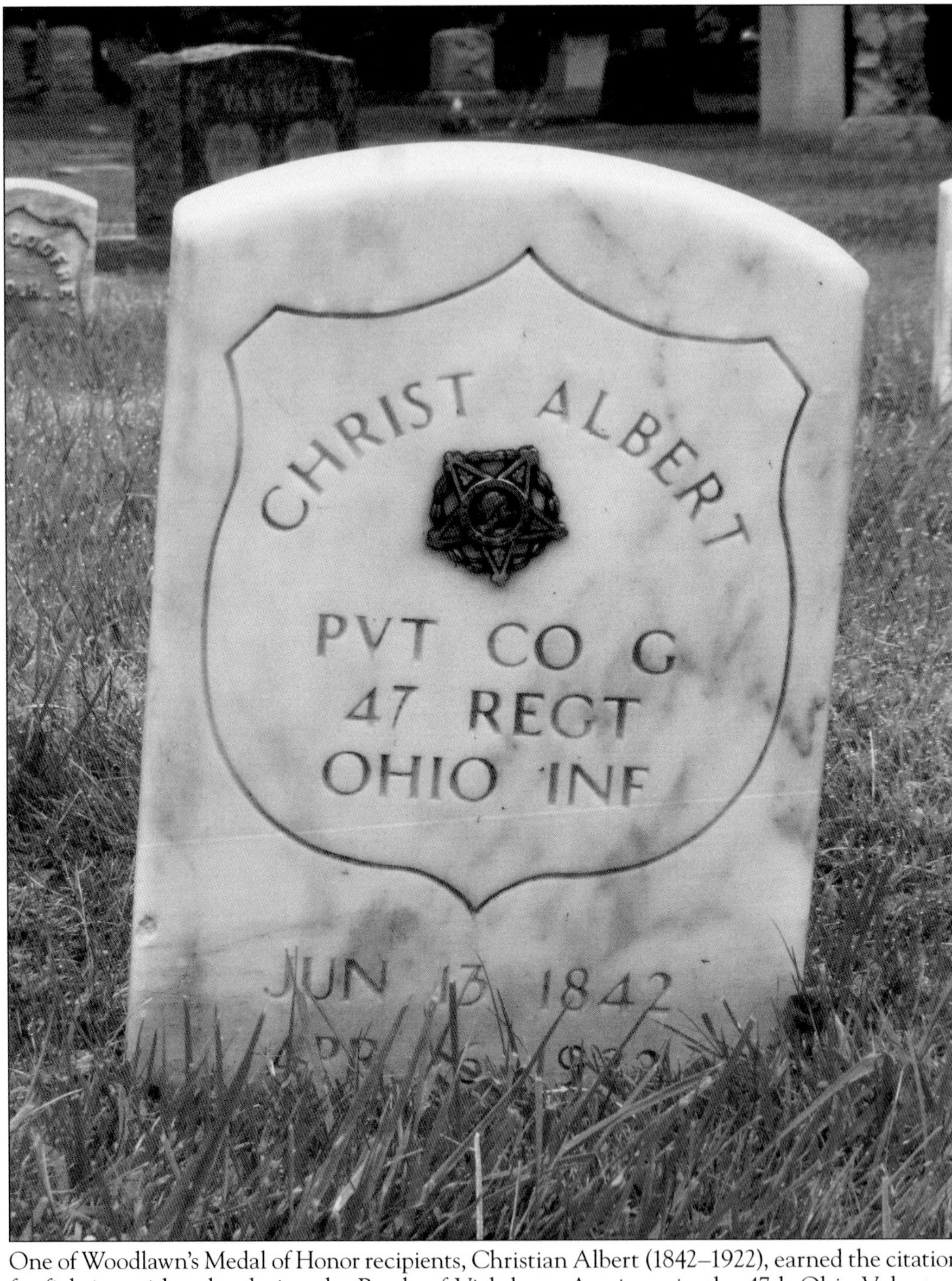

One of Woodlawn's Medal of Honor recipients, Christian Albert (1842–1922), earned the citation for fighting with valor during the Battle of Vicksburg. A private in the 47th Ohio Volunteer Infantry, Albert participated in a suicide mission, along with 150 other unmarried men, to divert enemy fire. One of the few survivors, Albert received his medal 32 years later for "gallantry in the charge of the volunteer storming party." Today, this government-issued Civil War–era headstone marks his gravesite. (DB.)

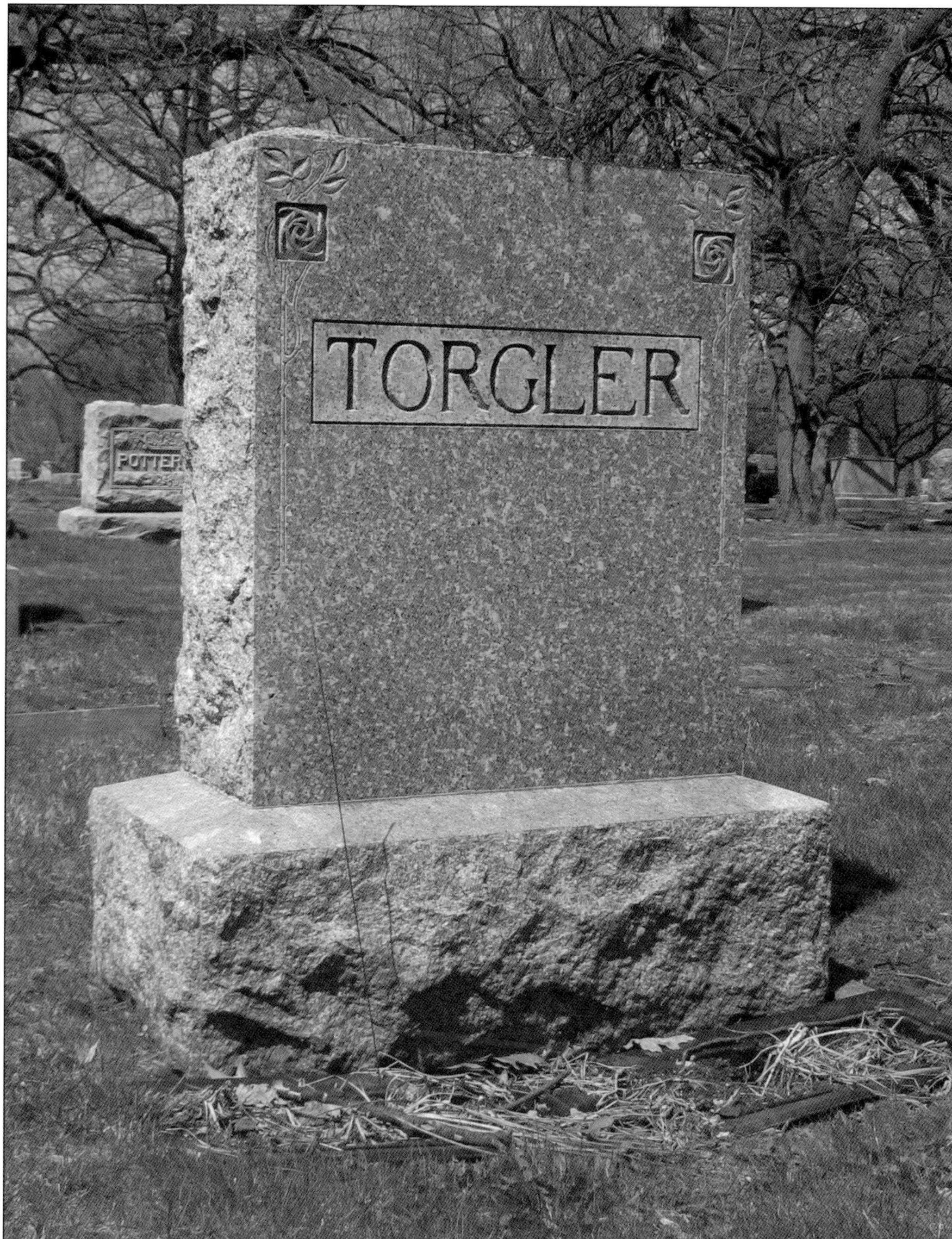

At great risk to himself, Sgt. Ernst R. Torgler saved the life of his wounded commander at the Battle of Ezra Church during the siege of Atlanta. For this heroic deed, Torgler received the Congressional Medal of Honor. German born, Torgler (1840–1923) served his adopted country as a member of the 37th Ohio Volunteer Infantry. The Medal of Honor was first proposed by an act of Congress during the Civil War. Christian Albert and Ernst Torgler are two of the earliest recipients of this medal, which honors the bravest of the brave.

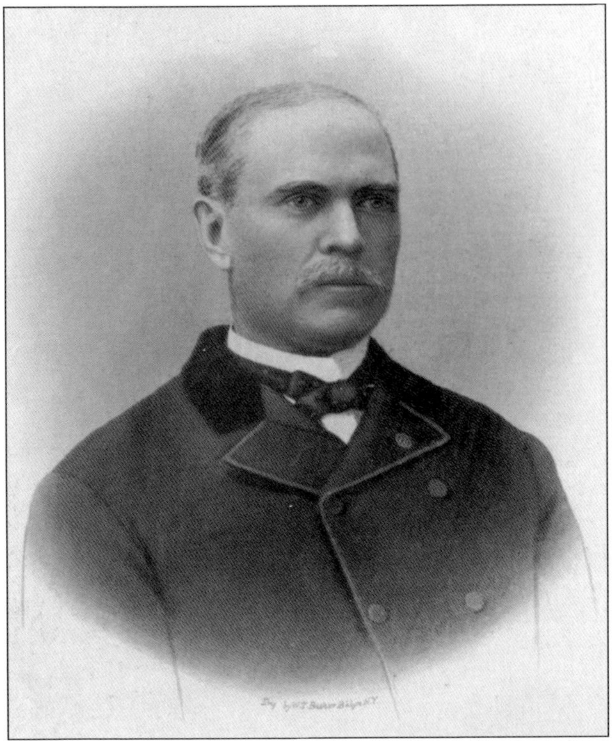

A newspaper editor and politician, Isaac R. Sherwood (1835–1925) served as an officer in the US Army during the Civil War. Later, he was elected to the US Congress for seven straight terms (1907–1921) and was the last Civil War veteran to serve in the US House of Representatives. At the start of World War I, his pacifist views made him very unpopular. Ohioans considered his beliefs to be unpatriotic and turned their back on him when he ran for reelection in 1920. Today, he rests beside his wife, journalist Kate Brownlee Sherwood, under the family monument. (Left, TPL; below, DC.)

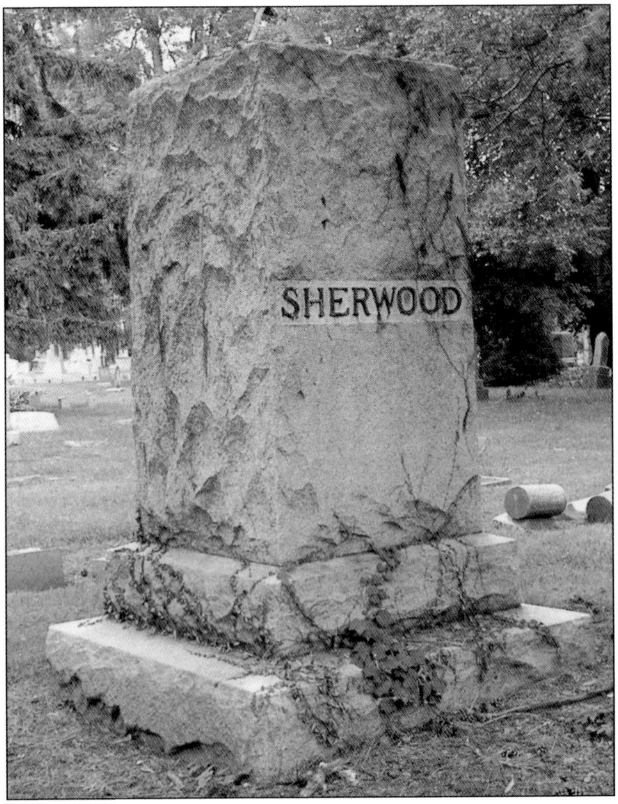

Four

The Industrialists

The United States was marked by unprecedented industrial growth during the last quarter of the 19th century and the early 20th century. As a major contributor to this development, Toledo factories began producing a multitude of items for homes, farms, and businesses, including wagons for all purposes, intricately carved glass punch bowls, and bicycles with wheels made of wire spokes.

Milburn Wagon Works, one of the world's largest and most prosperous wagon factories, was an early Toledo operation, established in 1875. Edward Libbey relocated his glass-manufacturing plant to Toledo in 1888 and spurred so much interest in that industry that Toledo gained the nickname "Glass Capital of the World." The DeVilbiss family contributed to the industrial growth with the manufacturing of many of their inventions, including the springless scale and the atomizer. By the 1920s, the automotive industry had a commanding influence on Toledo's economy.

Part of the success of these manufacturing businesses was due to Toledo's location on the Great Lakes. Toledo served as the northern terminus of the Miami and Erie Canal and later became a hub for several railroad companies, making the city easily accessible for travel and transportation of goods. By 1880, Toledo was the center of trade in the Midwest.

The ease with which people could reach Toledo and the increasing number of available factory jobs caused Toledo's population to surge. Eager to escape tyrannical rulers, poverty, and the lack of opportunities in their homeland, vast numbers of immigrants came to Toledo from southern and eastern European countries during this period. These newcomers embraced the democratic ideals of their adopted country, worked in the factories, and lived nearby, creating a sprawling urban landscape in Toledo.

In true democratic style, Woodlawn Cemetery was open to anyone who could afford a plot. Many of these factory workers and their families were laid to rest with simple headstones to mark their graves alongside the grand mausoleums and massive monuments erected for Toledo's captains of industry.

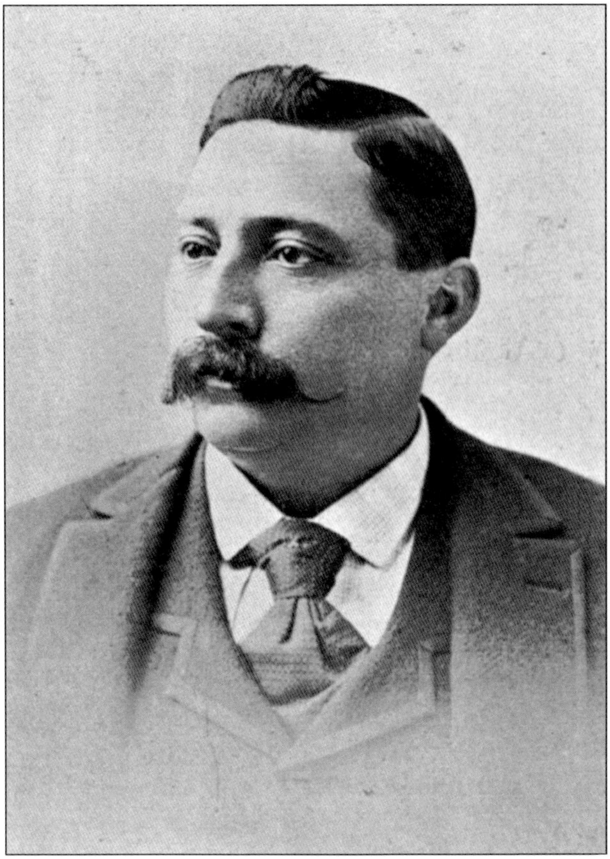

As a young man, John J. Huebner (1854–1910) learned the art of brewing under his father's guidance and while training at famous breweries in Germany. Upon his return to America, he became the brewmaster of Lenk's Brewery, a well-known Toledo firm. Later, he established the Huebner Brewing Company, a merger of several local breweries. (JM.)

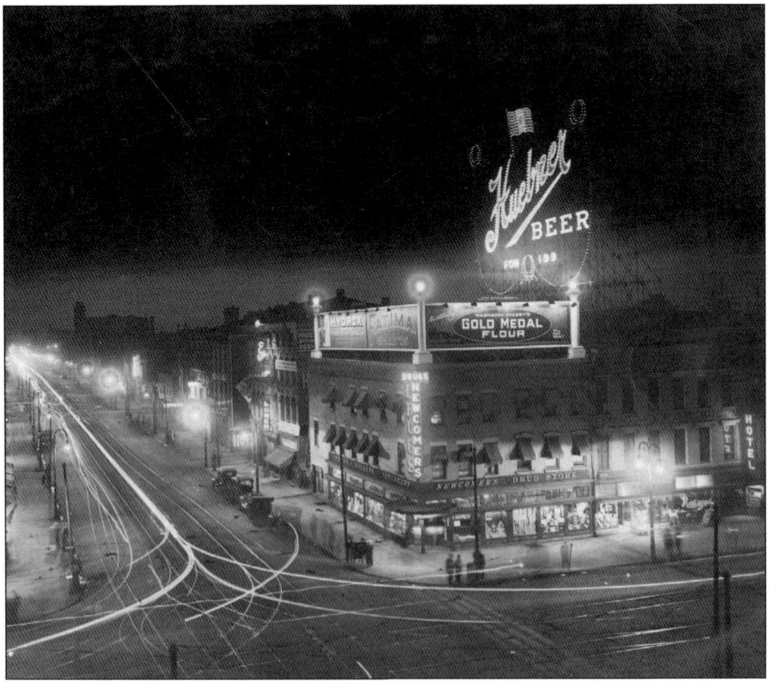

The Heubner Brewing Company became the largest brewing operation in Northwest Ohio. Prominent advertisements such as the one at this intersection were familiar sights around Toledo. Another advertising tactic was the use of the slogan "Pure Without Drugs or Poison," embossed on Huebner-Toledo beer bottles, most likely in response to those pushing for prohibition. (TPL.)

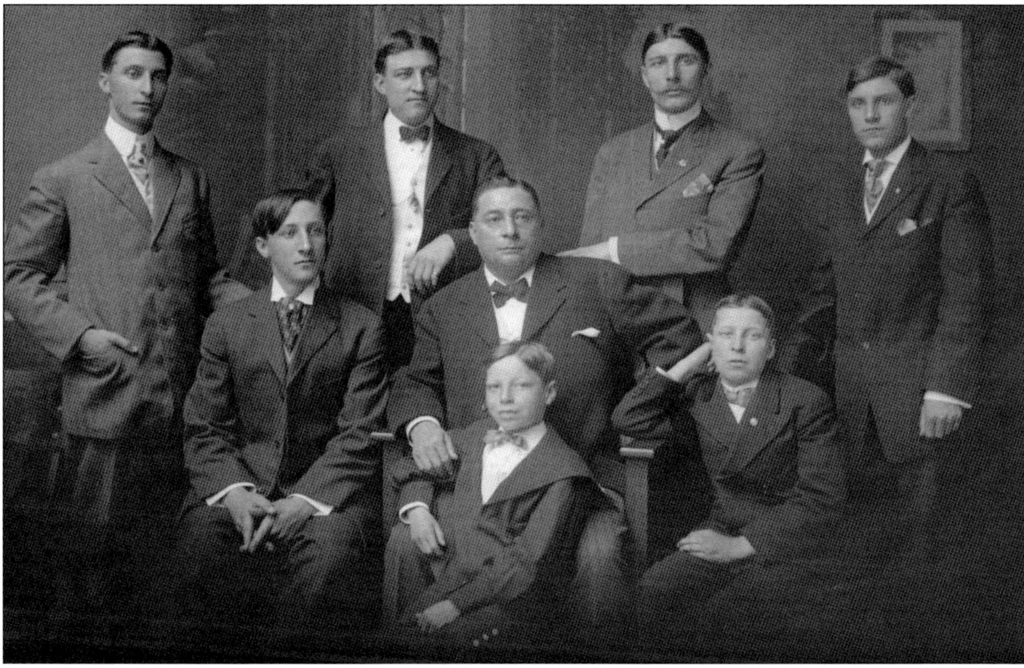

John Huebner and his wife, Catherine, were the parents of 11 children. Huebner is surrounded by seven of his sons in this photograph taken at his 50th birthday celebration. Many of these young men joined the business as brewmasters. They continued to successfully run the family brewery for several years, but the contentious 18th Amendment, instituting Prohibition, caused the Huebner Brewery to close its doors forever in 1921. (JM.)

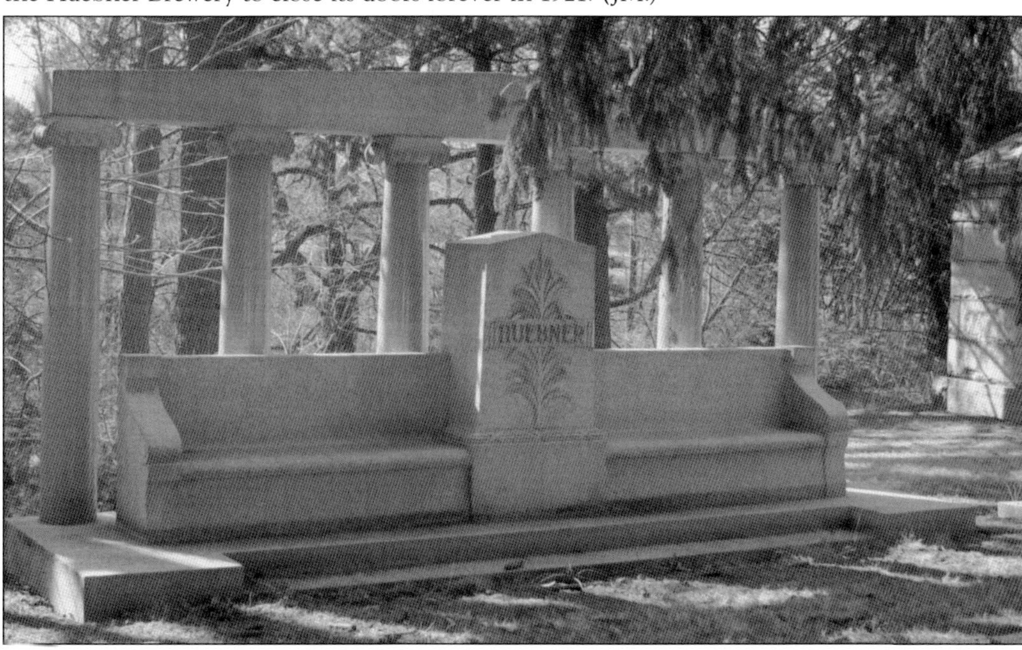

With six columns forming the backdrop, this stately monument features the Huebner name on the central tablet. John Huebner is buried at this site, along with his wife, several of his children, and other family members.

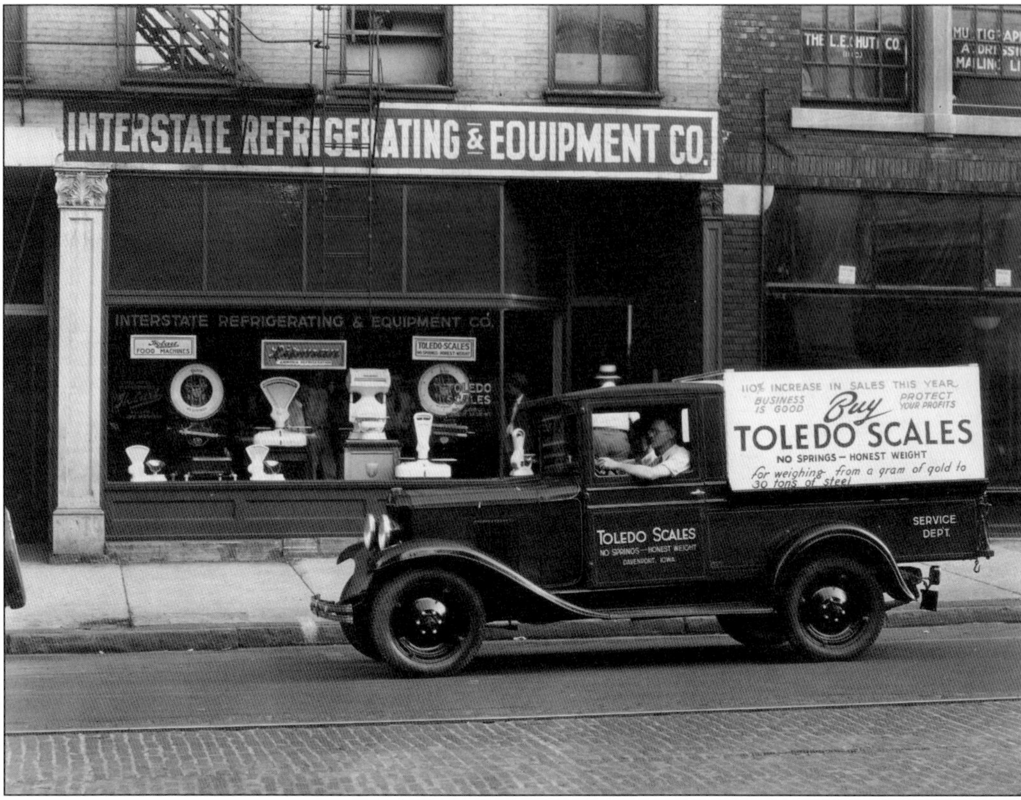

A Toledo businessman and inventor, Allen DeVilbiss Jr. (1873–1911) developed and patented the springless pendulum scale. His invention resulted in the establishment, in 1897, of the DeVilbiss Computing Scale Company. Within a few years, the company was purchased by the Toledo Computing Scale & Cash Register Company, of which DeVilbiss was the factory manager. This company, whose familiar slogan was "No Springs, Honest Weight," sold its product to markets around the world. The name "Toledo" was prominently featured on the front of each scale. (Above, TPL.)

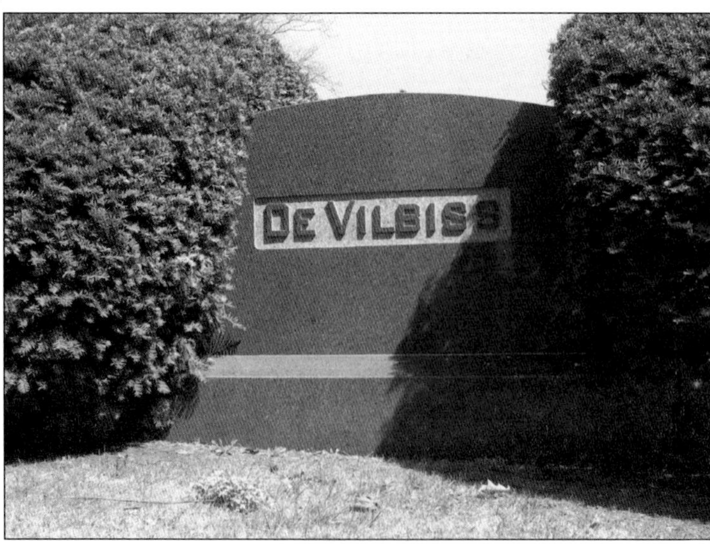

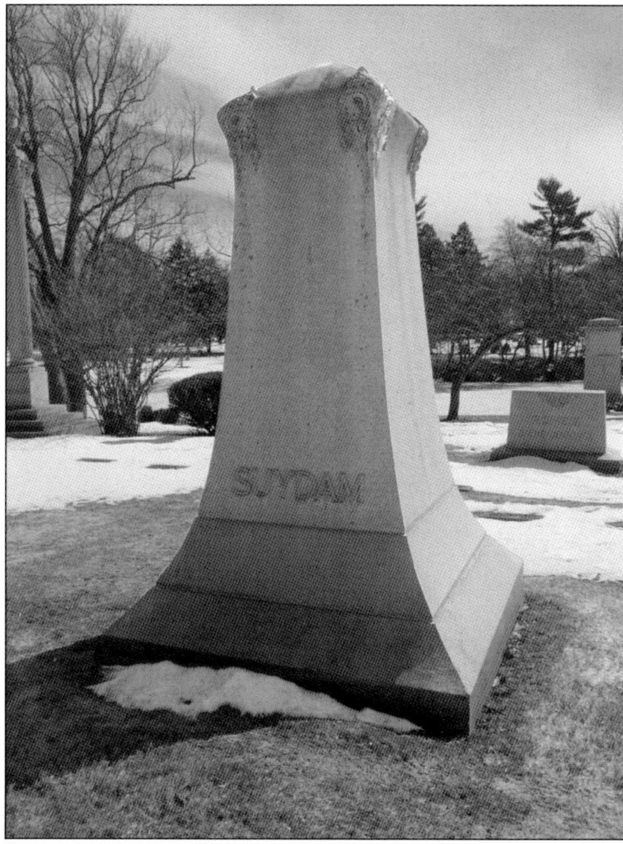

In his 40 years of commercial life, Frank D. Suydam (1845–1911) is said to have employed more workers than any other man in Toledo. A tireless worker, he was president of both the Milburn Wagon Works (pictured below), the first modern factory in Toledo, employing more than 700 workers, and the Toledo Bending Company. (Below, TPL.)

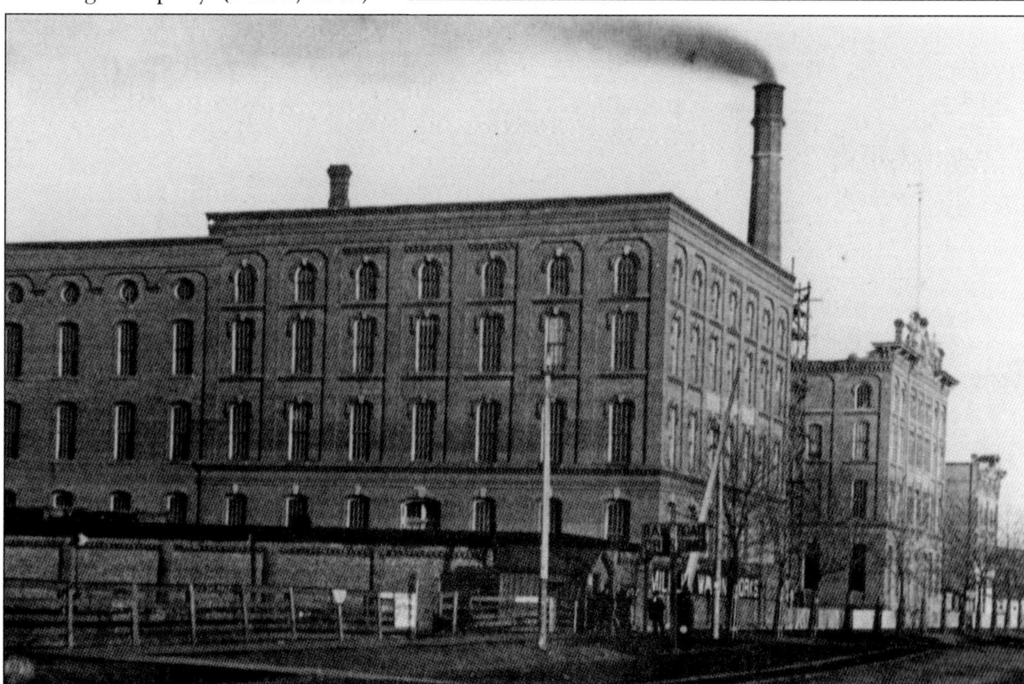

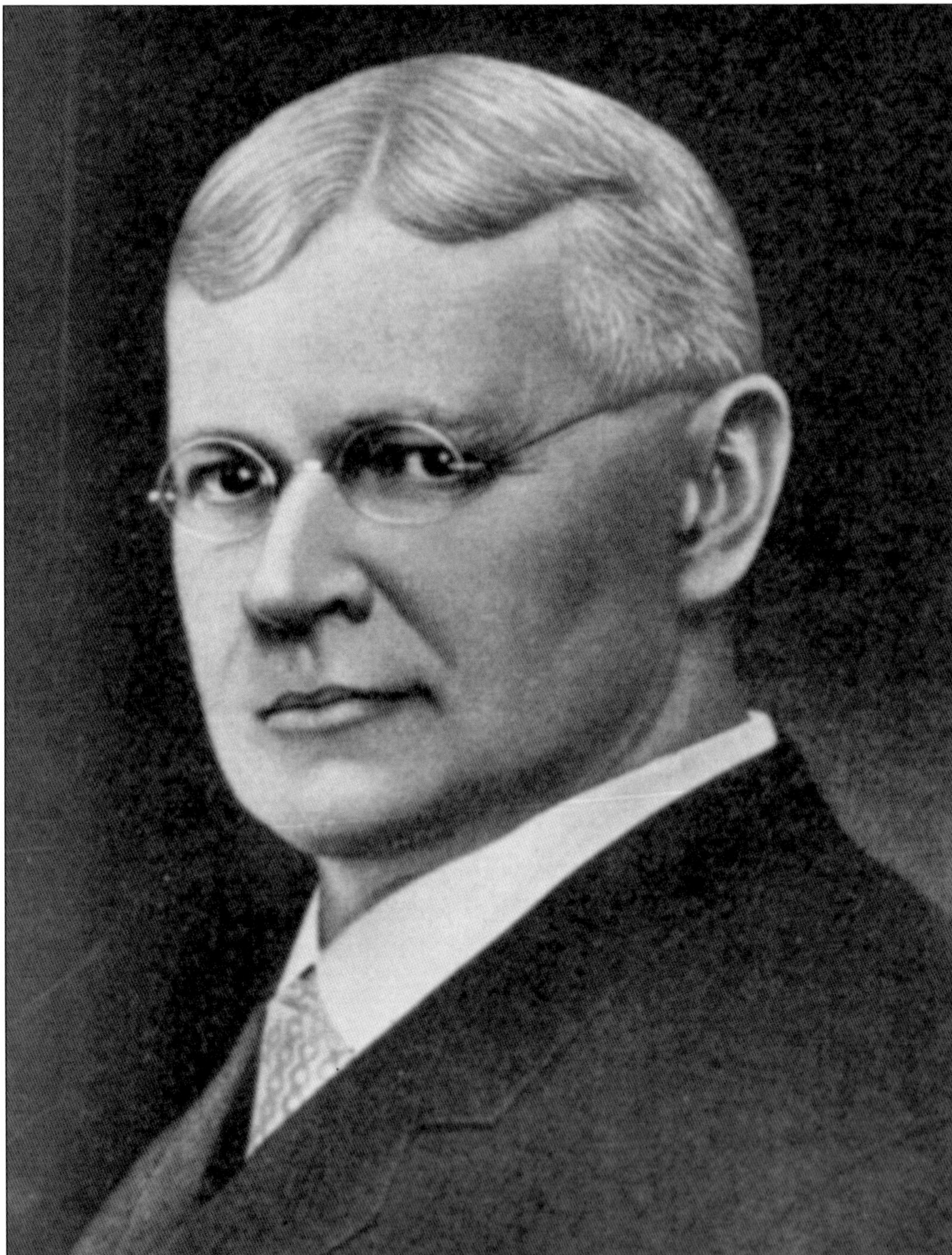

A mechanical engineer and inventor, Irving W. Colburn (1861–1917) was a pioneer in the glass industry. He established the Colburn Machine Glass Company in 1906. The firm worked on flat-glass technology, but was bankrupt by 1911. Colburn joined the Toledo Glass Company in 1912 when it bought his patents. Along with partner Michael Owens, Colburn developed a process for the production of flat glass. The Libbey-Owens Sheet Glass Company revolutionized the sheet-glass industry. (TPL.)

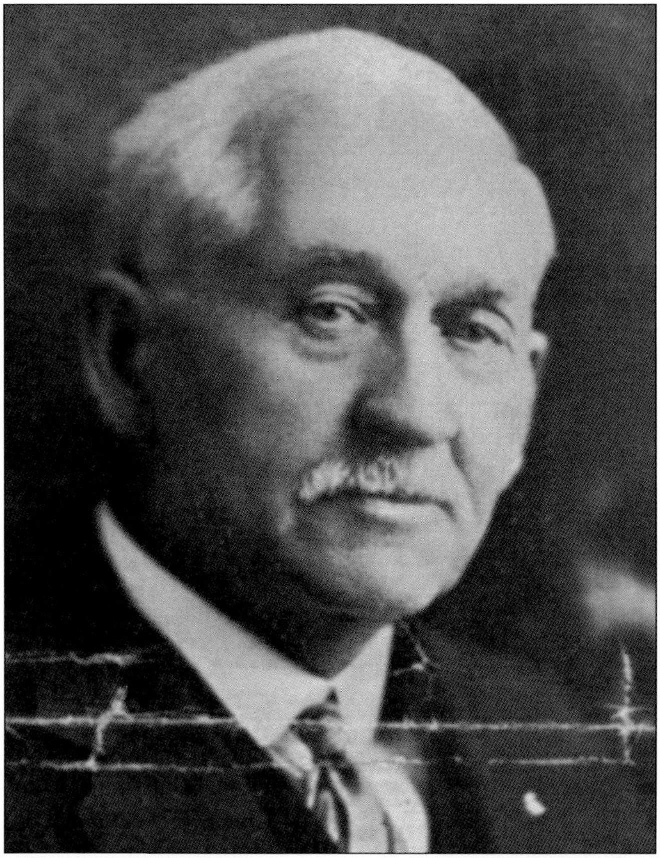

Dr. Allen DeVilbiss Sr. (1840–1917), the area's first ear, nose, and throat specialist, was also an inventor who perfected and patented a spray atomizer that provided an easier and more sanitary way to apply medicated oils to his patients' throats. It was later used for other applications as well. His invention was so lucrative that he was able to discontinue his medical practice. In 1888, he founded the DeVilbiss Manufacturing Company. DeVilbiss's sons, Thomas and Allen Jr., followed in their father's footsteps as successful inventors and Toledo businessmen. (Right, TPL; below, CAC.)

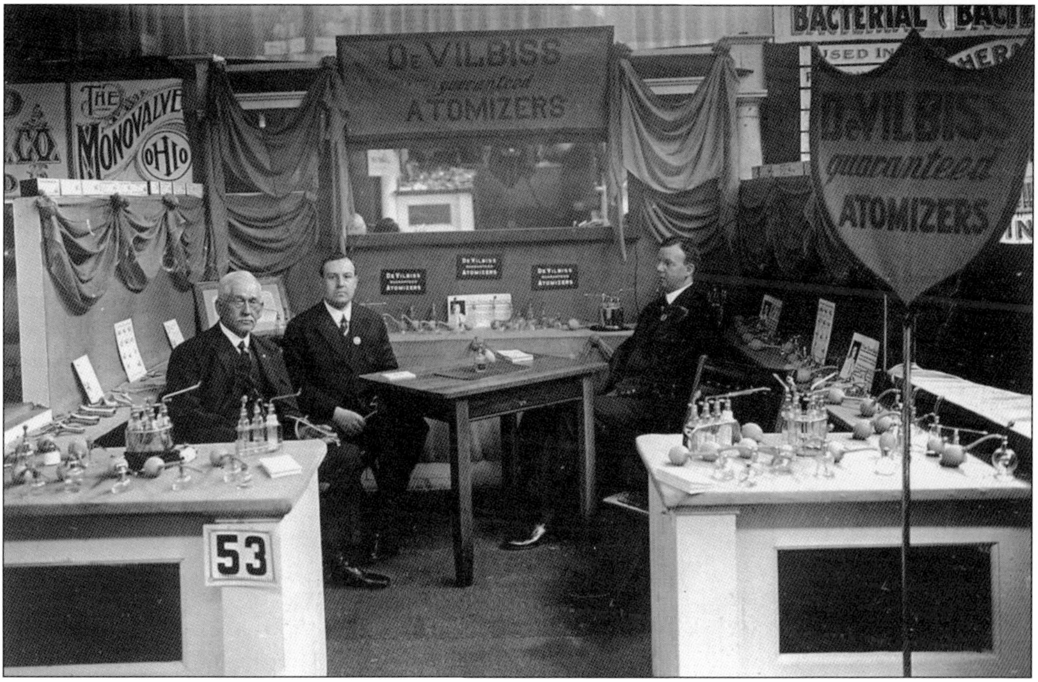

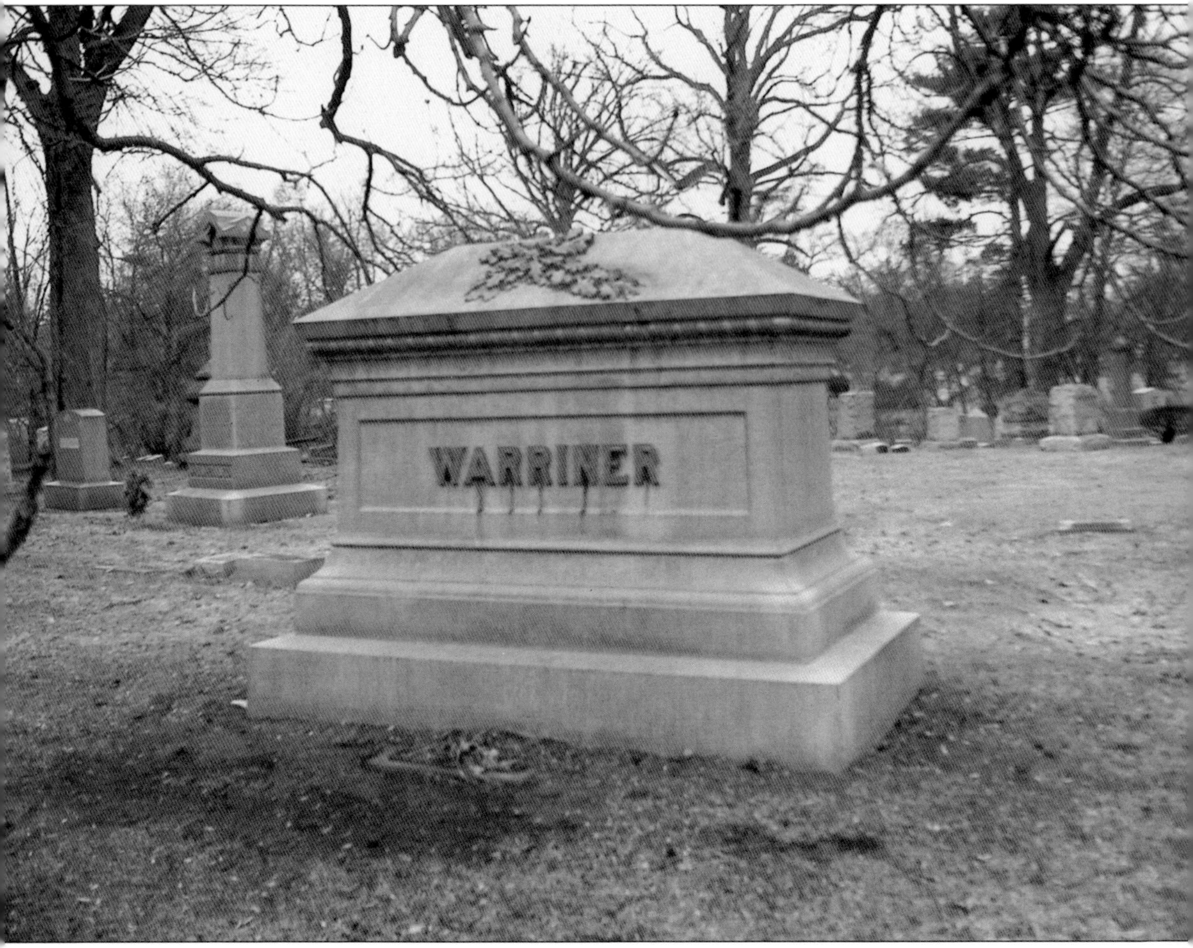

The Warriner Monument features a cross designed with intricately hand-carved oak leaves, symbolizing strength and endurance. It commemorates the lives of Harrison Arms, Reuben Warriner, and their family members. The two mens' burial together in the Warriner family plot honors their deep friendship.

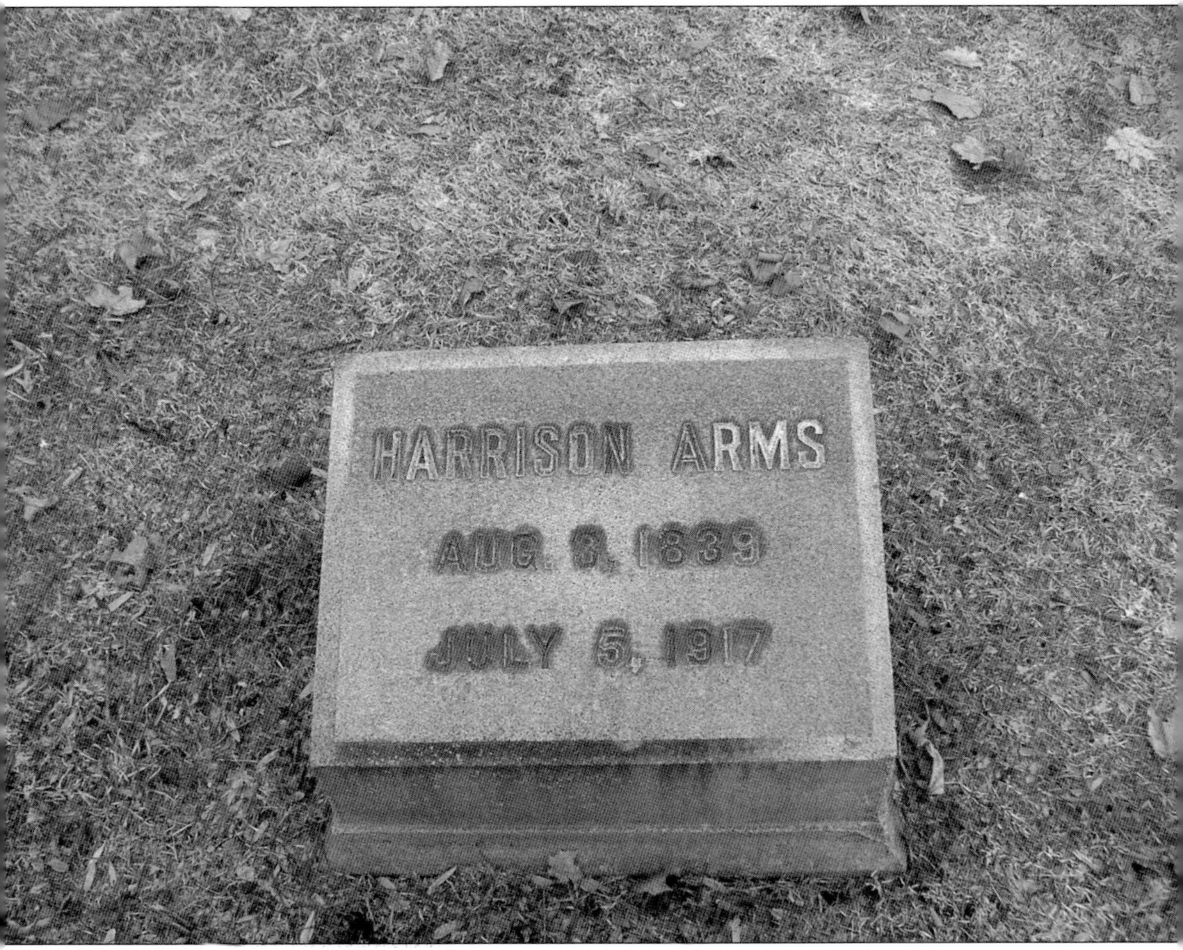

Harrison Arms ran a sizable sale, livery, and coach stables, with room for 65 horses, on St. Clair Street in Toledo near the city center for many years. Arms is credited with patenting a railway transport car for thoroughbred horses while living in Toledo. Based on this and his other innovations, he established and served as president of the Arms Palace Horsecar Company in Chicago, which, according to his obituary, resulted in great personal wealth. Arms was nationally known throughout the horse world. Upon his death, his body was cremated in Detroit, and his ashes were buried at Woodlawn Cemetery.

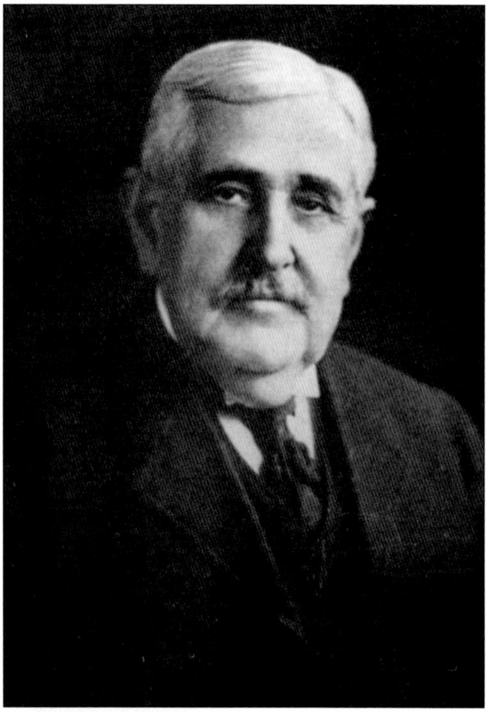

At the start of his business career, Edward Ford (1843–1920) worked as a clerk on a steamboat for several years. Later he went into the glass industry, working for various companies, and was involved in the development of several plate-glass factories. He finally built his own plant on 173 acres of farmland on the Maumee River. It included the most modern machinery and appliances available. Upon the construction of the world's largest plate-glass factory in 1898, Ford became a leader in Toledo's glass industry. (BB.)

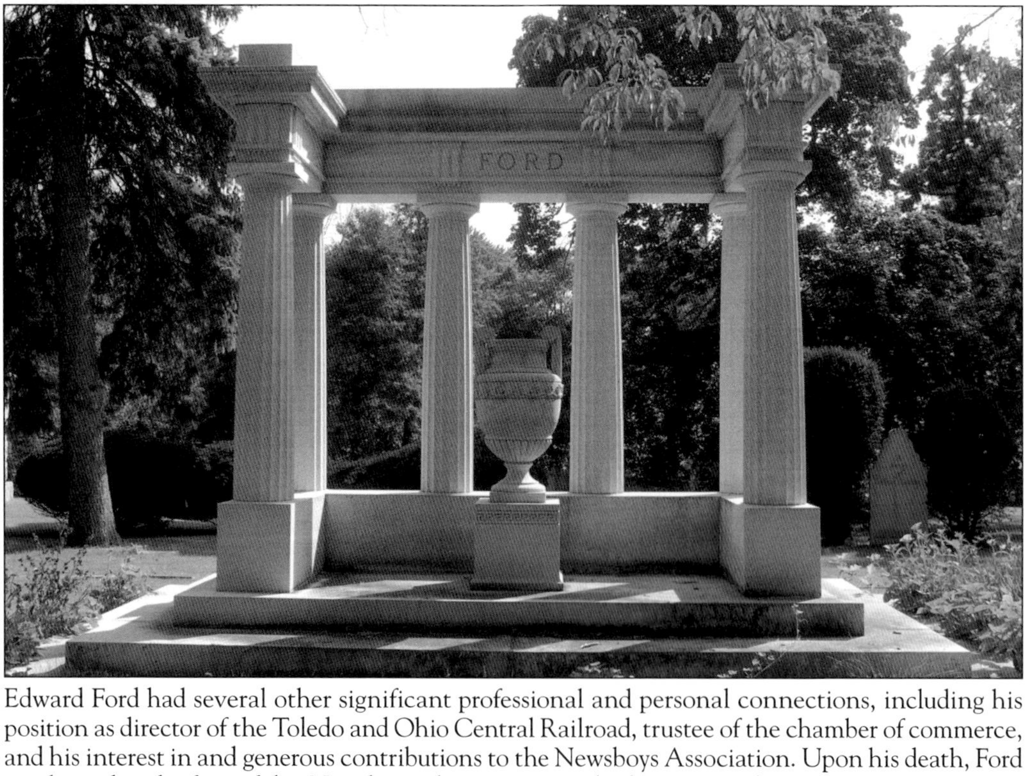

Edward Ford had several other significant professional and personal connections, including his position as director of the Toledo and Ohio Central Railroad, trustee of the chamber of commerce, and his interest in and generous contributions to the Newsboys Association. Upon his death, Ford was buried at the foot of this Neoclassical monument, which serves as the memorial for Ford and his family. A colonnade of imposing granite frames the large urn that sits on a pedestal. (GLF.)

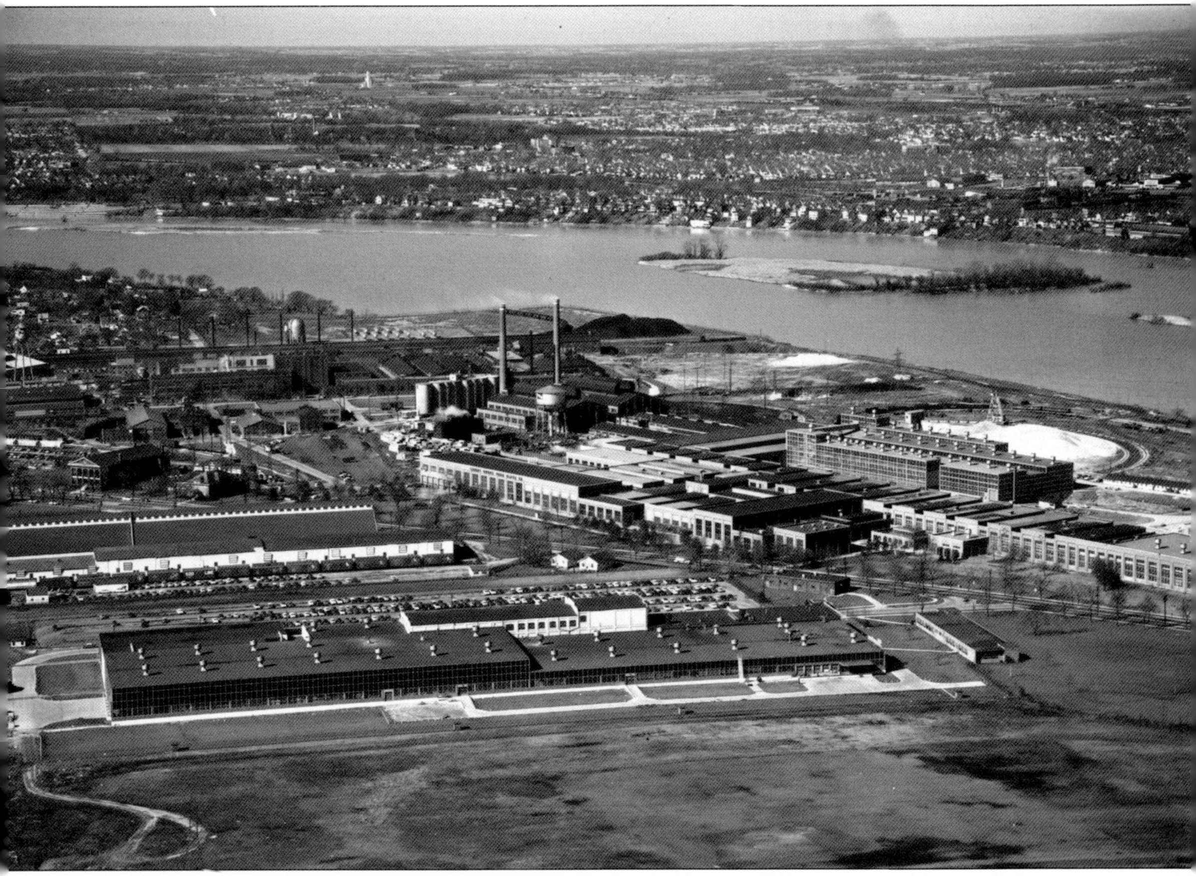

Surrounding his plate-glass factory, Edward Ford also built a model company town with housing and services for his workers, many of whom had formerly worked with Ford at other glass plants. The construction of model company towns by more enlightened industrialists during the late 19th century ensured that the surrounding village developed in a sanitary and uncongested manner. In addition to other amenities, Ford constructed the Ford Club, which was used as a place for his workers and their families to meet and socialize. He named his new town Rossford, a combination of his wife, Caroline Jane Ross's, maiden name and his own. For years, Ford's presence was felt throughout the town, as he was often seen walking through the village, stopping in at the shops and sharing a friendly greeting with residents. (TPL.)

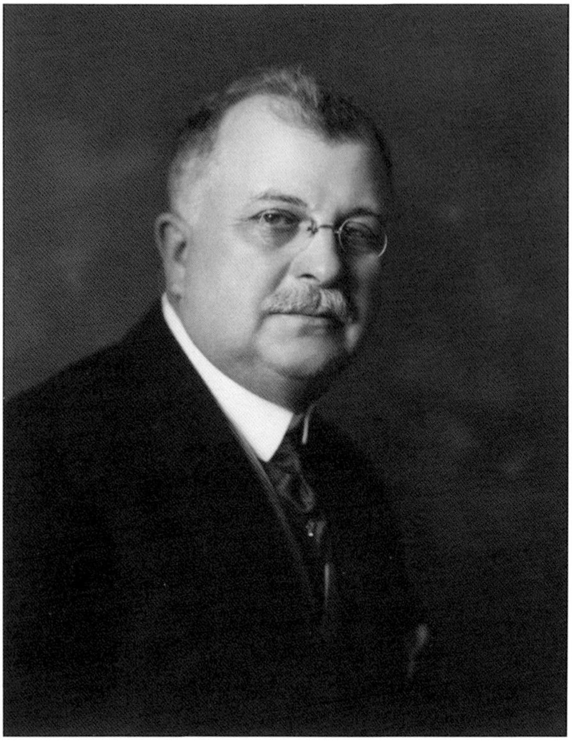

Edward Drummond Libbey (1854–1925), a glass industry pioneer, moved his company from Massachusetts to Toledo in 1888. The company struggled in the early years, but its glass exhibition at the Chicago World's Fair in 1893 allowed the Libbey Glass Company to gain international recognition. Gradually, his success and work with innovator Michael Owens resulted in the creation of several glass businesses, including the Libbey-Owens Sheet Glass Company, allowing Toledo to gain the title "Glass Capital of the World." (BB.)

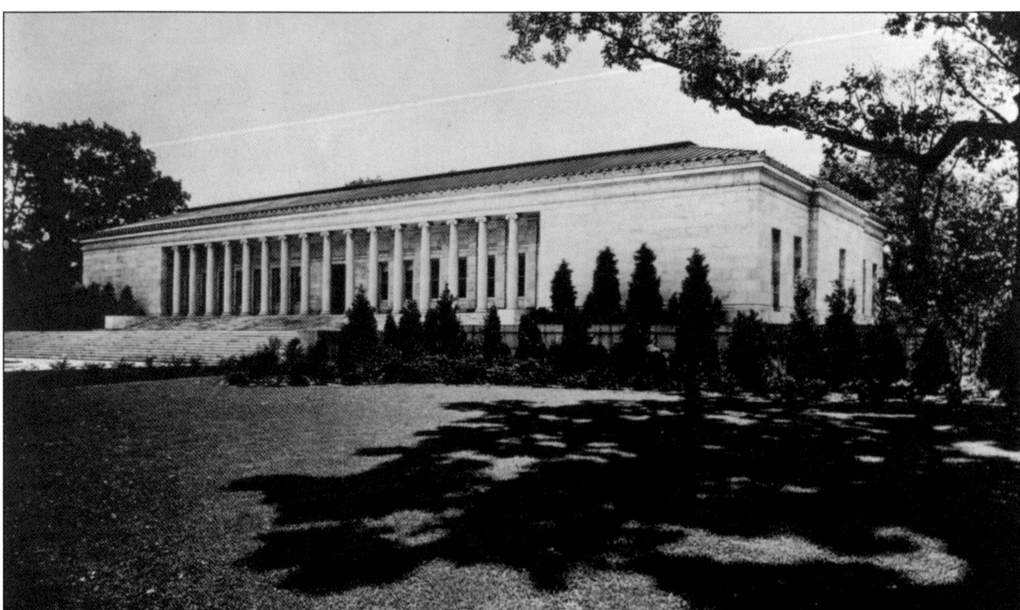

In 1901, Edward Libbey founded what became a first-rate art museum. Libbey and his wife, Florence, frequently traveled to Europe and Africa, visiting museums and collecting artifacts to exhibit in Toledo. In keeping with his belief that the museum should benefit all, rather than only members of the upper class, Libbey promoted a catalog of art and music study for the masses. Additionally, he insisted that the new institution be named for Toledo rather than for himself, as others suggested. To this day, the Toledo Museum of Art maintains its world-class status. (TMA.)

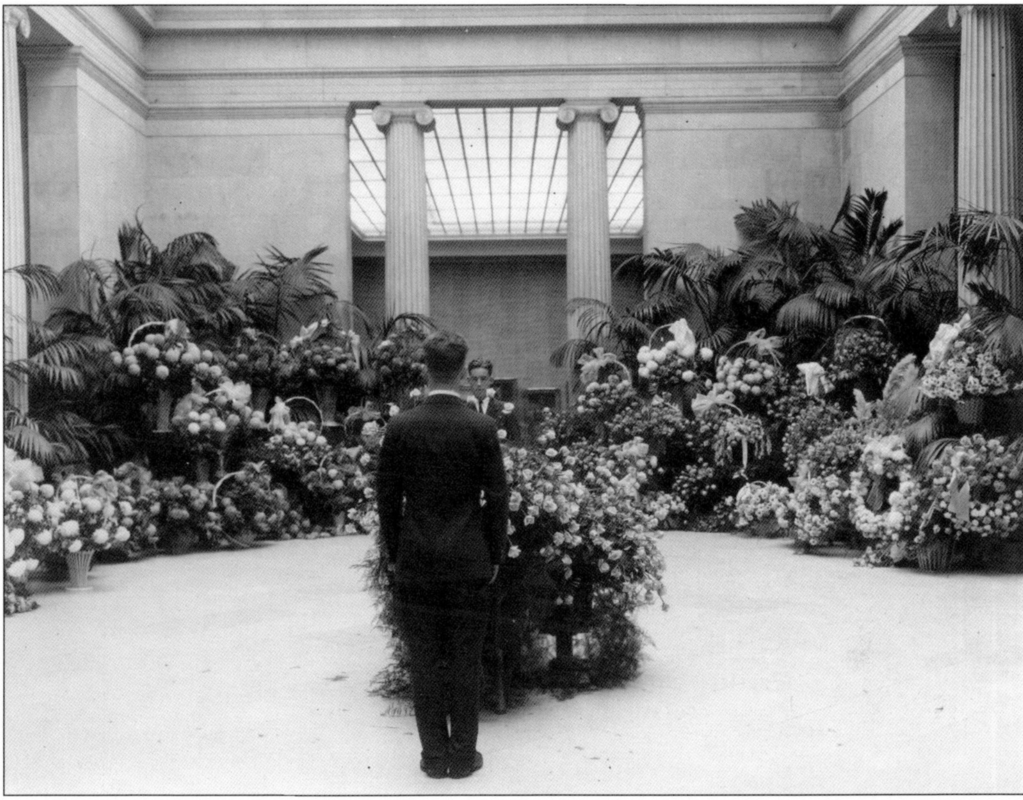

Upon his death, Edward Libbey's coffin was placed in the Sculpture Court of the Toledo Museum of Art, where thousands of mourners passed by to pay their final respects prior to his burial. (TMA.)

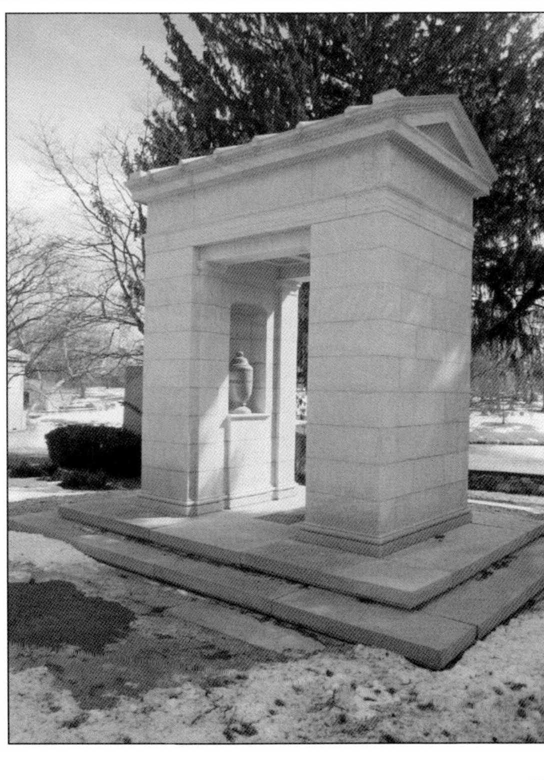

Libbey, his wife, Florence Scott Libbey, and their only son, William, all rest at this Lloyd Brothers monument in view of the cemetery's lake. Matching urns sit within alcoves on opposite sides of the memorial, where the Libbeys' monograms can be found high up on the wall.

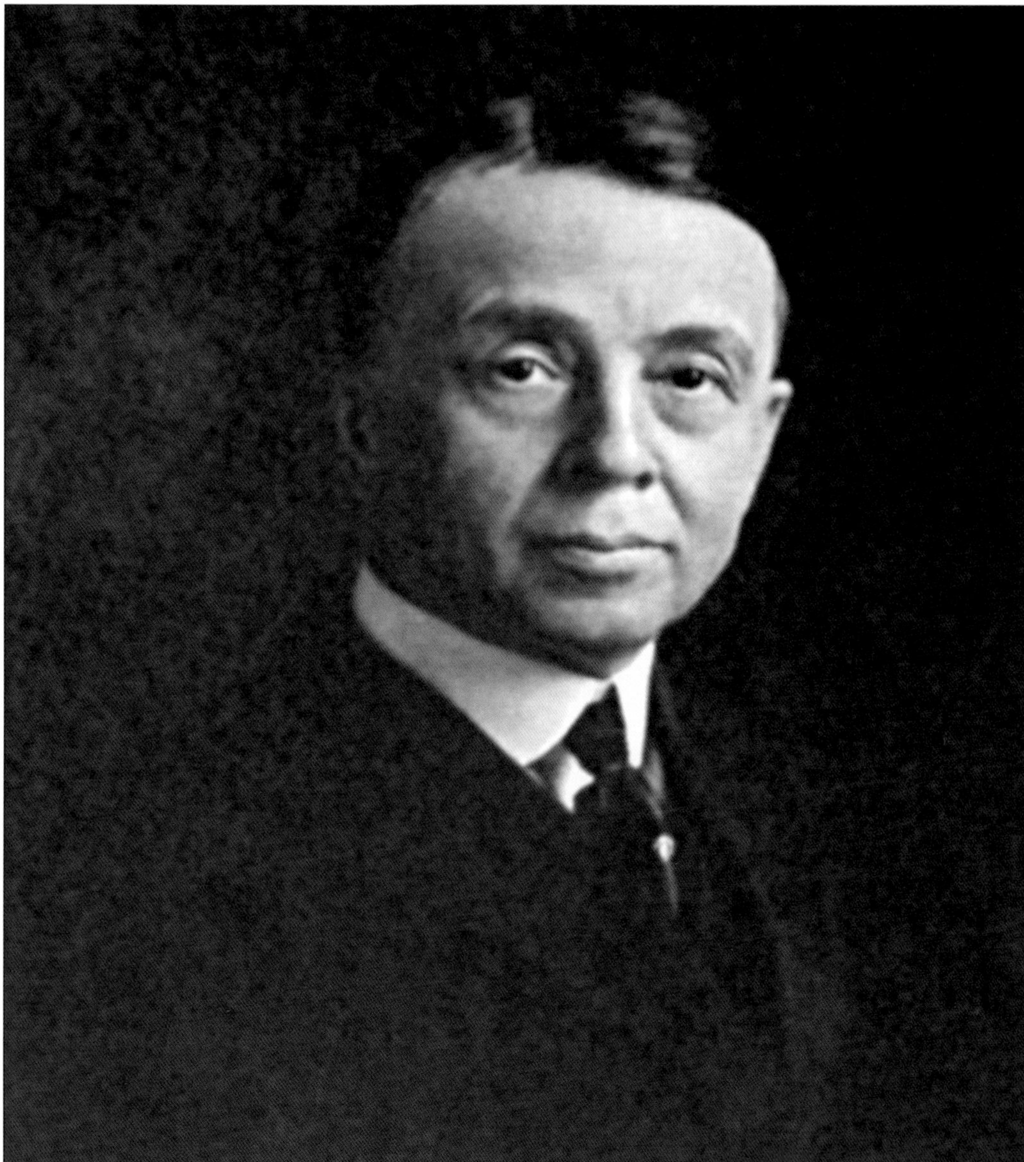

George Butler Storer (1866–1920), founder and president of the Standard Steel Tube Company, also served as the secretary of the Toledo Chamber of Commerce. Under his strong leadership, the chamber increased its support of local charities, educational programs, and civic activities. Camp Storer, a summer camp in Michigan, was named in his honor because of his work with the Young Men's Christian Association and his love of nature. (STF.)

Five

Lawyers, Politicians, and Social Advocates

Toledo, as the seat of Lucas County, drew many lawyers to live and work within its boundaries. Local politicians generally came from the legal field; however, some were also newspaper editors who had strong opinions regarding individual rights, city management, and community affairs. One local lawyer, Morrison Waite, went on to serve as chief justice of the US Supreme Court for 14 years. Others served as federal, state, and local politicians in a variety of capacities. Interestingly, Toledo supported a large German-speaking population that managed to elect several German immigrants to the position of mayor during the last quarter of the 19th century.

As industrialization advanced throughout the country, enthusiasm for the remarkable achievements of this period soon became tarnished by the development of slums, poor working conditions in the factories, and other social problems. This gave rise to Progressive-era reformers and social advocates. Toledo's progressive spirit was evident in the work of several men and women who acted on their concerns for those whose lives were hindered by the excesses of "Gilded Age Grandeur." Their actions not only improved the day-to-day lives of many fellow Toledoans, but at times attracted the eyes of the nation.

One individual who gained national acclaim for the innovative programs and reforms that he instituted was John Gunckel. His great empathy for Toledo's street children prompted him to guide Toledo's newsboys and, later, those of the nation, to "do better." So beloved and respected was Gunckel at the time of his death that his hearse was escorted by his family, friends, local and state dignitaries, members of the Toledo Newsboys Association, and thousands of active and former newsboys from all over the country. The entire entourage walked the full three miles from his funeral site to his final resting place at Woodlawn Cemetery.

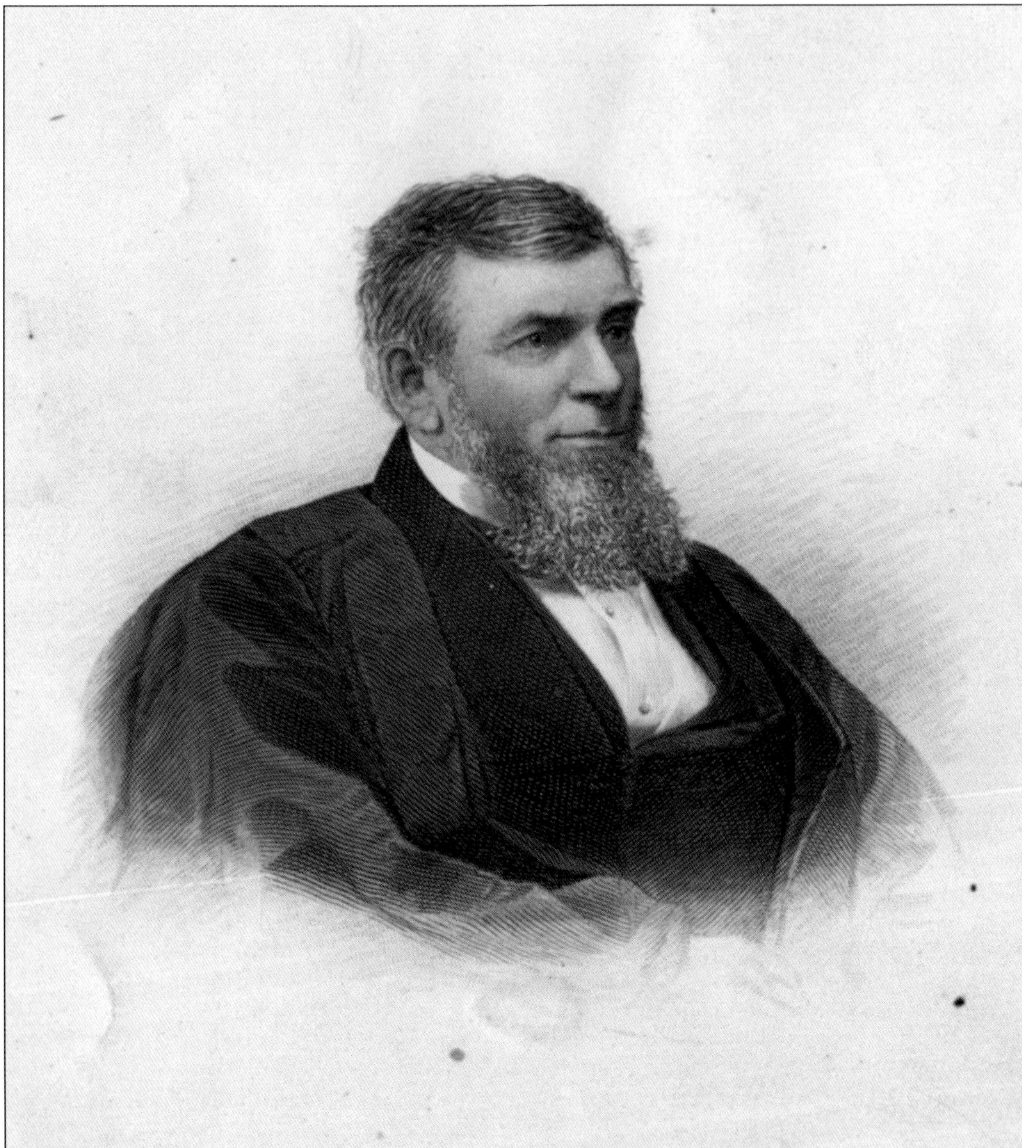

Morrison Remick Waite (1816–1888) graduated from Yale University before setting up practice as an attorney in Maumee, Ohio, and later in Toledo. After the Civil War, President Grant appointed him to serve on a three-member legal team to seek damages from Great Britain for losses of American shipping. His success led to his appointment as chief justice of the US Supreme Court in 1874, a position he held until 1888. Waite is one of only 17 men to have held the office of chief justice in the nation's history. (TPL.)

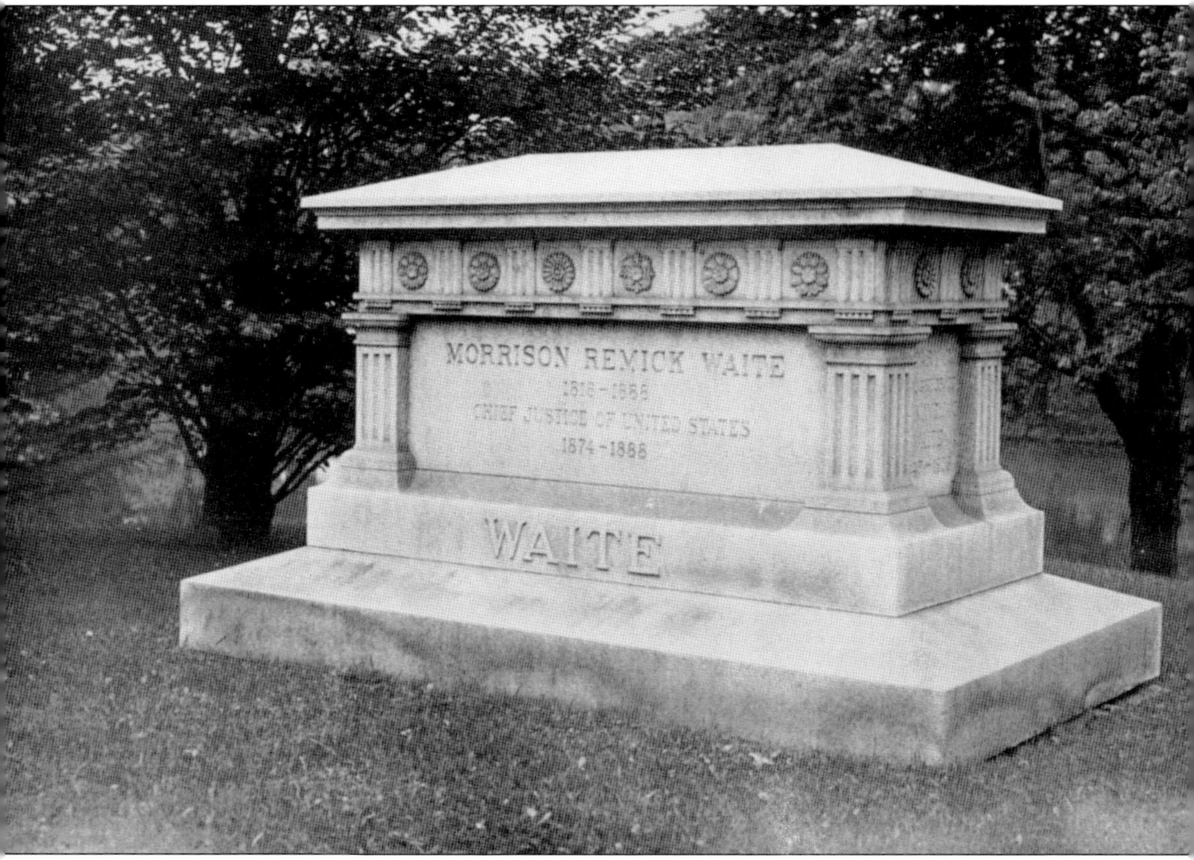

The Waite sarcophagus, designed and constructed by Lloyd Brothers, sits upon a gentle rise in Section 42. This handsome monument features a band of rosettes, each separated by three vertical bars. (WC.)

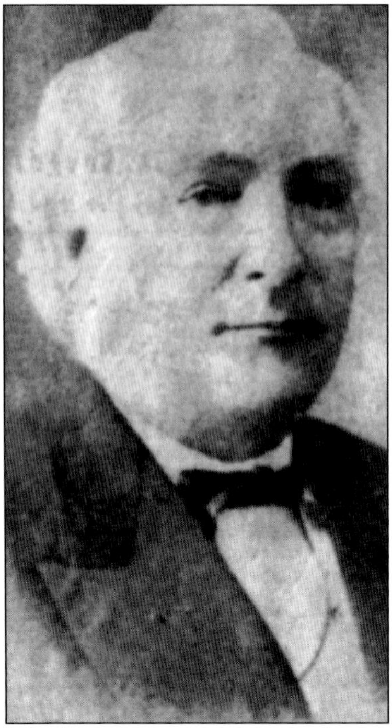

William Kraus (1813–1883) arrived in New York City from his home in Bavaria as a young man. His travels led him to Toledo, where he became a successful banker. Later, Kraus was elected to the police board. After that, he served as mayor of Toledo. (Left, TPL.)

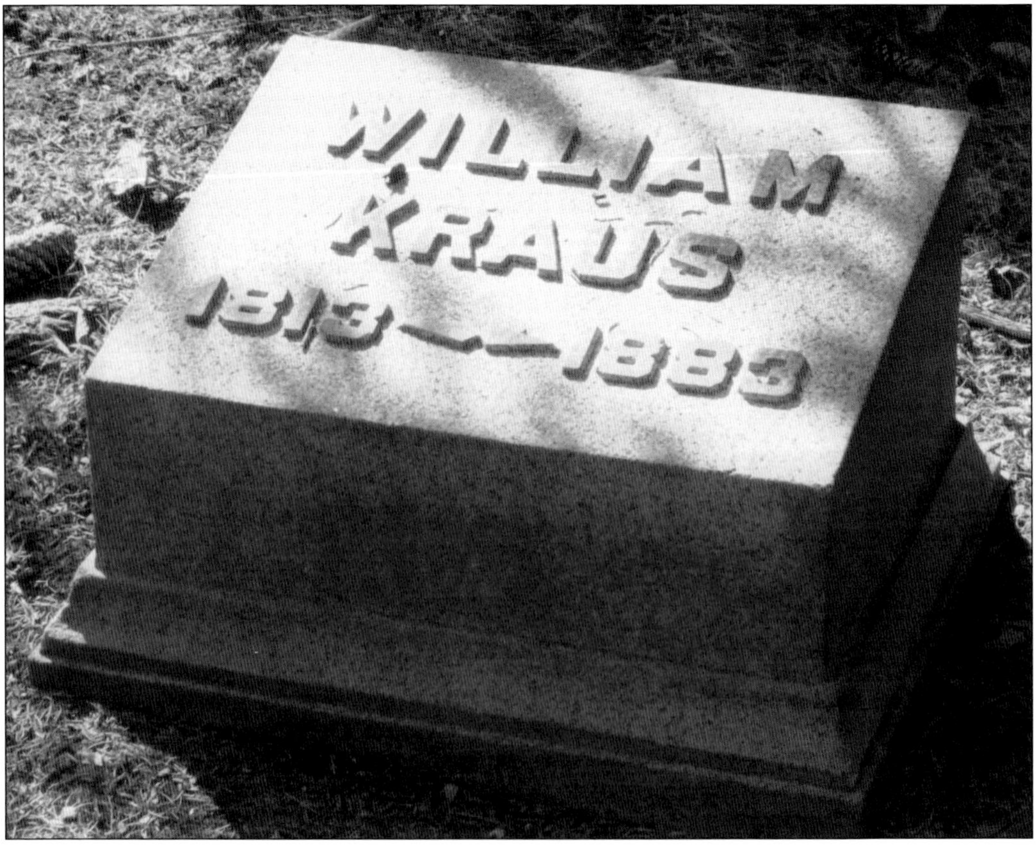

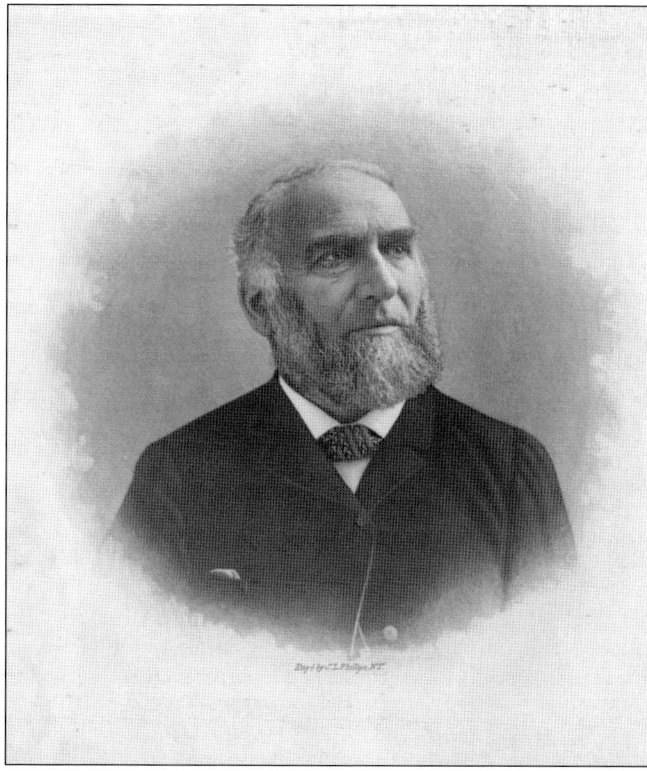

Guido Marx served as Toledo's mayor from 1875 to 1877. As a young man, Marx (1827–1899) fled from Germany when his involvement in political agitation threatened his safety. His continued interest in civic affairs allowed him to serve the public as editor of the German newspaper the *Toledo Express*. He was a police board member and a Toledo University trustee. A huge boulder marks his gravesite. (Right, TPL; below, WC.)

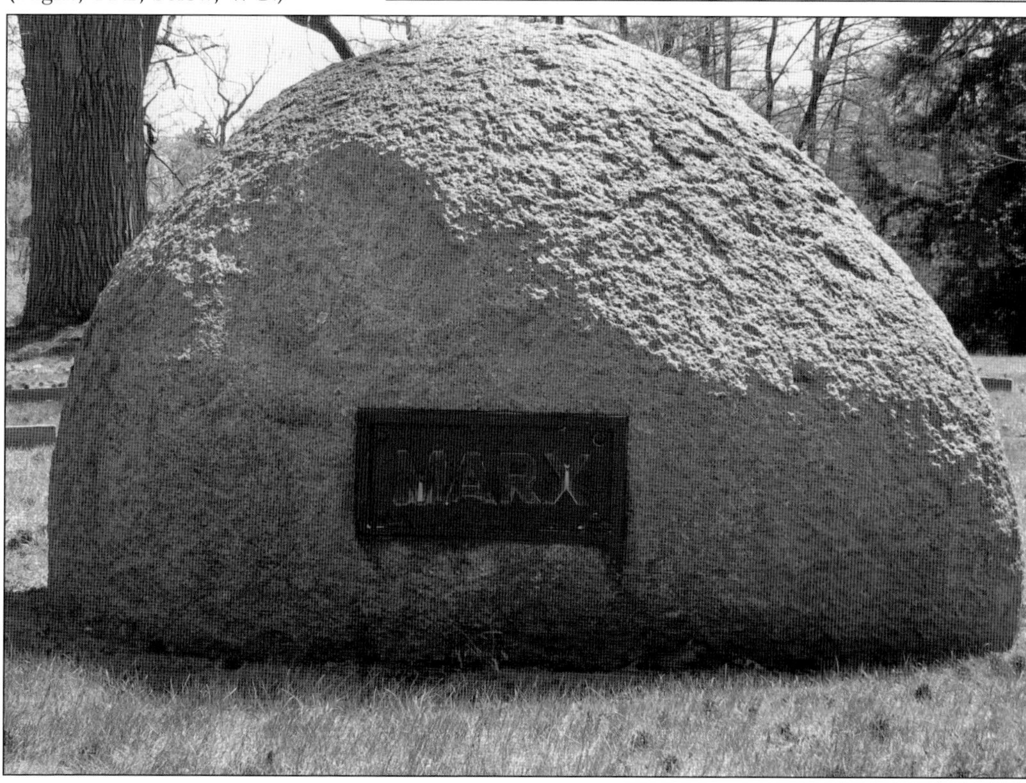

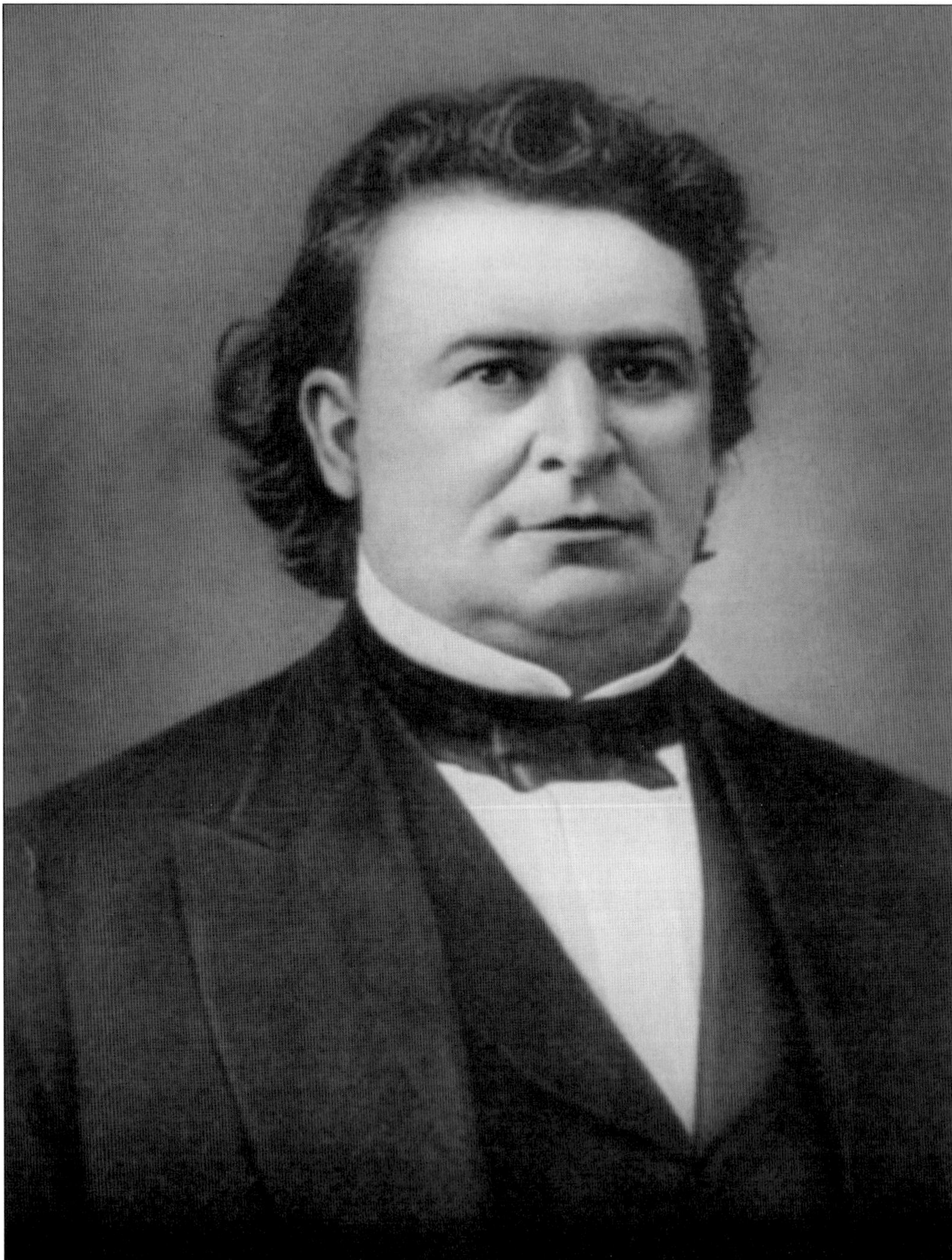

As an Ohio newspaper editor, James M. Ashley (1822–1896) advocated his strong abolitionist views. Elected to the US Congress in 1859, he fiercely promoted the abolition of slavery and was a key figure in the passage of the 13th Amendment in 1865. A close friendship developed between Ashley and President Lincoln, and Ashley served as a pallbearer at the slain president's funeral. After the Civil War, Ashley served as governor of the Montana Territory. He was president of the Toledo, Ann Arbor & Northern Railroad until his retirement in 1890. (WC.)

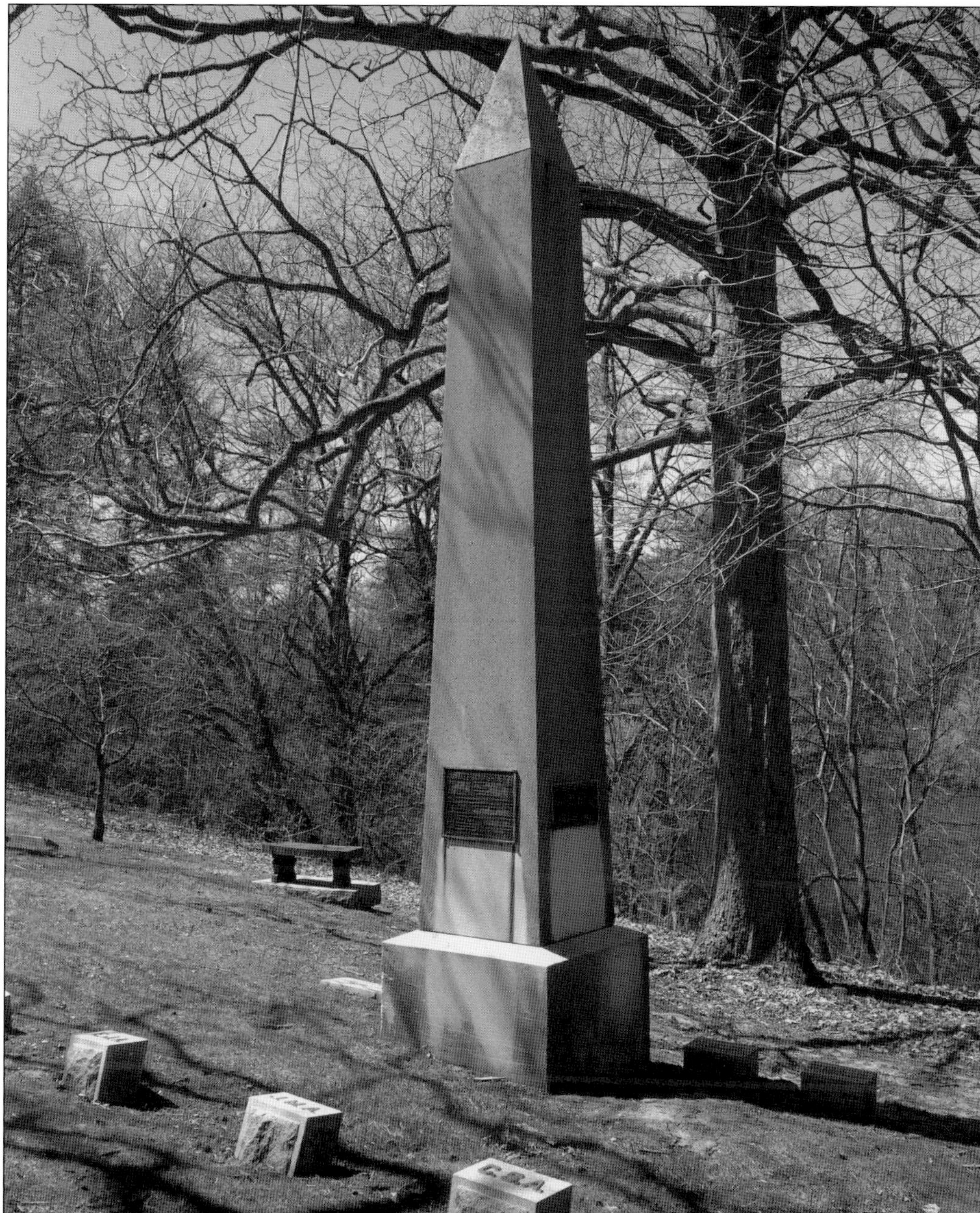

Emma S. Ashley (1836–1912) and her husband, James, settled in Toledo after fleeing from their southern Ohio home due to harassment for their abolitionist activities. Later, Emma Ashley served as the first president of the Toledo Women's Suffrage Association, the forerunner of the Toledo League of Women Voters. As president of this association, she was permitted to speak before legislative committees, stressing the need for women to have the privileges of full citizenship. On a local level, in her work with the suffrage association, she cooperated with the City of Toledo to shelter homeless girls, as many were viewed as unworthy of charitable assistance. Her gravesite lies at the foot of this obelisk, which serves as the Ashley family monument.

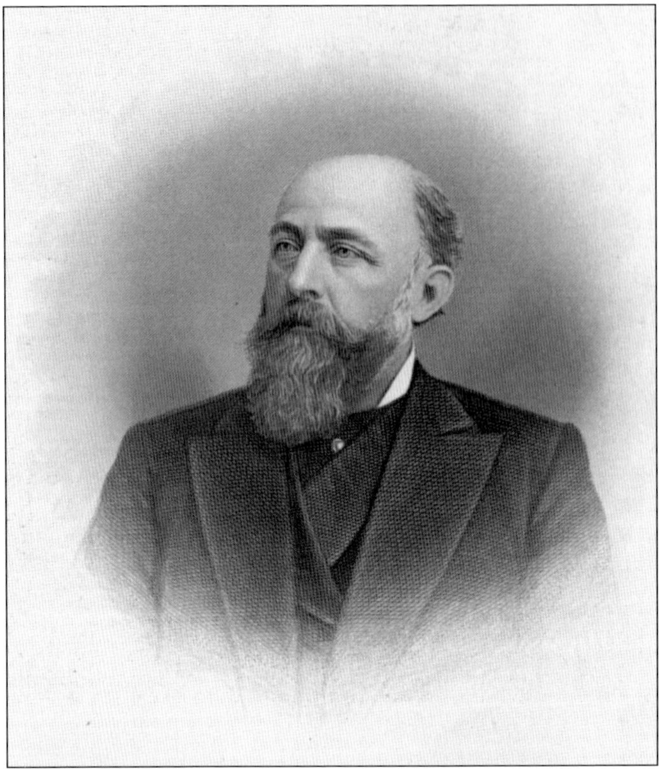

Jacob Romeis (1835–1904) arrived in America from Germany as a teenager and found work as a cabin boy on a steamship. He progressively worked his way into more important positions until he became depot master of Toledo. A member of the Republican Party, he served as Toledo's mayor from 1879 to 1885 and later was elected to the US House of Representatives. (Left, TPL.)

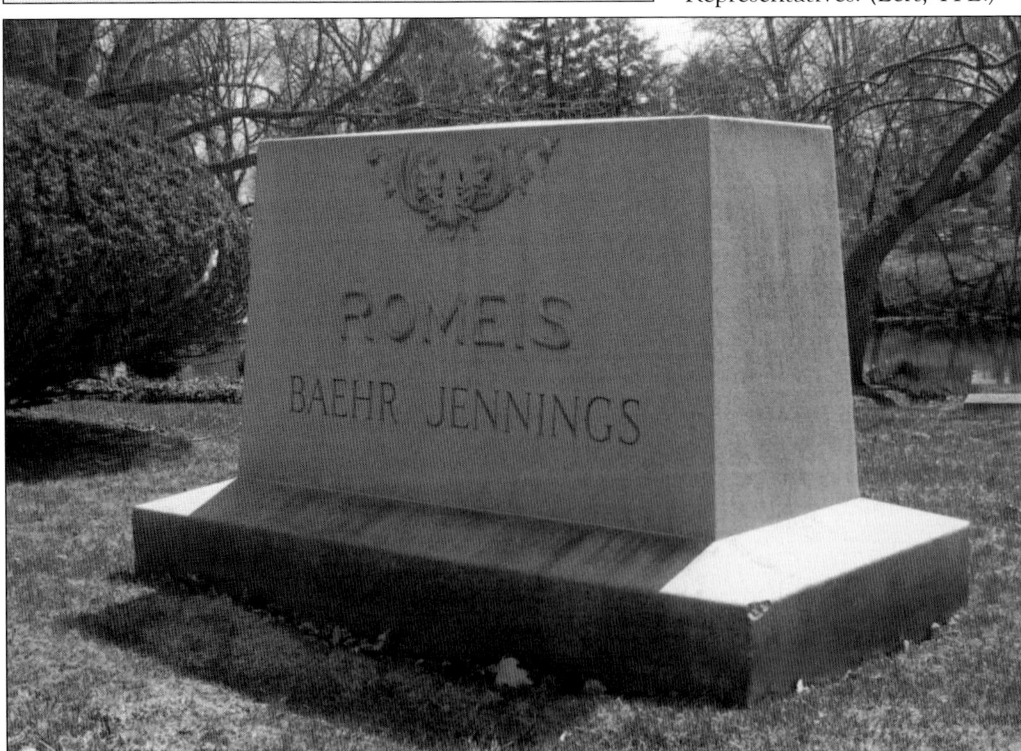

Joseph W. Cummings started his professional life in Indiana, where he worked as a lawyer and then as prosecuting attorney for five Northwest Indiana counties. At the outbreak of hostilities during the Civil War, Cummings (1839–1899) enlisted, but his company was never used due to its lack of weapons.

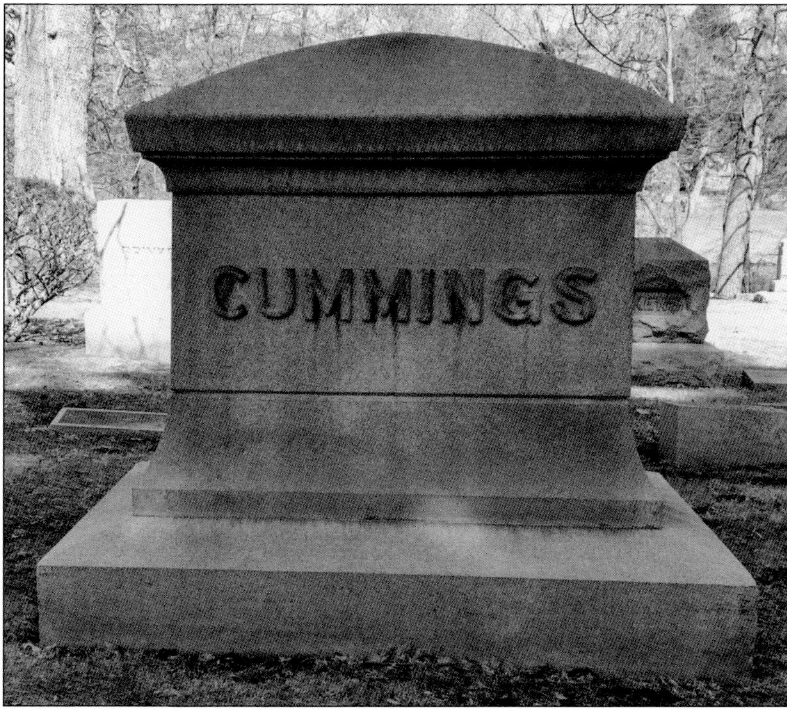

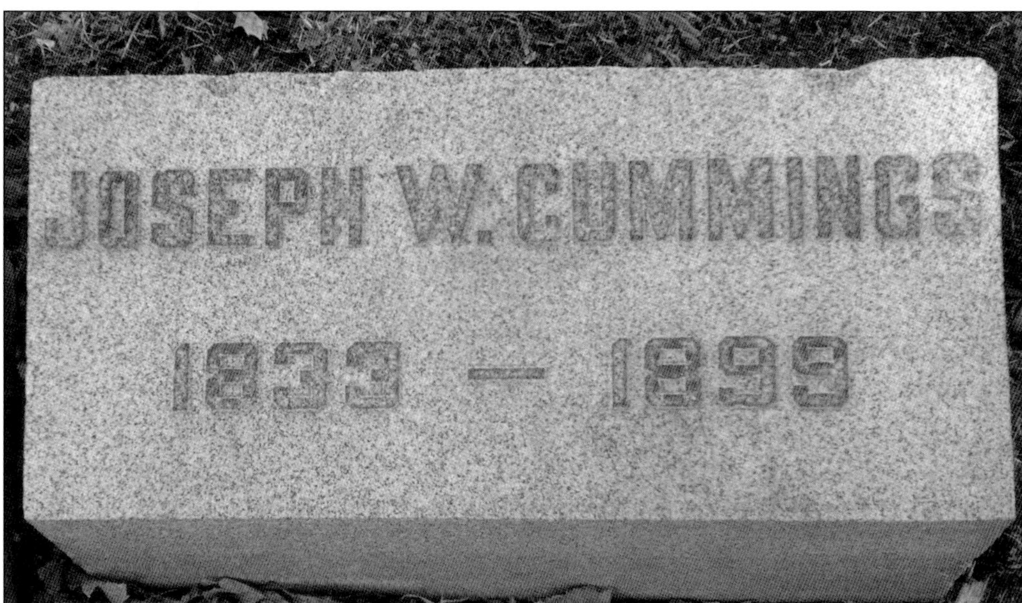

After moving to Toledo, Cummings served as the police judge and later as a probate judge.

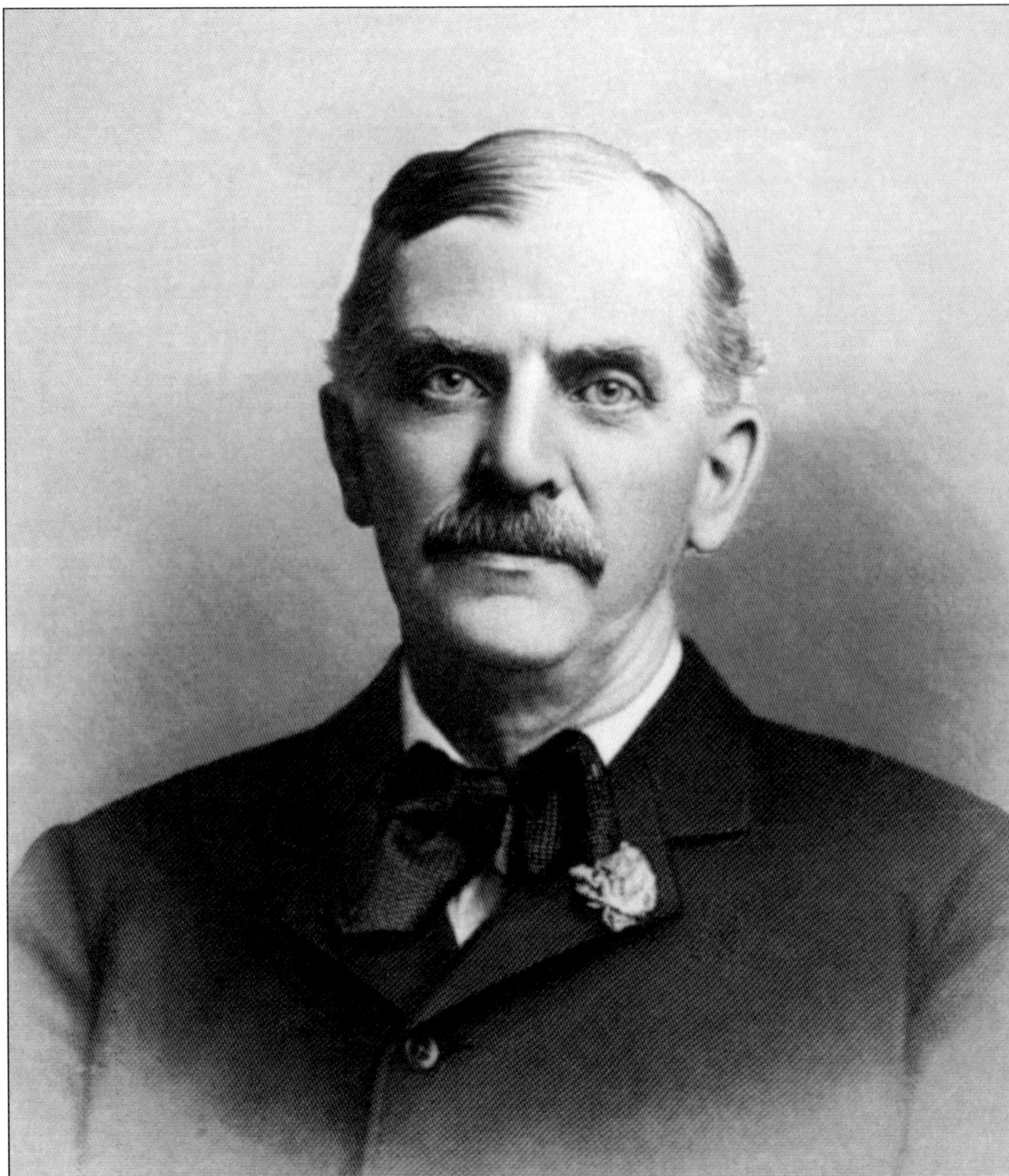

Early in his career, Samuel Milton Jones (1846–1904) spent several years investing in the Pennsylvania oil fields. Later, he moved to Lima, Ohio, where he continued working in the oil industry. He finally gained great wealth by selling his business interests to Standard Oil. With this fortune, he established the Acme Sucker Rod Plant in Toledo to manufacture a new type of drilling tool he had invented. Rather than display a list of rules for his workers to follow, as was customary, Jones simply posted one rule on the company notice board. The simple mandate was, "Do unto others as you would have others do unto you," the Golden Rule. Jones introduced several employee benefits unimaginable at the time, including an eight-hour workday, profit sharing, and paid vacations. As an employer, Jones's popularity grew to legendary proportions, earning him the nickname "Golden Rule Jones." (TPL.)

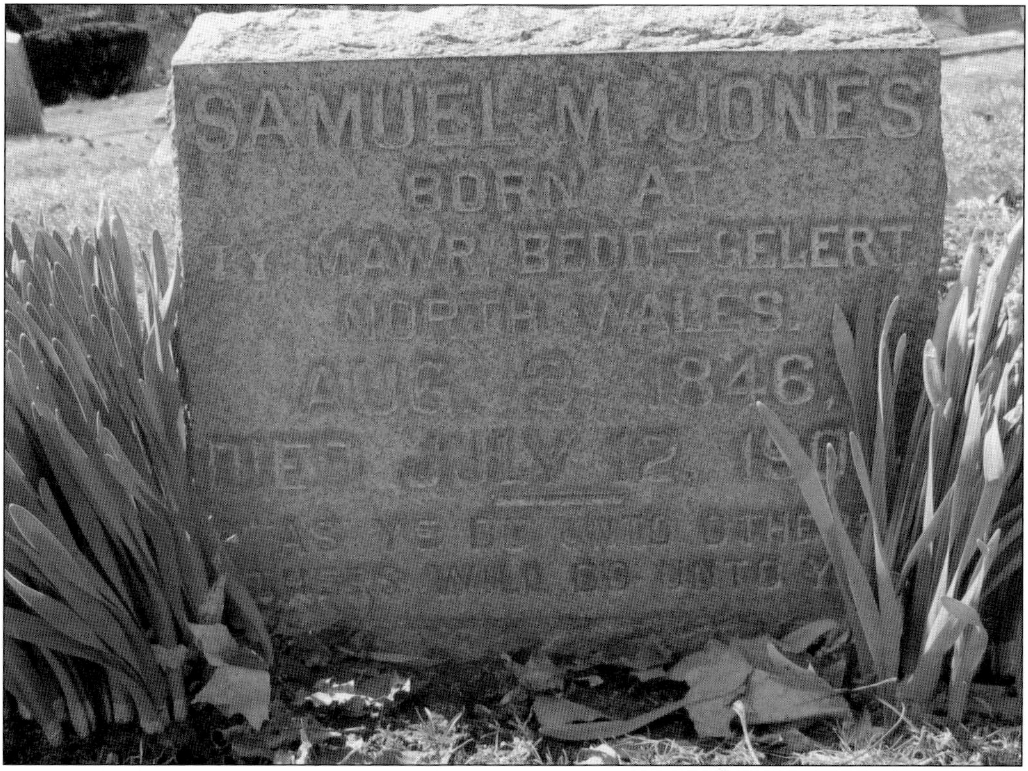

Etched at the base of Samuel Jones's marker is the Golden Rule, reminding all viewers of their duty toward their fellow man. A progressive reformer, Samuel Jones was elected mayor of Toledo in 1897. His popularity remained strong with the working class as he instituted several changes, including the establishment of free kindergartens and playgrounds, refusal to enforce laws prohibiting Sunday liquor sales, and the reform of city government. However, his uncompromising implementation of the Golden Rule to all constituents caused his Republican supporters to drop him in favor of a more traditional politician after his first term. Surprisingly, Jones went on to win the city's top position three more times as an independent. Upon his sudden death during his fourth term, his funeral was the city's largest up to that time. Today, political experts list him as the fifth best big-city mayor in US history.

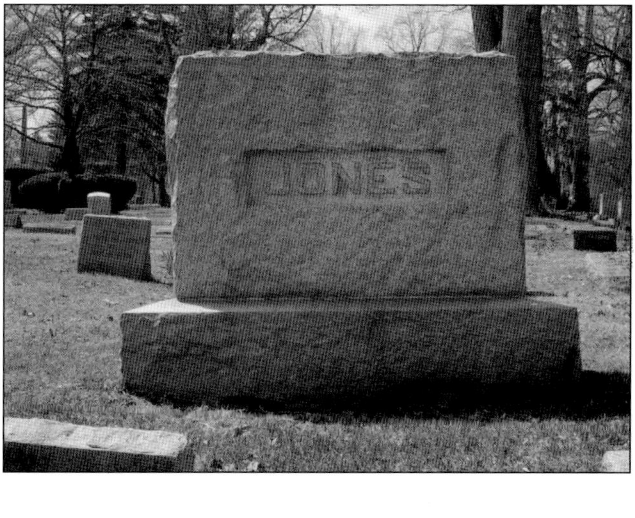

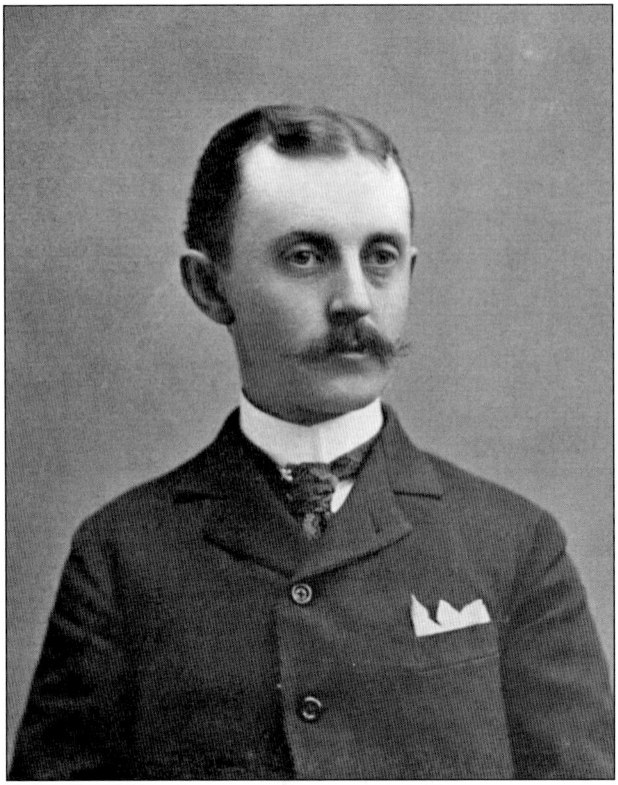

Guy G. Major (1859–1912) served two terms as a Republican mayor of Toledo, from 1893 to 1897. Prior to this, he was president of the American Linseed Company. He also organized the Major Linseed Oil Company, which became one of the largest linseed and castor oil companies in the United States. (TPL.)

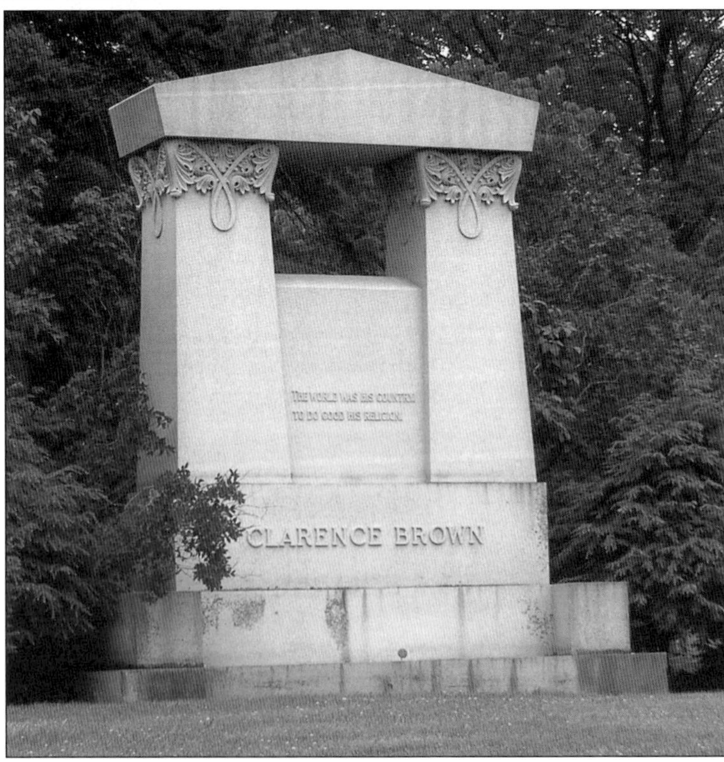

In his early career, Clarence Brown (1852–1918) worked for the city as clerk and then as city solicitor. He eventually opened his own law office and developed an impressive client list, including railroad companies and glass manufacturers. For several years, Brown was also a lecturer on medical jurisprudence at the Northwestern Ohio Medical College. The bold lines of his monument are softened by the floral embellishments at the top of each pillar.

John R. Doyle (1844–1919) practiced law in Toledo for several years, and in 1873 was elected judge of the US District Court for Northern Ohio. He was appointed to the Ohio Supreme Court 10 years later. Upon his return to private practice, Doyle served as president of the American Bar Association and the Ohio Bar Association. (TPL.)

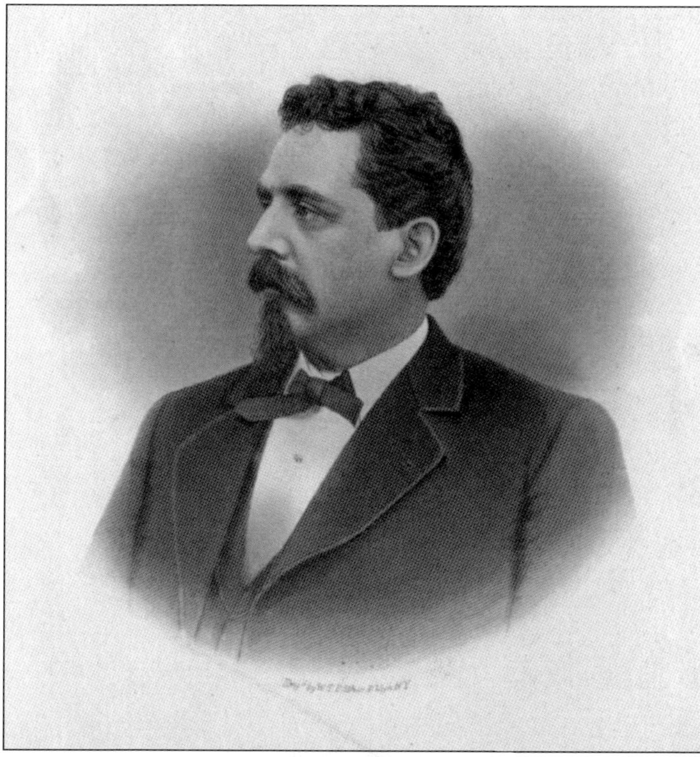

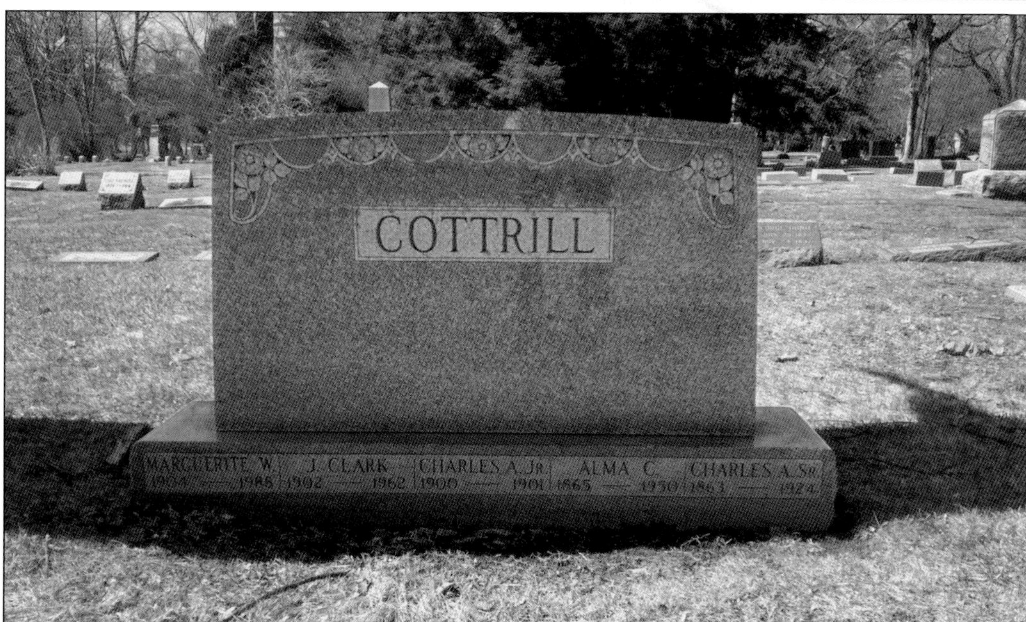

Charles A. Cottrill (1863–1924) was a nationally known politician, a leader of Toledo's African American community, and a realtor in the early 1900s. Later, he served as president of the Toledo branch of the National Association for the Advancement of Colored People. In 1911, Pres. William Howard Taft appointed him to the position of collector of revenue in Honolulu, Hawaii, making him the first African American appointed to a federal position in Hawaii.

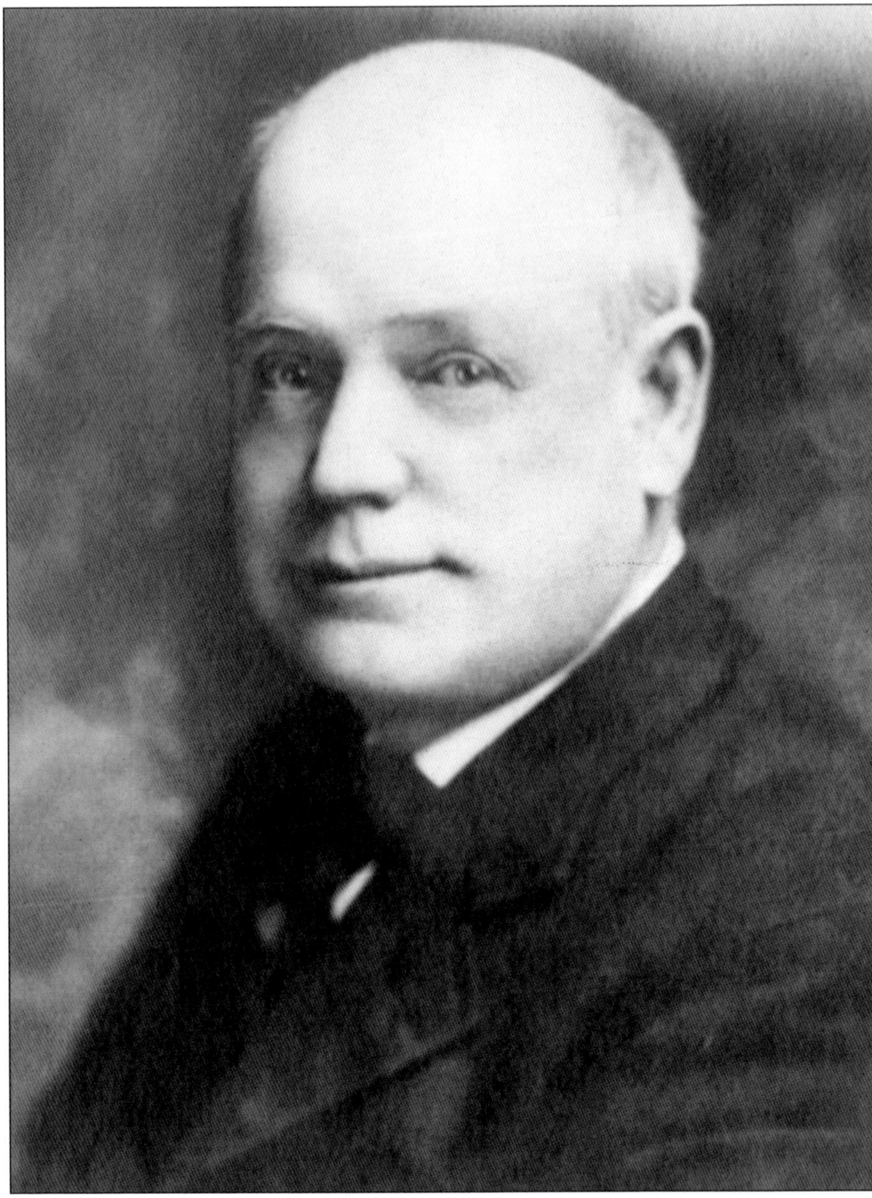

John E. Gunckel (1846–1915), an unassuming railroad ticket agent, rescued many unruly boys from the streets and almost single-handedly solved the city's "boy problem" by founding the Toledo Newsboys Association. In an agrarian society, a boy's character developed under the watchful eye of caring parents and supportive neighbors. As America became more urbanized, a boy's development was often shaped more by negative influences beyond the family. As a result, big cities were confronted with large numbers of boys who roamed the streets looking for fun, often resulting in behaviors ranging from simple annoyance to disruption in commerce and even criminal activities. The Newsboys Association assisted in character development by using the natural energy, talents, and skills of these youngsters to engage in purposeful activities that benefited each young man personally as well as the entire community. Gunckel's unique program helped Toledo's newsboys reach their full potential by focusing on training the boys, from an early age, in business skills and responsibility. (BGI.)

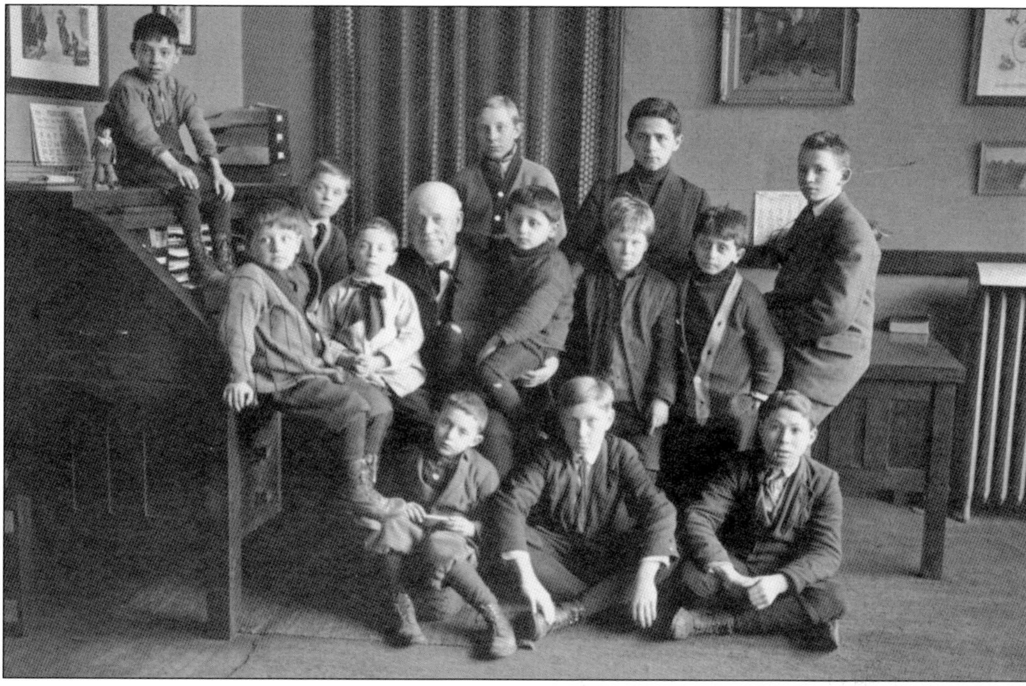

Throughout his adult life, John Gunckel was often seen walking along the streets of Toledo surrounded by several excited boys. These sightings prompted promotional photographs, such as the one shown here, which were often printed in national publications to promote his program. His organization was so well-received that city leaders convinced him to quit his job with the railroad and devote all of his time to work with Toledo's boys. Upon his death, the Newsboys honored John Gunckel by assisting in the development of one of Woodlawn Cemetery's most outstanding monuments. Shaped as a pyramid, it is composed of thousands of stones contributed by newsboys, ex-newsboys, and schoolchildren. Upon the pyramid is a copper plaque that begins with the following inscription: "The newsboys' friend John Elstner Gunckel, 1846–1915. There was a man sent from God whose name was John." (Both, BGI.)

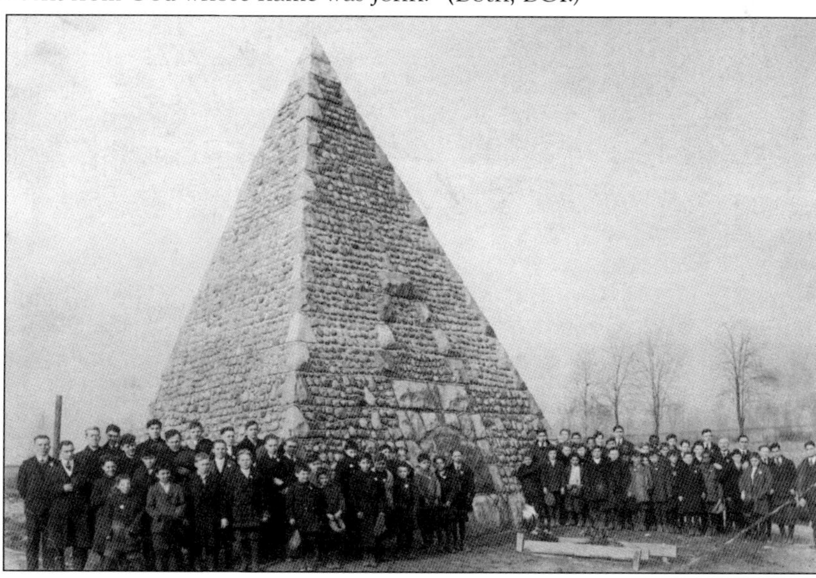

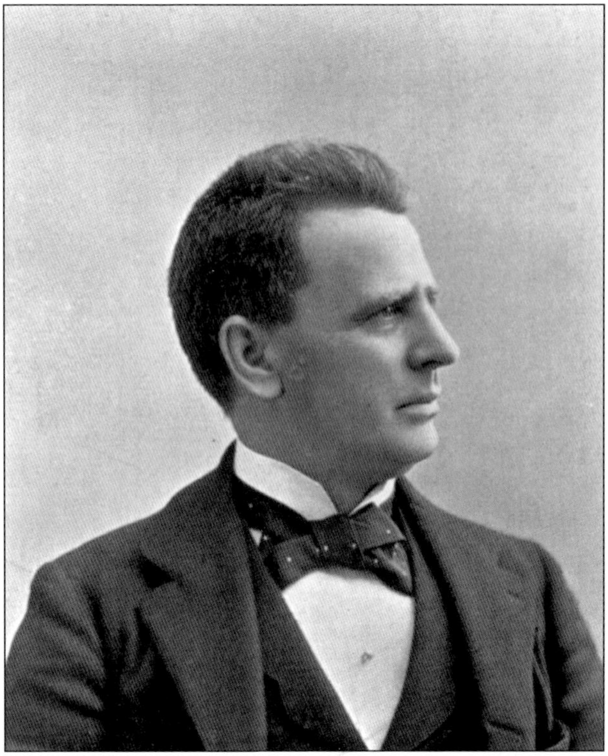

A graduate of Cornell University, James Harding Southard (1851–1919) served six terms as a Republican member of the House of Representatives from Ohio. While in Congress, Southard chaired the Committee on Coinage, Weights, and Measures. Earlier, he practiced law in Toledo and served as the Lucas County prosecutor for six years. (TPL.)

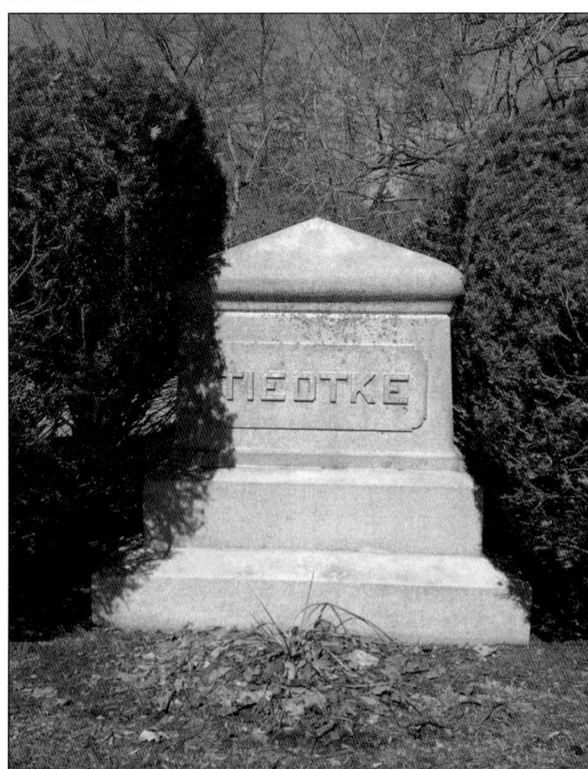

Harry Tiedtke, brother of the well-known retailers, achieved prosperity in his own right in the printing and, later, real-estate business. In his private life, Tiedtke (1870–1924) promoted better living and social conditions through his church work and philanthropic efforts. He assisted in the establishment of the Toledo Newsboys Association and was an organizer of the Toledo City Mission.

As the wife of a successful businessman and a young mother, Charlotte Steele Secor (1840–1926) could have lived a life of ease. However, her commitment to children and the less fortunate inspired her to become active in social work. She helped found Toledo's first day nursery, the Toledo Industrial School, and served as a trustee of Toledo Hospital.

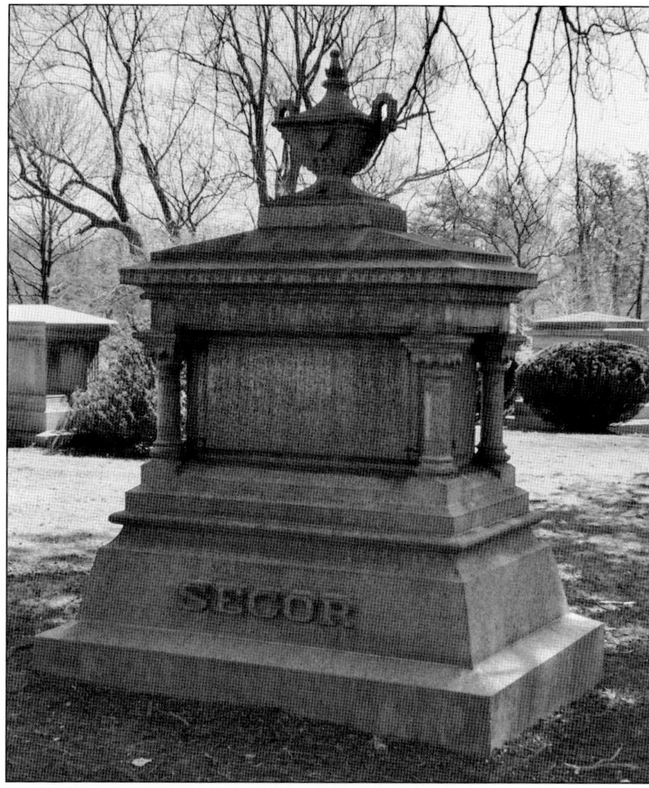

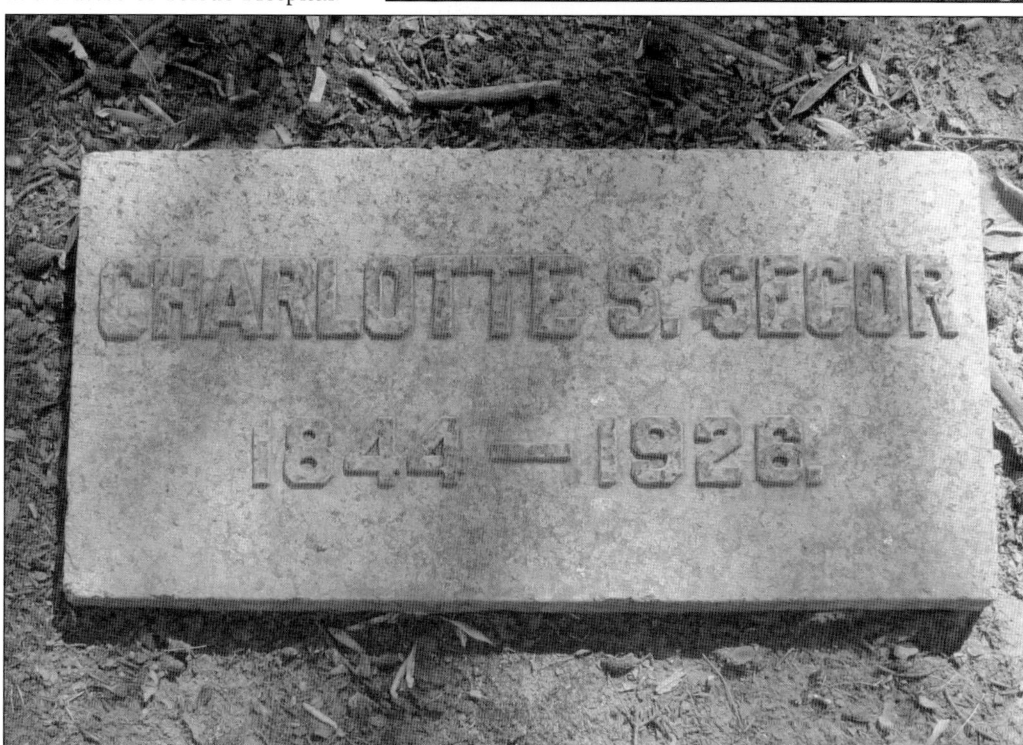

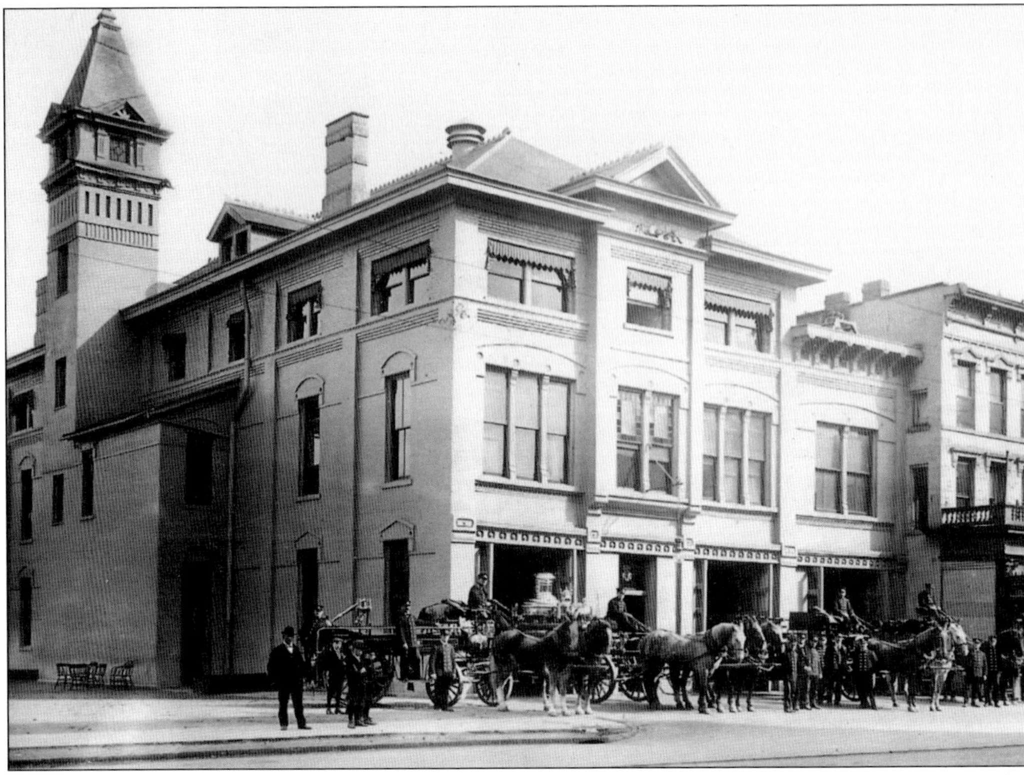

A native of Switzerland, John Nagely (1844–1922) was appointed fire chief in 1885. During his tenure, the first hook-and-ladder truck was purchased by Toledo Fire Station No. 3. The station (above) stood on the corner of Jefferson and Ontario Streets. The hose wagon shown below was an earlier purchase by the city. (Both, TFM.)

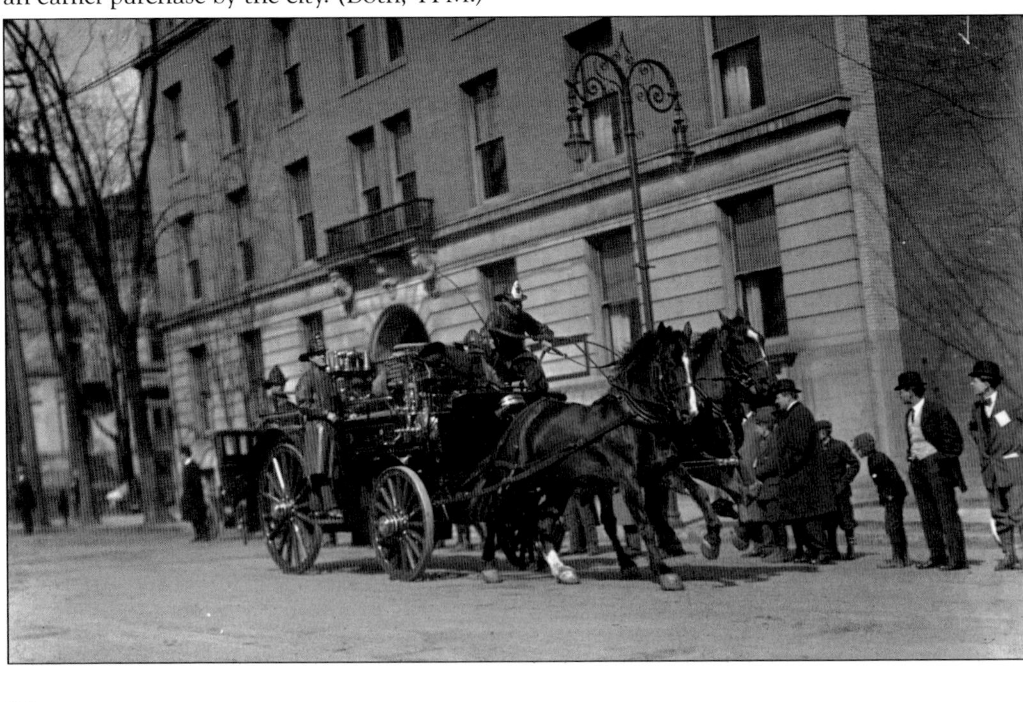

Perry D. Knapp served as the chief of police in Toledo from 1902 to 1914. During his tenure, he adopted the philosophy of former mayor Sam Jones, who relied upon the Golden Rule in dealing with others. Knapp (1856–1923) believed that punishment should fit the criminal, not the crime. (TPM.)

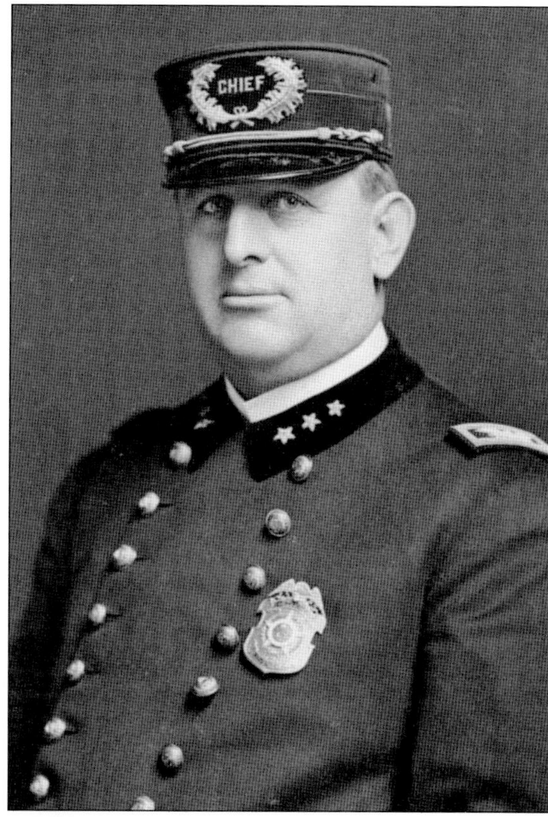

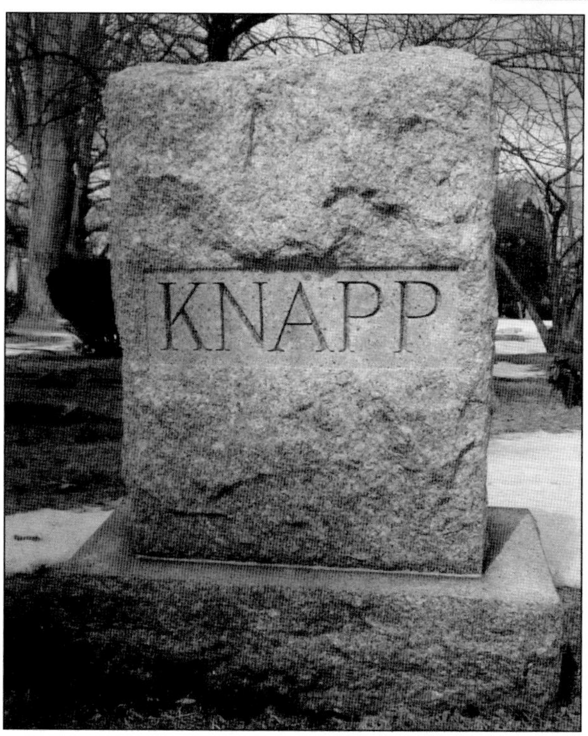

During Knapp's years as police chief, the percentage of crime was lower in Toledo than in any other city of its size in the country.

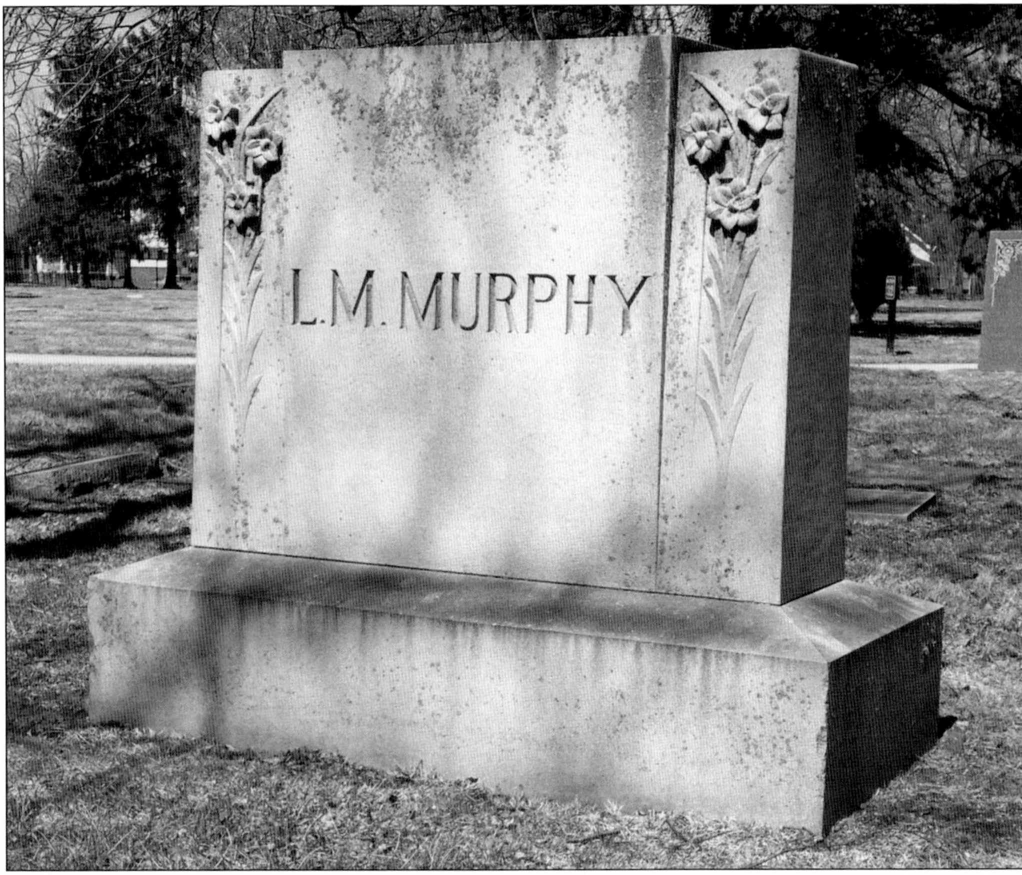

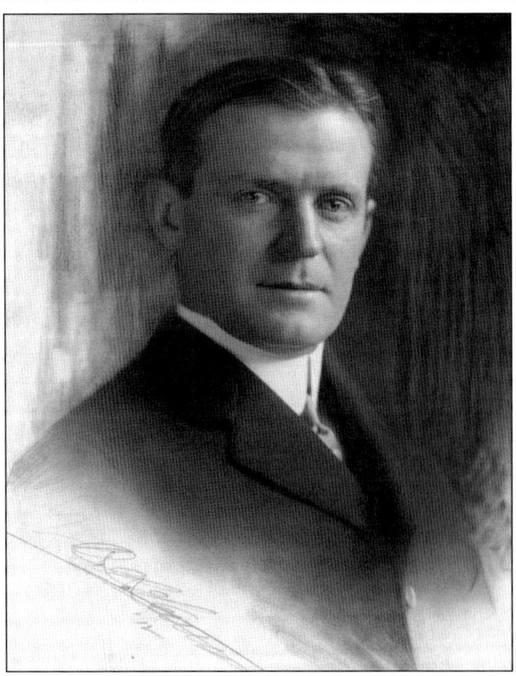

L.M. Murphy (1849–1926), a Civil War veteran, became a Toledo attorney who took cases for the weak and the poor. His skills were so admired that other attorneys and laymen would fill the courtroom beyond capacity to hear the "Sage of the Maumee" address the court.

Bernard F. Brough (1871–1926) was a prominent Toledo attorney who served as a judge of the Common Pleas Court. A member of the Republican Party, he was elected mayor in 1921 and, two years later, was reelected by one of the greatest majorities ever given a mayoral candidate. (TPL.)

Six

Educators and Other Interesting Toledoans

While the individual lives of many Toledoans found in this chapter do not fit neatly into any specific category, their contributions to the larger story of Toledo's development during the 50 years covered in this book are just as important as those found in the other chapters. The men and women of this chapter received recognition in their lifetime or upon death for a wide variety of interests and activities.

One of the youngest persons mentioned in this book, Exeria Wheeler, represents the typical American of this period. Like most others, he attended the local schools for several years, then found full time employment in his teen years. Exeria's experience and early death was one example of many that contributed to the reformers' cry for child labor laws and to amend workplace safety standards.

Kate Brownlee Sherwood was not only a great asset to her husband's political career; she made a name for herself as a writer. In one of her most famous poems, "Democratic Salad," Sherwood leaves the reader with a mixed feeling of patriotism, optimism, and lightheartedness. This salad, she wrote, was composed of "a handful of hospitality, a heartful of good cheer, a headful of common sense; mix with the oil of joy, flavor with faith, hope and charity; serve liberally at the festive board, and keep the door wide open to all comers."

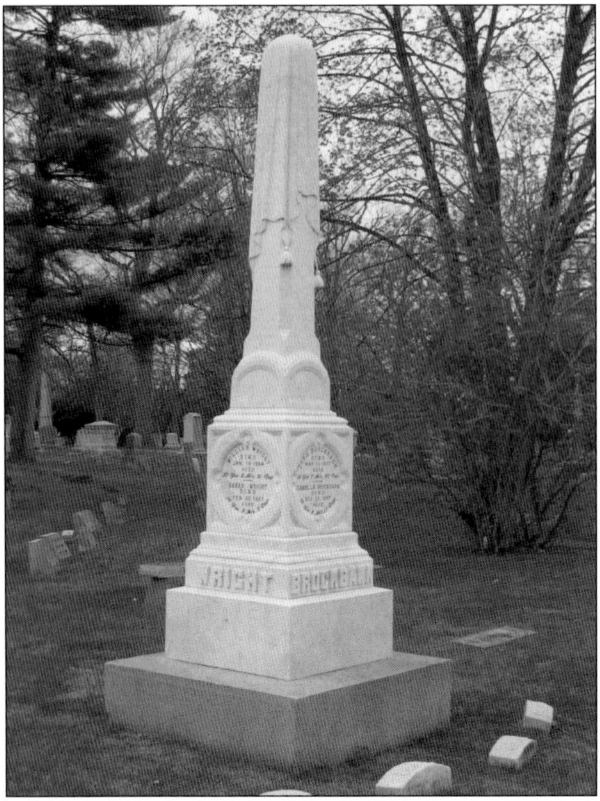

The Brockbank memorial is an early Lloyd Brothers monument in Woodlawn Cemetery. John Brockbank, a farmer in Washington Township, died in 1877; the monument was refurbished in 1978. Made of white marble, and cleaned and re-lettered in recent years, it stands out among the other stones in its section.

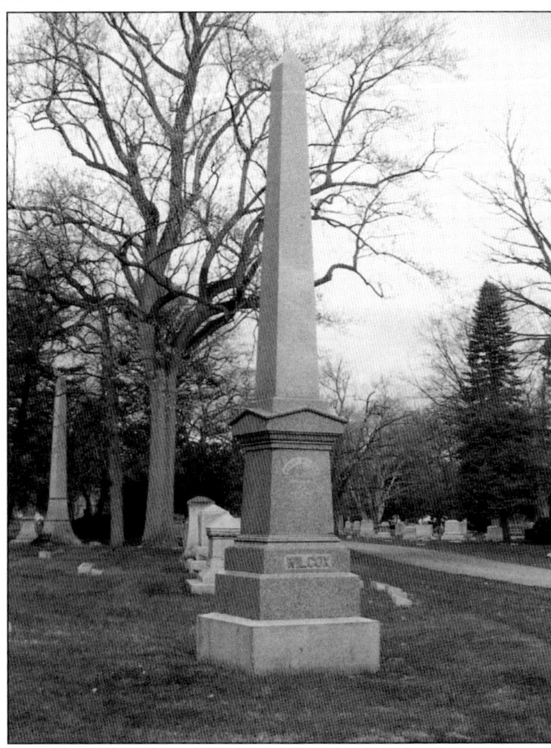

Henry Wilcox (1802–1880) was a boot- and shoemaker who moved to Toledo in the early 1830s from England. His obelisk is one of the early Lloyd Brothers stones in Woodlawn. His daughter, Matilda, married Edward Lloyd, one of the Lloyd brothers, in 1869. The clean lines of the obelisk are in contrast to many of the more ornate stones in Woodlawn.

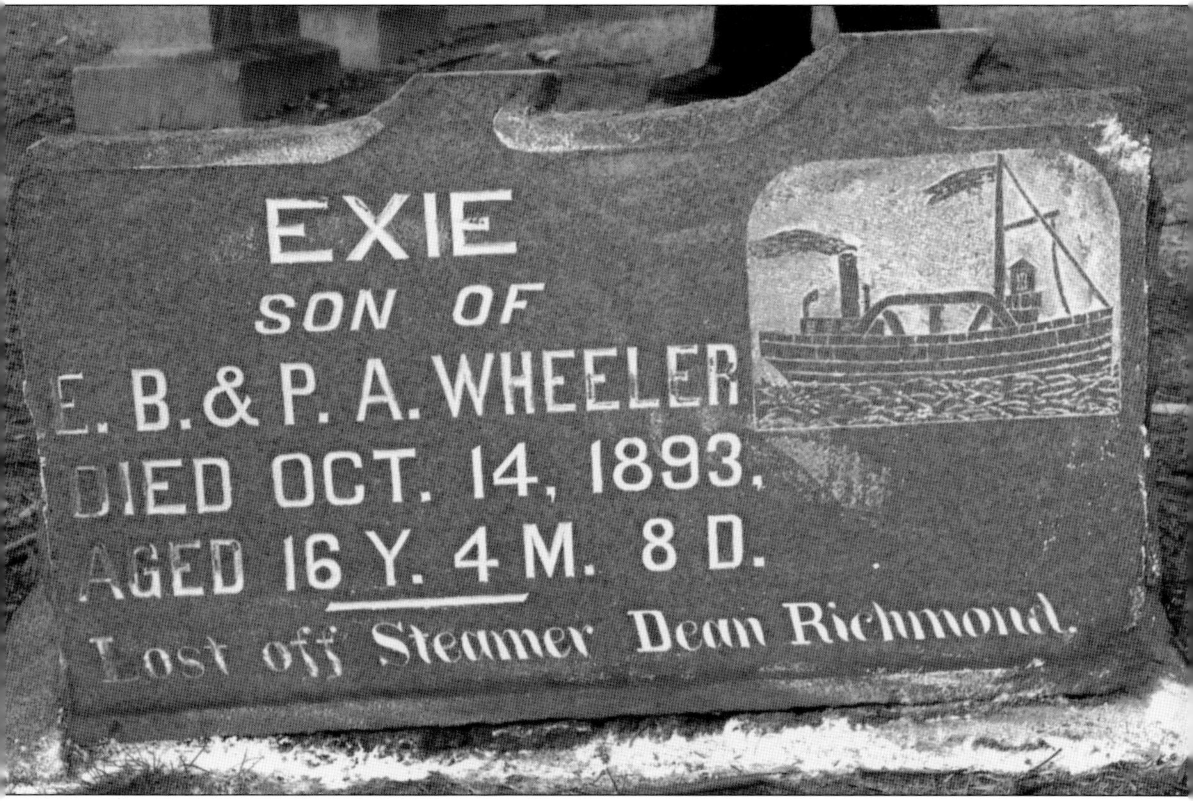

Little is known of George Boyson (1867–1893) and Exeria Wheeler (1877–1893), except that they were among the crew of the *Dean Richmond* when it sank to the bottom of Lake Erie in a terrible storm. A freight carrier, the *Dean Richmond* left Toledo for Buffalo, New York, as a storm was just beginning. On late Saturday, October 14, 1893, it was sighted and reported as completely disabled by the gale-force winds and towering waves. A rescue attempt was impossible. Early Sunday morning, debris and bodies from the ship were discovered along the shore near Dunkirk, New York. There were no survivors; however, several of the bodies of the 18 crewmembers were recovered. Boyson, age 26, lived with his wife in East Toledo and served as second mate. At 16 years old, Wheeler held the position of lookout. He was survived by his parents and younger brother. His grave marker, seen here, is inscribed with his nickname, "Exie," and an image of the *Dean Richmond*.

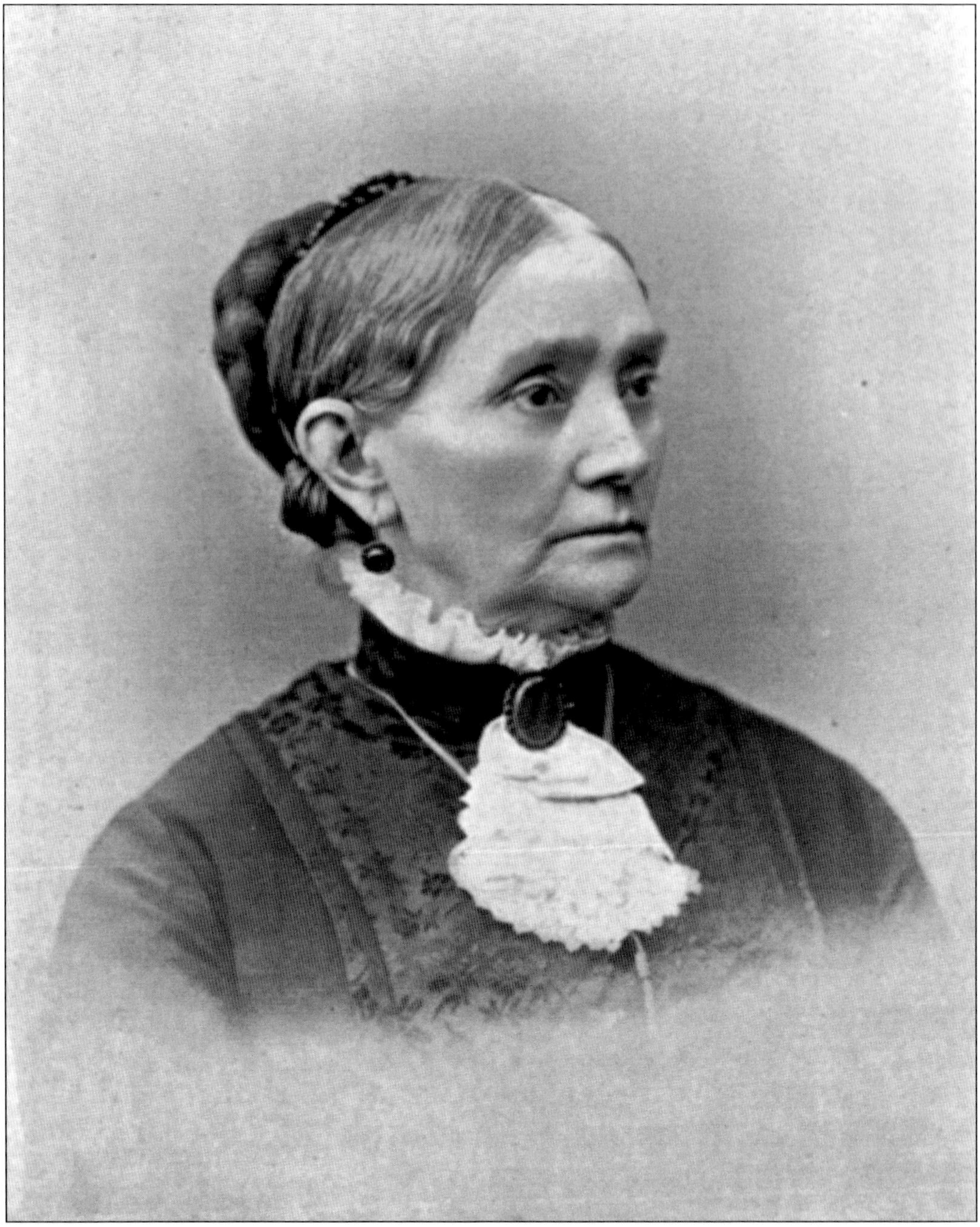

In her autobiography, Harriet Whitney Collins (1814–1903) detailed her life story alongside the evolution of Toledo from a pioneer settlement to a bustling Great Lakes community. As a child of eight, her family joined a wagon train traveling from New York to Michigan, a four-week trek. They moved to Toledo two years later, where, at the age of 12, Collins finally began her formal education in a one-room schoolhouse. She was hired as Toledo's first female teacher four years later. To this day, Harriet Whitney Collins is the only woman for which a Toledo high school has ever been named. (TPL.)

This monument memorializes the life of Ransom Richards (1833–1886), who grew up on the cemetery property when it was his family's farmstead. His monument, which is High Victorian in style, resembles a miniature church, featuring arched openings and Classical columns.

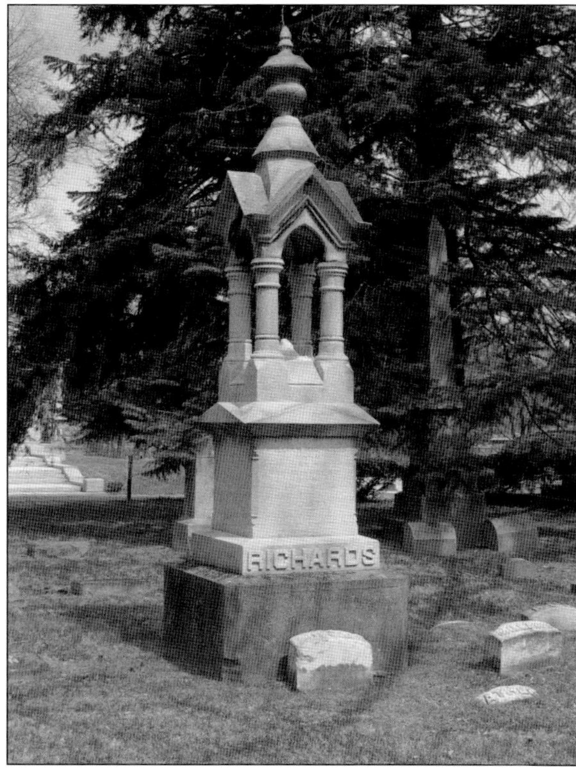

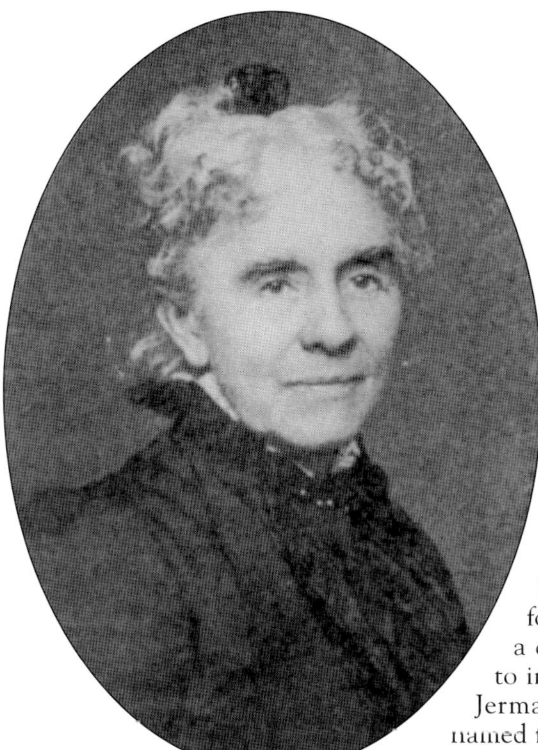

Forced to seek employment upon the death of her husband, Frances D. Jermain (1829–1905) found work at the Toledo Public Library. For a quarter of a century, she worked tirelessly to implement improvements in the library. The Jermain Branch of Toledo's library system was named for her and served the city's north end from 1918 to 1974. (TPL.)

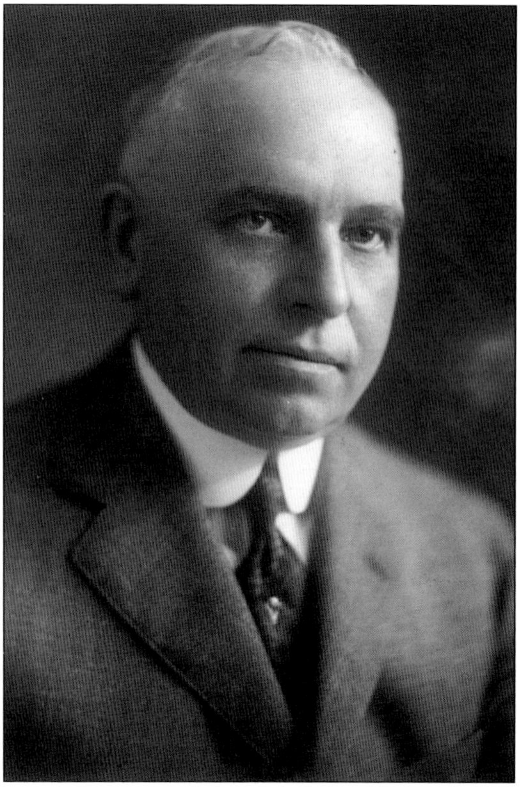

Charles Feilbach (1862–1924) operated a successful wholesale grocery business and was also actively devoted to the care of physically disabled children. As president of the Toledo School Board, he was instrumental in the development of Toledo's School for Crippled Children. Upon his death, the name of the school was changed to the Charles Feilbach School for Crippled Children. (BGI.)

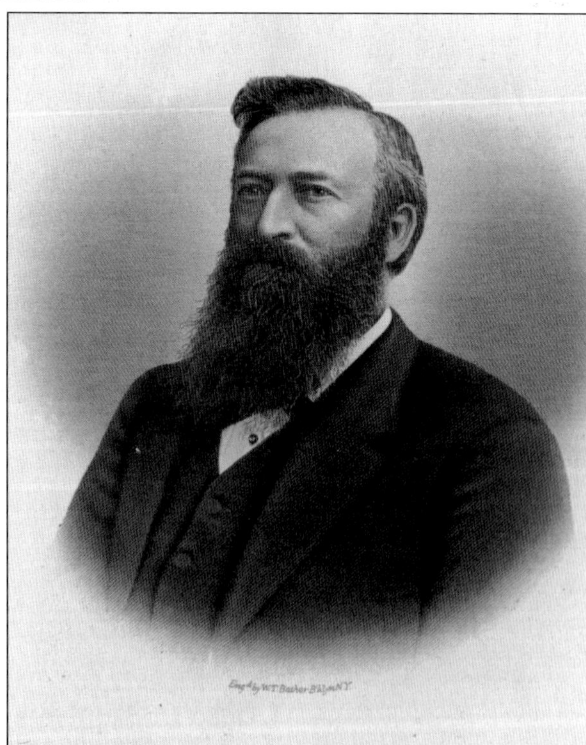

A member of the 86th Ohio Volunteer Infantry during the Civil War, Calvin Hamilton Reed (1840–1915) became a distinguished general practitioner of medicine. He was later elected to the chair of professor of obstetrics at the Northwestern Ohio Medical College and cofounded the Toledo School of Medicine. (TPL.)

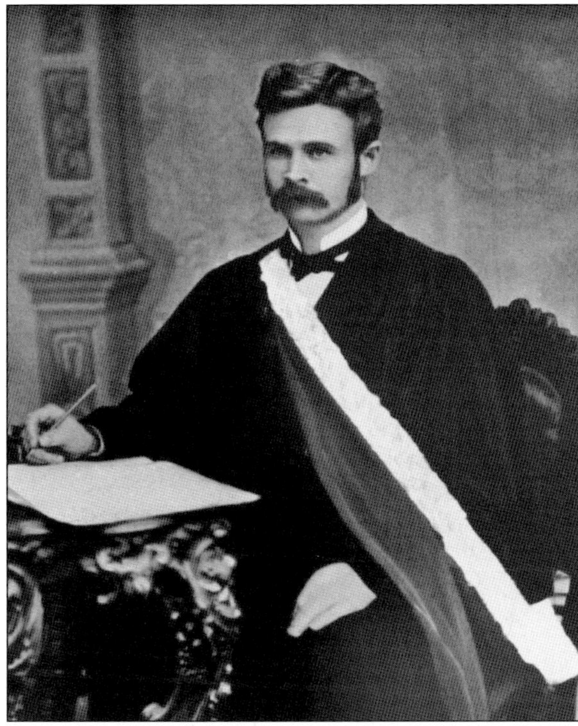

Matthew H. Davis (1849–1904) became director of the Toledo Business College in 1858. During his tenure, the student population grew rapidly and the college absorbed four other schools. As a result of his skillful leadership, the name was changed to Davis Business College. This institution has been in continuous operation for over 150 years in the Toledo area. In the early photograph below, several students are gathered in front of the college. (Both, DBC.)

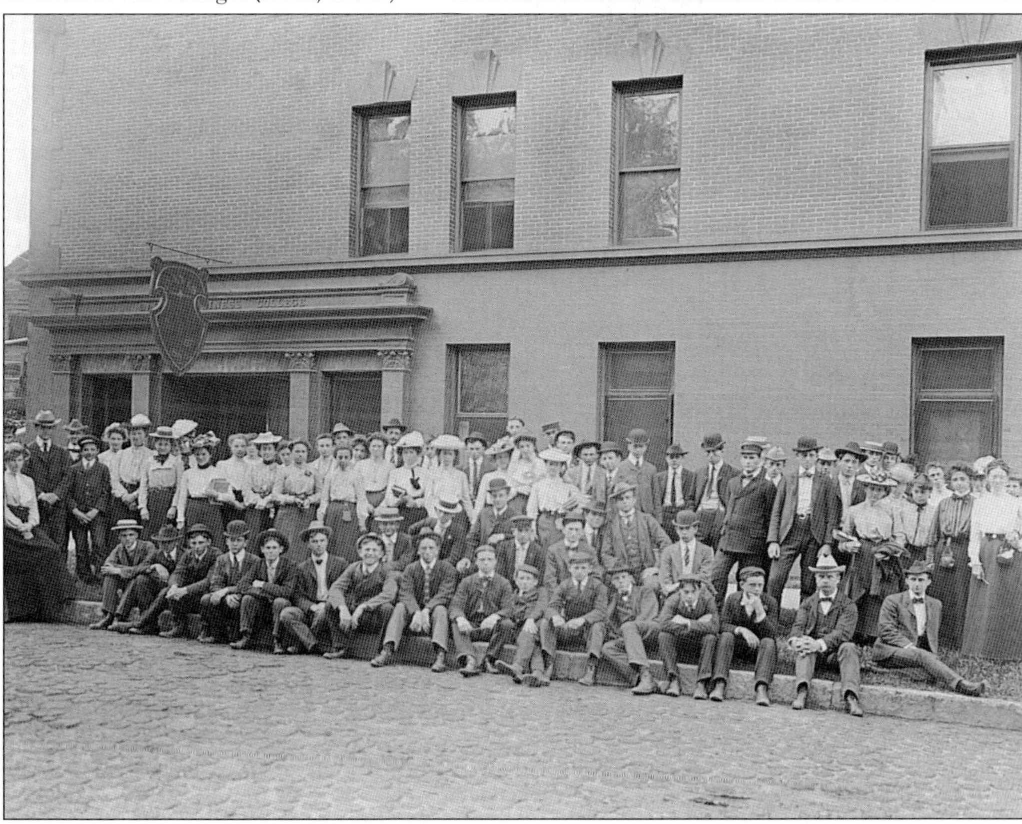

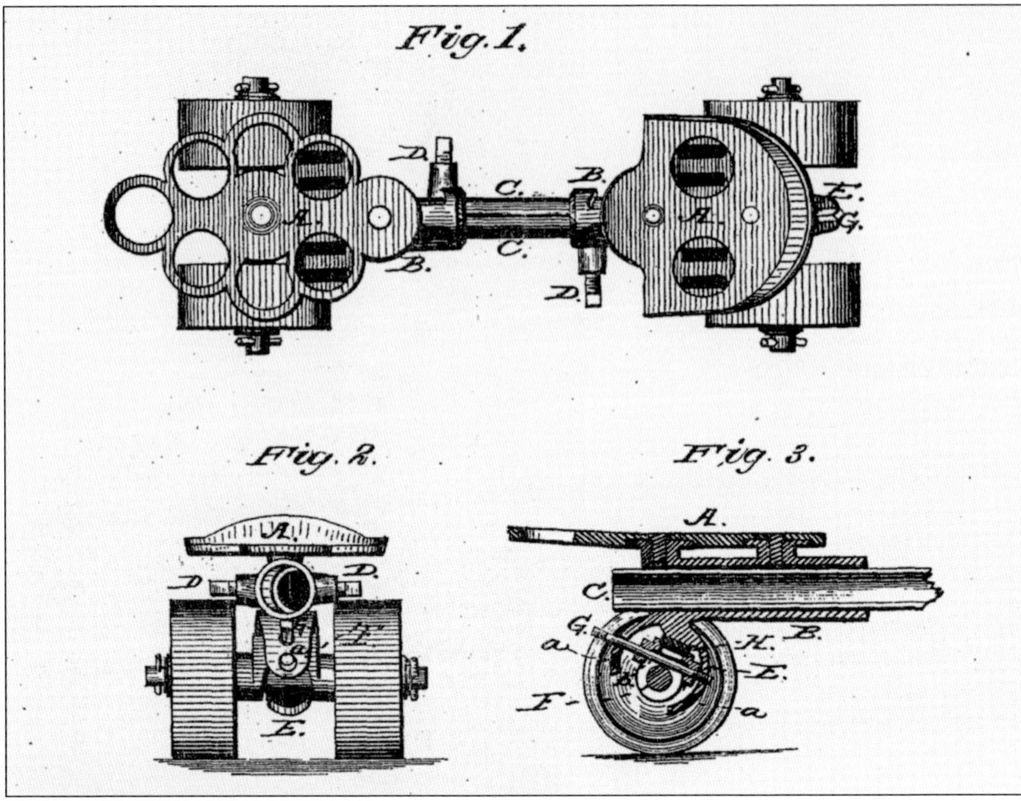

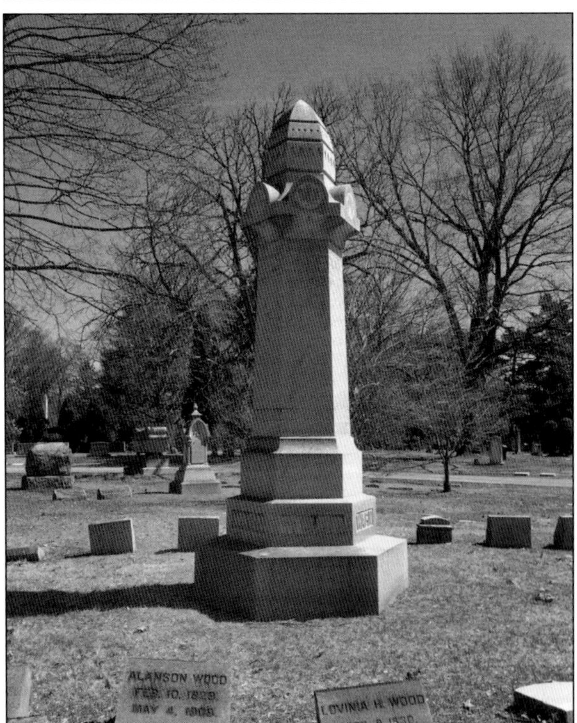

Alanson Wood (1829–1909) arrived in Toledo and worked as a carpenter until he sold his invention of an improved roller skate (illustrated above) for a large sum in 1881. He developed the first modern roller coaster two years later, one that thrilled the rider with high speeds, as opposed to the more traditional coaster that provided a slow and scenic ride. His first crude attempts at a roller coaster ran on several dozen old roller-skate wheels strung together. Today, his monument can be seen high above the others from distant points within the cemetery. (Above, WC.)

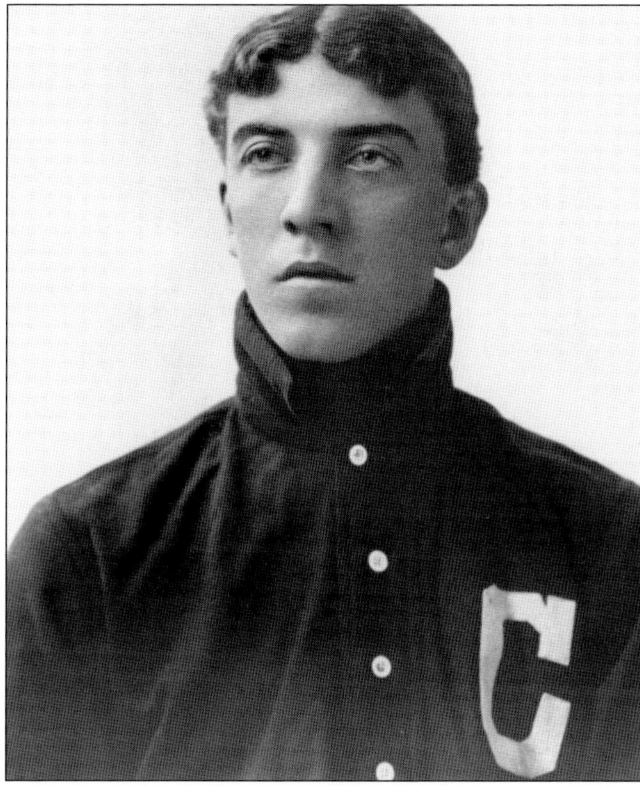

Known as "The Human Hairpin" because he pitched with a pinwheel motion, Adrian "Addie" Joss (1880–1911) began his baseball career with the Toledo Mud Hens. He then moved to the Cleveland Broncos. Joss pitched the fourth perfect game in baseball history and most likely would have gained greater glory had his life not been cut short at the age of 31 by tubercular meningitis. His funeral was well attended, with nationally acclaimed evangelist Billy Sunday presenting the eulogy. Joss was posthumously elected to the National Baseball Hall of Fame in 1978. (Right, JH.)

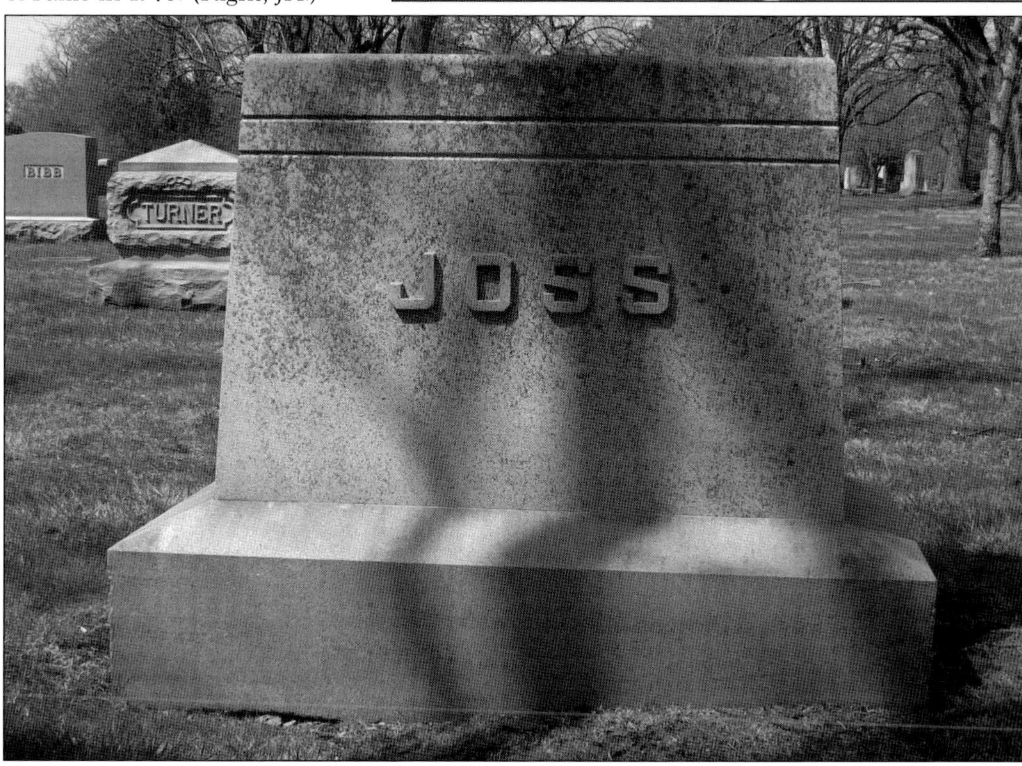

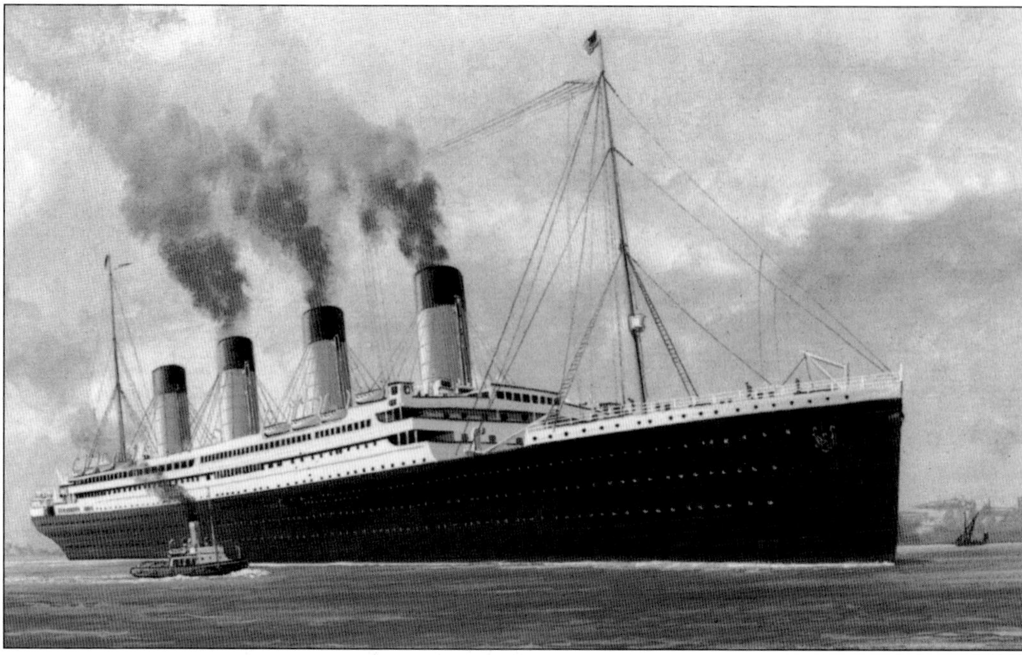

Son of a Lucas County sheriff, William H. Harbeck (1868–1912) became a pioneer documentary motion picture photographer. He was the first to film the aftermath of the San Francisco earthquake in 1906. He was on board the *Titanic* for its maiden voyage. Soon after the iceberg ripped open the side of the majestic ship, it was discovered that the young lady traveling with him was not his wife, but a 24-year-old model Harbeck had met in Paris. When his wife traveled to Halifax to recover his body, she was almost turned away as an imposter, as it was believed that his wife had drowned in the tragic sinking. Harbeck's body was returned to Toledo and, at first, was placed in an unmarked grave. Today, however, he rests under a simple marker at Woodlawn Cemetery. (Above, TPL.)

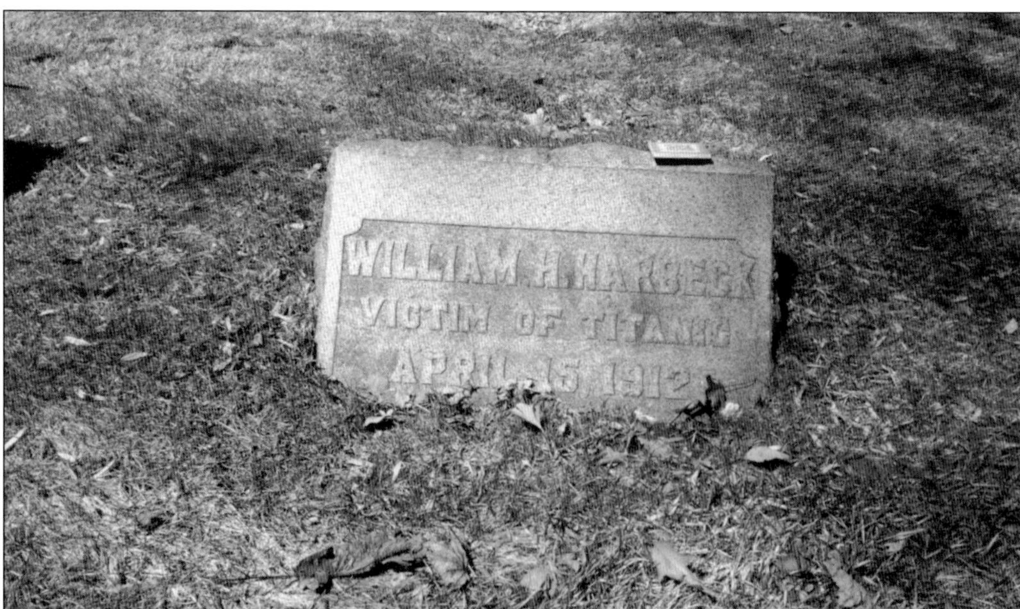

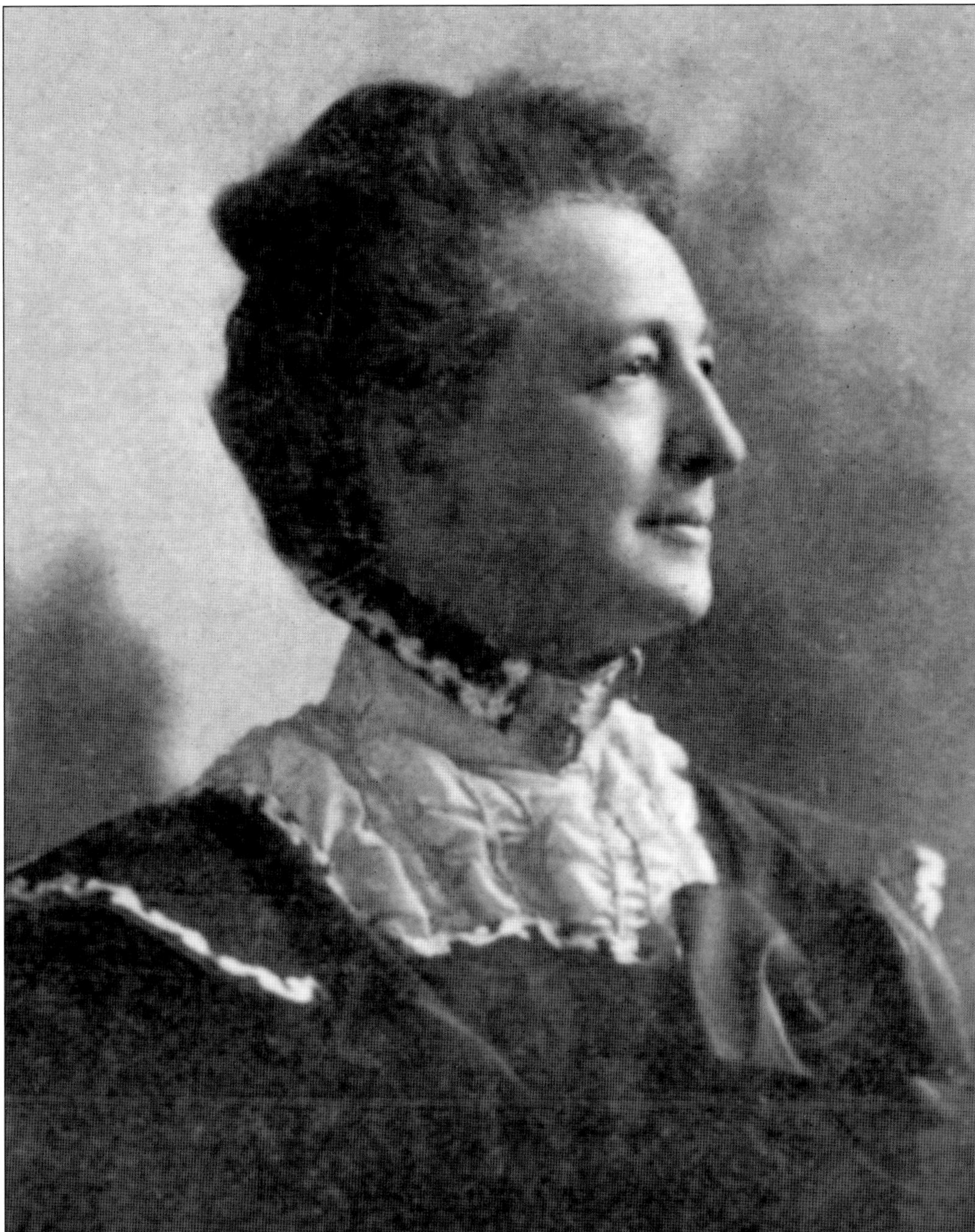

Kate Brownlee Sherwood (1842–1914), a prolific writer, published many sentimental poems commemorating fallen heroes and tragic events of the Civil War, making her one of the nation's most beloved women of that era. During the war, Sherwood volunteered her nursing services on the field and in military hospitals. She founded the Women's Auxiliary of the GAR and edited its official publication, the *National Tribune*, for many years. Meanwhile, she supported many other causes and was said to have been a member, officer, or founder of more organizations than any other woman in Toledo. So revered was she in life and long after, that during World War II, a Liberty ship was named in her honor. (TPL.)

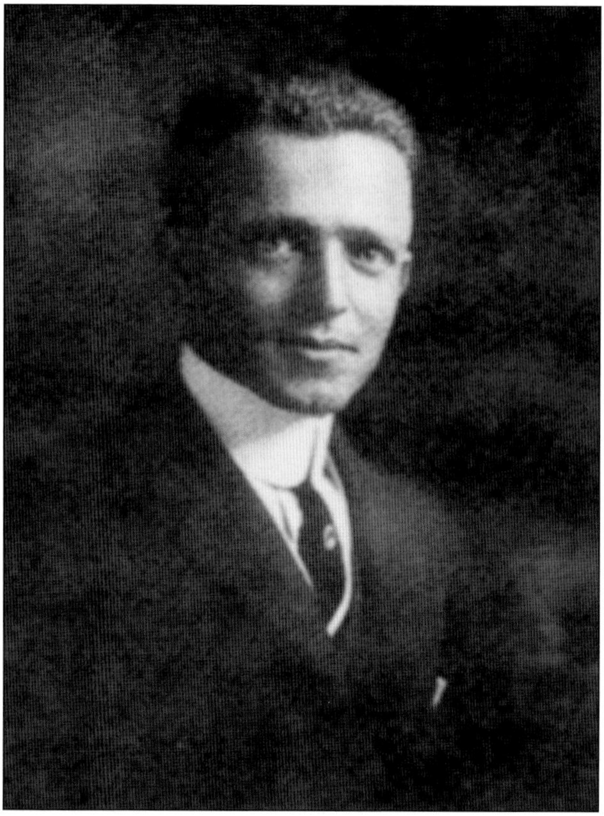

While in college, Roland A. Spitzer (1885–1916) captained the Yale cross-country team, where his record-breaking speed allowed him to compete in the 1908 Olympics in London. Upon graduation, he returned to Toledo and became treasurer of the Spitzer-Rorick Banking Company. He was active in the Boy Scouts movement in Toledo and served as a scoutmaster. After his death, Spitzer was laid to rest in the family vault. This grand mausoleum, designed in the Neoclassical style, is located along the cemetery's main roadway. The structure was built by Spitzer cousins, whose names are engraved above the two doors: Ceilan Milo on the left, and Adelbert Lorenzo on the right. (Left, TPL; below, FB.)

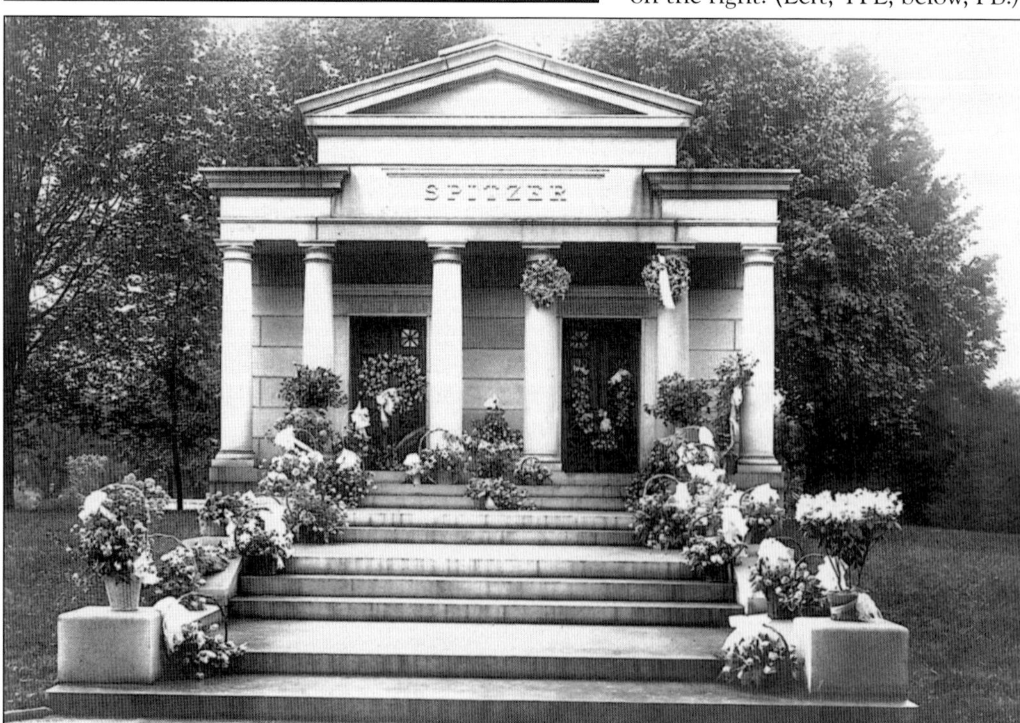

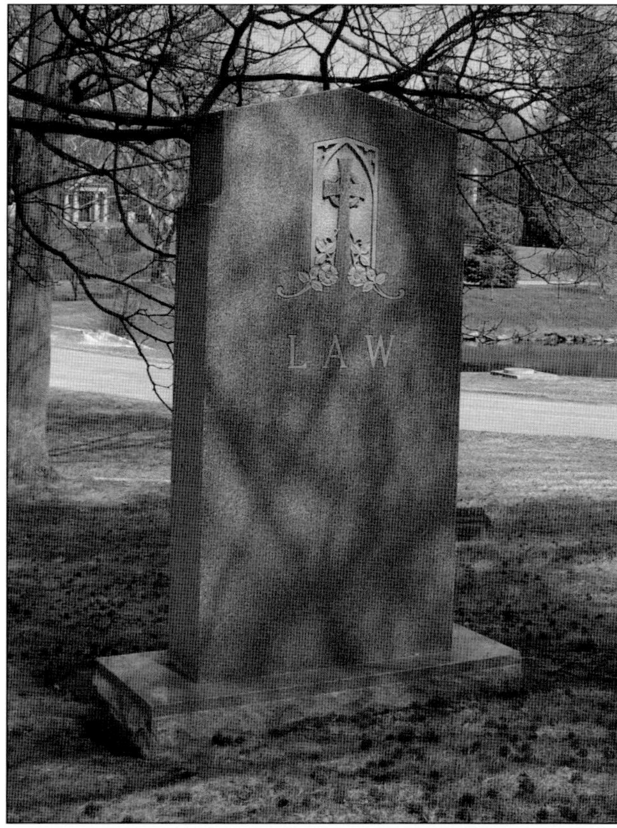

At a time when few women pursued a career outside the home, Mary E. Law (1853–1923) became a teacher and, later, a medical doctor. She taught in the Toledo Public Schools at first, but her interest in the new and progressive kindergarten movement prompted her to open a kindergarten with her sisters. So strong was Law's belief in education for the very young that she decided to start a kindergarten training school in Toledo, the Froebel School. Later, she earned a medical degree and was the only female to graduate from the Toledo Medical School in 1896. Her medical practice was short-lived, however, as she found that she preferred to train teachers. (Both, DB.)

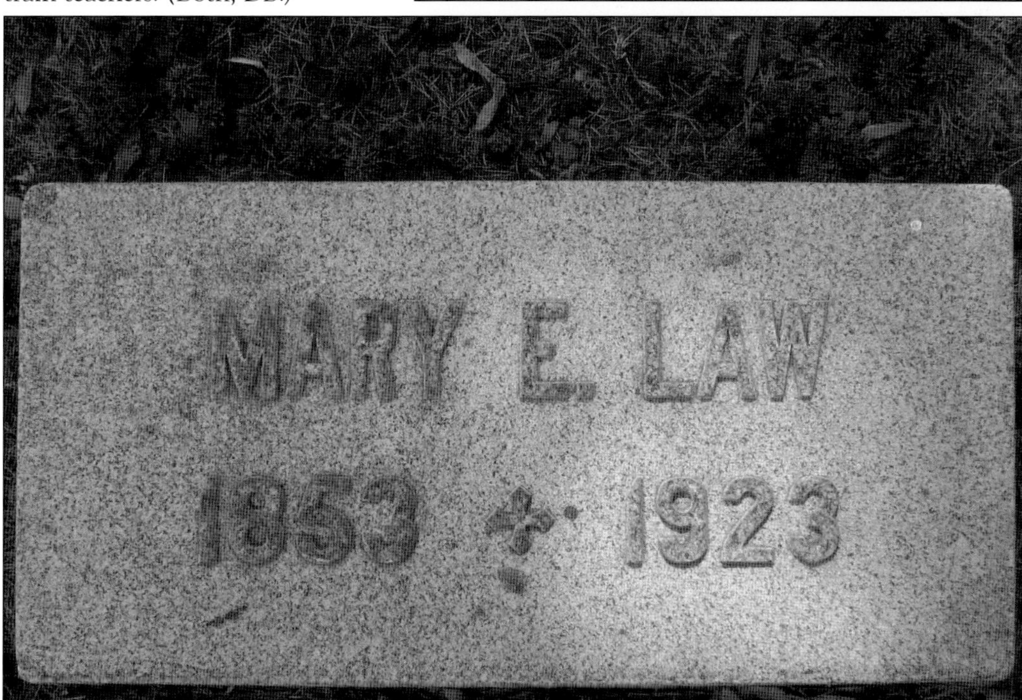

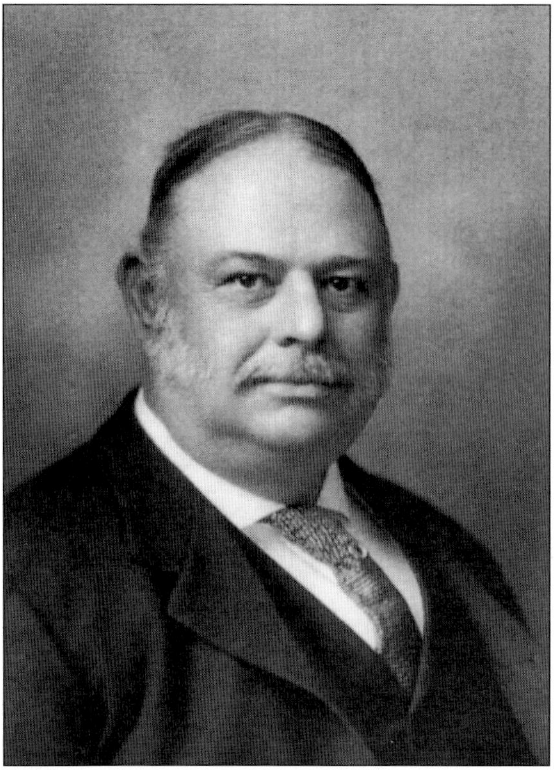

A prominent Toledo attorney, Noah Haynes Swayne (1848–1922) is credited with being the founder of professional baseball in Toledo. He donated the land on which Swayne Field was built, which served as the home of the Toledo Mud Hens for almost 50 years. Swayne's unusual monument features a triple headstone with Gothic arches. (Left, TPL.)

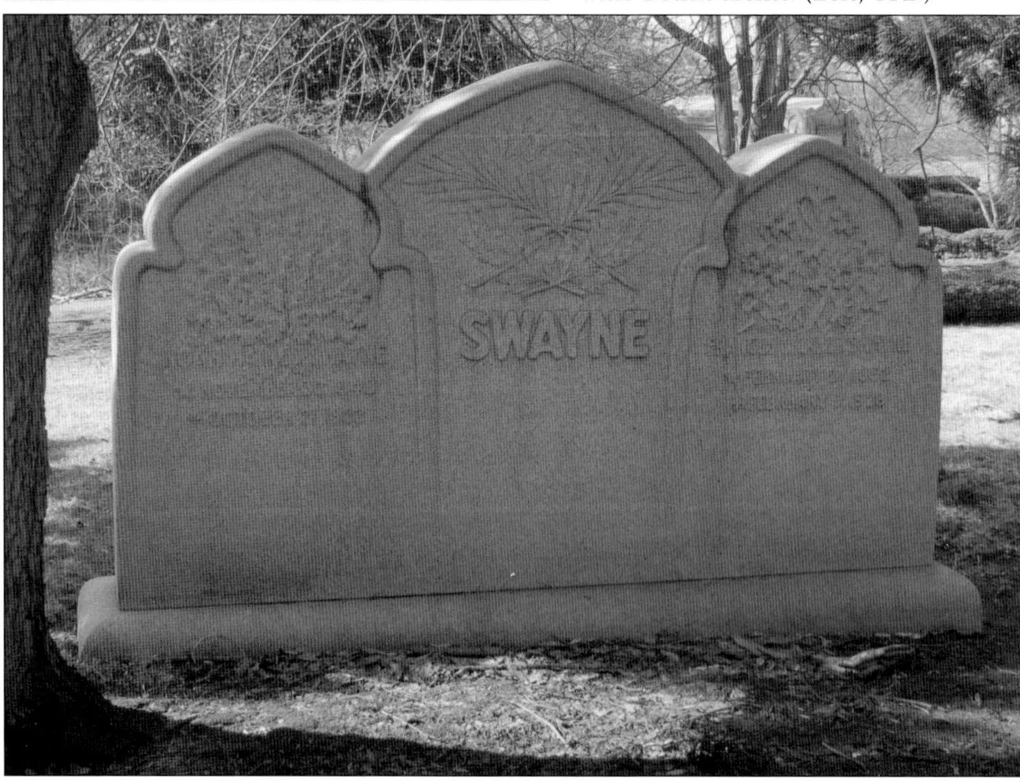

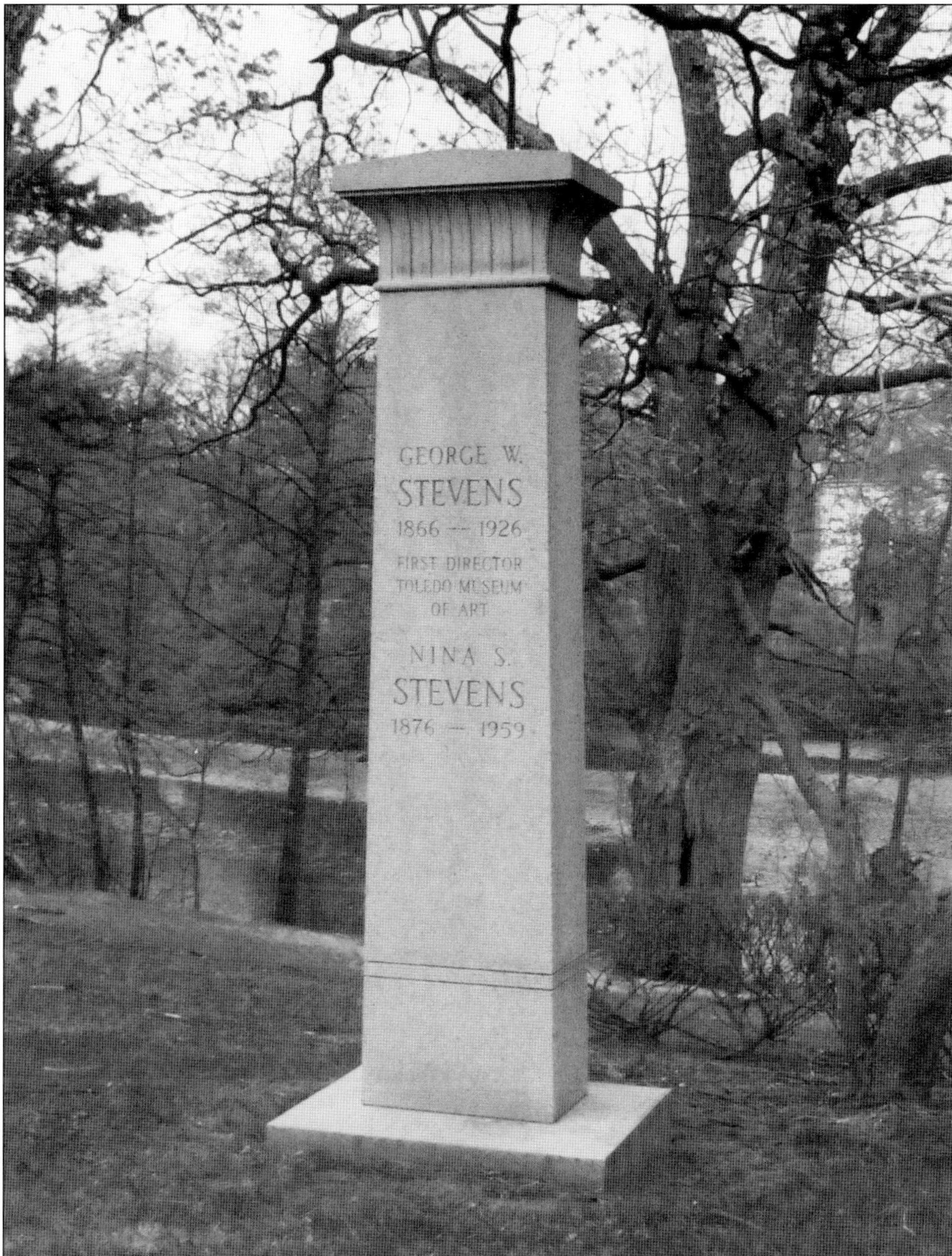

This pillar honors both George and Nina Stevens, cultural icons of Toledo who worked alongside Edward and Florence Libbey to achieve the early success of the Toledo Museum of Art. While this serves as George's burial site, Nina moved to Europe after his death and is buried there.

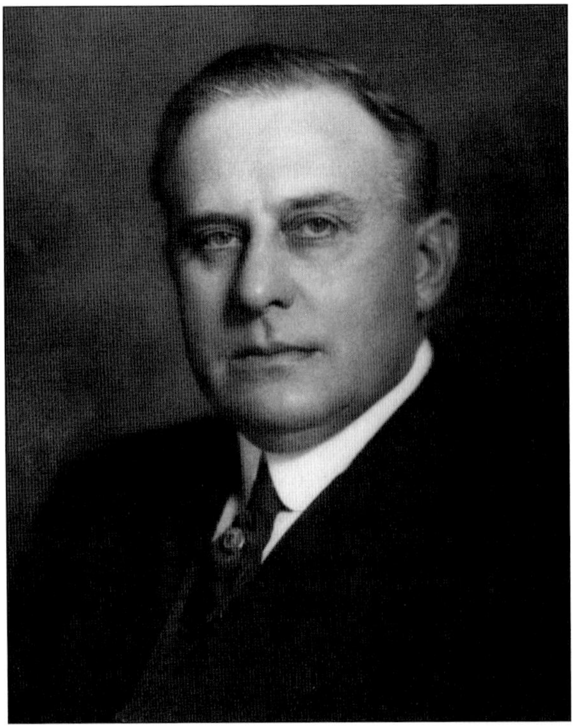

George W. Stevens (1866–1926) was the director of the Toledo Museum of Art from 1903 to 1926. Through hard work, a "can-do attitude," and the implementation of his progressive ideals in museum management and community outreach, Stevens's contribution to the early development of the museum into a world-class institution was invaluable. His wife, Nina, worked alongside George for several years, performing such duties as fundraising, custodial chores, teaching classes, and organizing events. She was eventually named assistant director of the Toledo Museum of Art. After George's death, Nina wrote his biography, *A Man and His Dream*, much of which provided a behind-the-scenes look at the early development of the Toledo Museum of Art. (Both, TMA.)

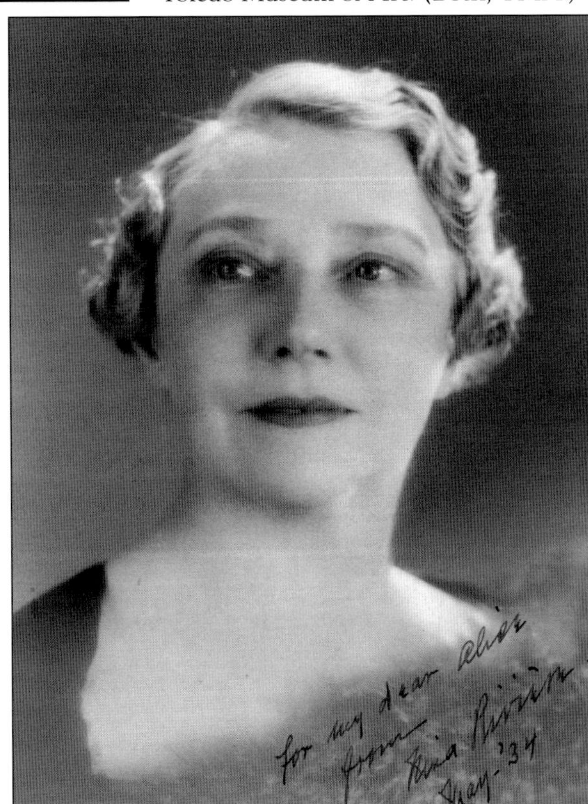

Seven

The Lloyd Brothers

Tombs are the clothes of the dead; a grave is but a plain suit, and a rich monument is one embroidered.

—Samuel Rogers (1763–1855)

Woodlawn is home to a variety of rich monuments from the Victorian period and into the early Art Deco movement. One sees stones with elements of Gothic, Classical, Neoclassical, and Egyptian styles along with the sleek lines of modern architecture. Lloyd Brothers Company played a major role in creating this outdoor art museum. The Rogers quotation paid tribute to John Lloyd when he died in 1938, age 79. He was president of Lloyd Brothers, working 66 years for the company his father founded in 1846.

Edward Lloyd, born in Wales, came to Northwest Ohio to work as a stonecutter on the Miami and Erie Canal. He stayed and began his business in Maumee, Ohio, in 1846. His sons, Edward, John, and Oliver, continued the business, moving to Adams and 11th Streets in Toledo in 1873. Edward left the business in 1880, and it was then incorporated as Lloyd Brothers Company. In 1894, the company moved to Auburn Avenue, opposite the entrance to Woodlawn Cemetery. Lloyd Brothers also had offices in Detroit, Michigan, and Washington, DC.

Lloyd Brothers designed innumerable tombstones and mausoleums in Woodlawn and other cemeteries, as well as private and public monuments throughout the United States. Locally, there are the Civil War monuments in Woodlawn, Willow, and Swan Creek Cemeteries; the McKinley monument at the county courthouse; the Fort Meigs monument; and the veterans monument in Toledo's Civic Center. Nationally, their monuments include the Zero Milestone at Washington, DC; Stonewall Jackson in Richmond and Charlottesville, Virginia; Robert E. Lee and the Lewis & Clark expedition in Charlottesville; Jay Cooke in Duluth, Minnesota; General Williams and Spanish War veterans in Belle Isle, Detroit; the Dodge mausoleum in Detroit's Woodlawn Cemetery; three of twelve monuments at the prison site at Andersonville National Historic Site in Georgia; and Booker T. Washington at the Tuskegee Institute.

A smaller segment of their work included stonework for public buildings and residences, including church altars, marble floors, fireplaces, and even marble bathtubs.

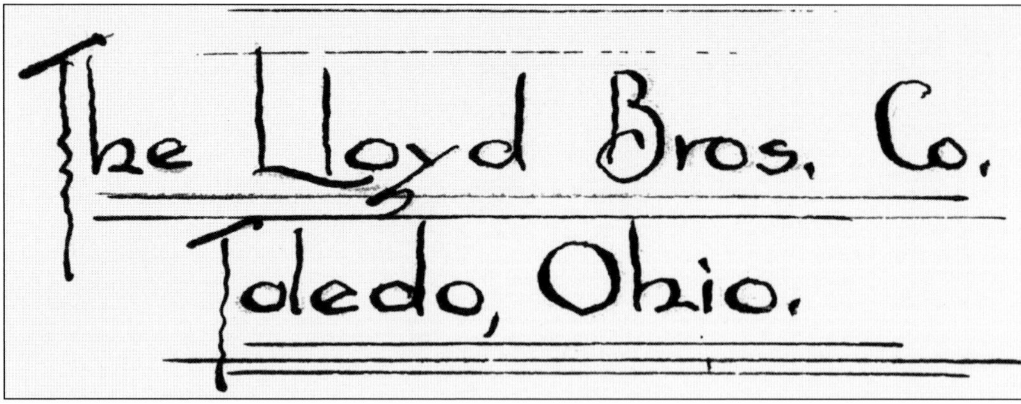

While the company name has been found on only some of their monuments, this distinctive signature was placed on all Lloyd Brothers designs. Their name, well known and respected throughout the monument industry, guaranteed excellent craftsmanship and high-quality products.

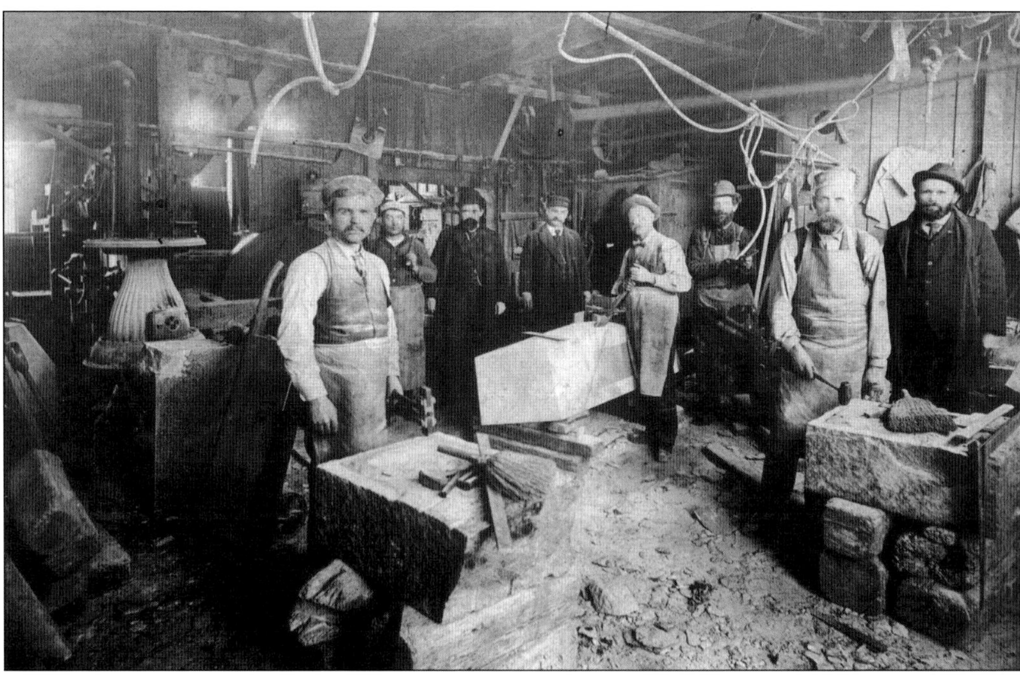

Ropes and pulleys hang in the background of this photograph of the Lloyd Brothers shop, located behind the company's office on Adams Street. The brothers are surrounded by the shop craftsmen as well as the tools of their trade. The slabs of granite, created by hammer and chisel handwork, are still beautiful today, 150 years later. (MW.)

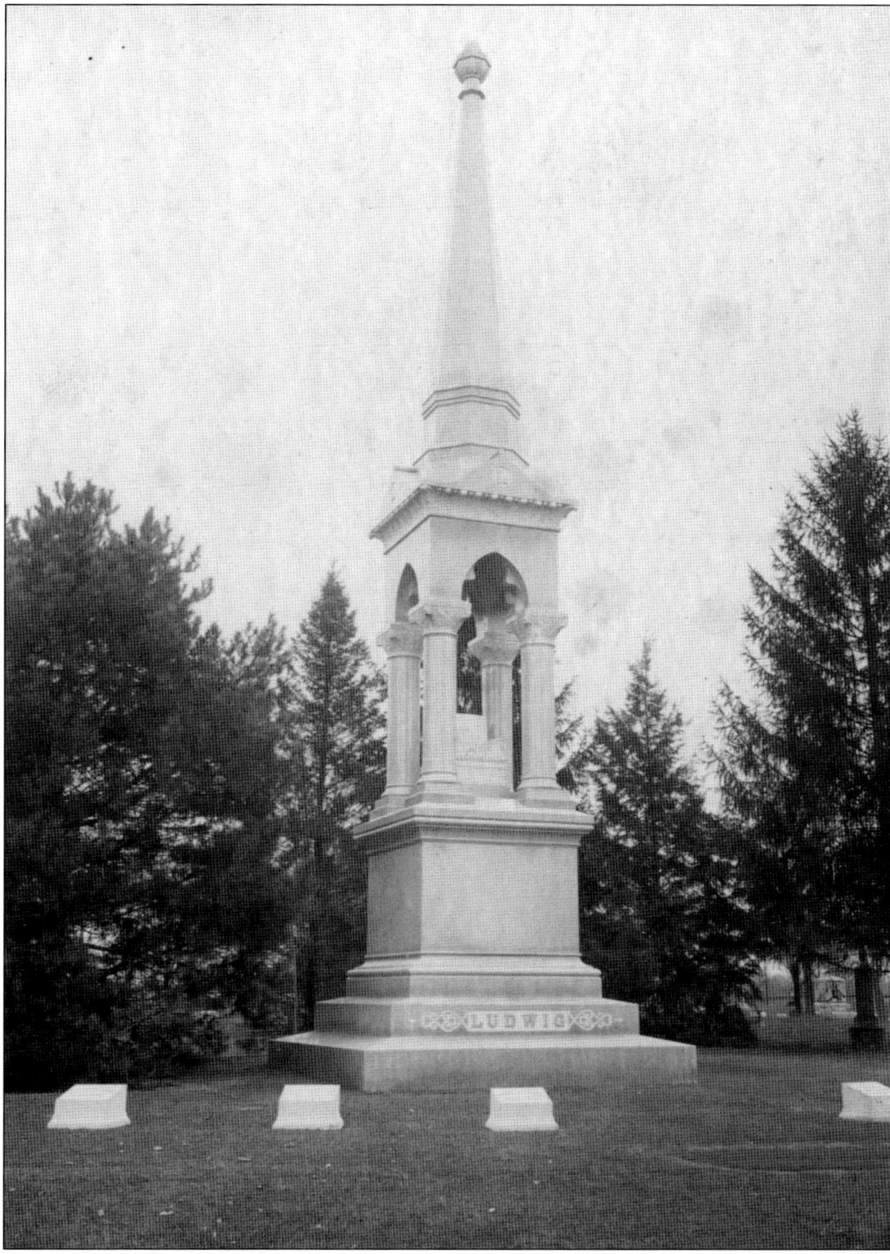

Leroy M. Ludwig (1848–1905) tried several different occupations before finding success in the oil fields of West Virginia. In 1893, he moved his family to Toledo, where they lived in one of the mansions on Collingwood Boulevard. After the death of his wife, Samantha, and son Theodore in 1899, Ludwig commissioned the largest monument in Woodlawn Cemetery. Located just inside the entrance, it is made of 13 sections of Vermont granite. Weighing approximately 185 tons and reaching 57 feet tall, the memorial, designed by Lloyd Brothers, was inspired by the Albert Memorial in London. Railroad track was laid to carry the granite to the site, and a special derrick was purchased to assemble the monument. When it was completed in 1900, Samantha and Theodore were interred. An unusual feature is the hand-carved replica of Samantha's chair in which she slept during the last years of her life. (MW.)

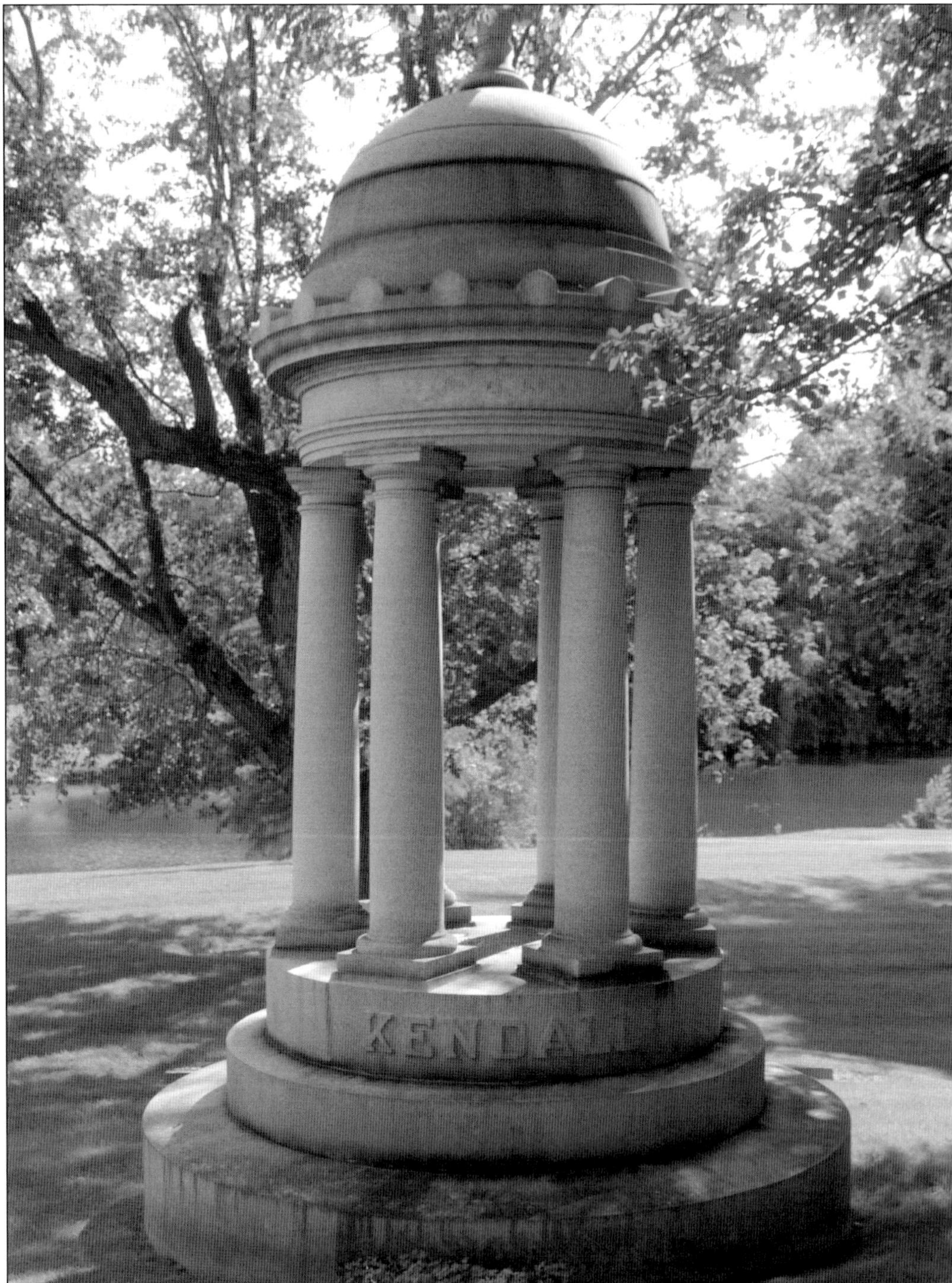

Cornelius Kendall (1839–1909) moved to Toledo from Chicago after the fire of 1871. He became a prominent businessman here as one of the founders of the National Supply Company and the Shaw-Kendall Engineering Company. His monument, designed by Lloyd Brothers, with its columns and magnificent circular canopy, suggests a Classical temple. Many of the Lloyd Brothers monuments, such as this one, were duplicated in other cemeteries throughout the country. (GLF.)

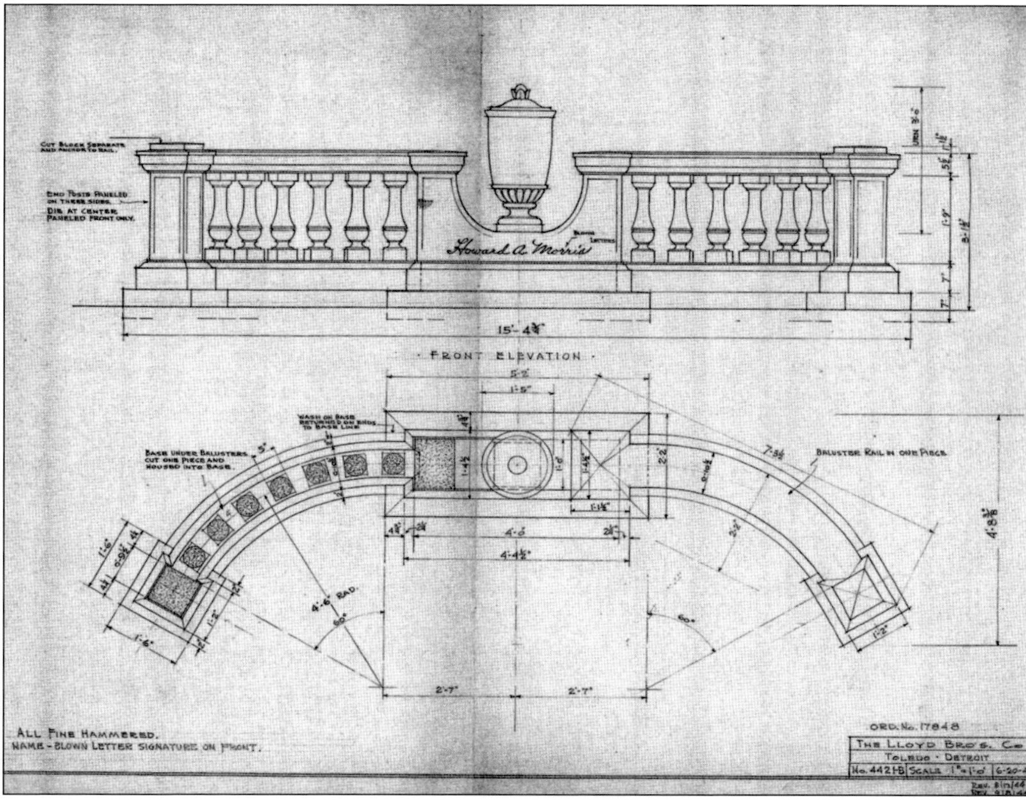

The drawings for Howard Morris's monument survive. They show the dimensions and detailed design of this beautiful monument.

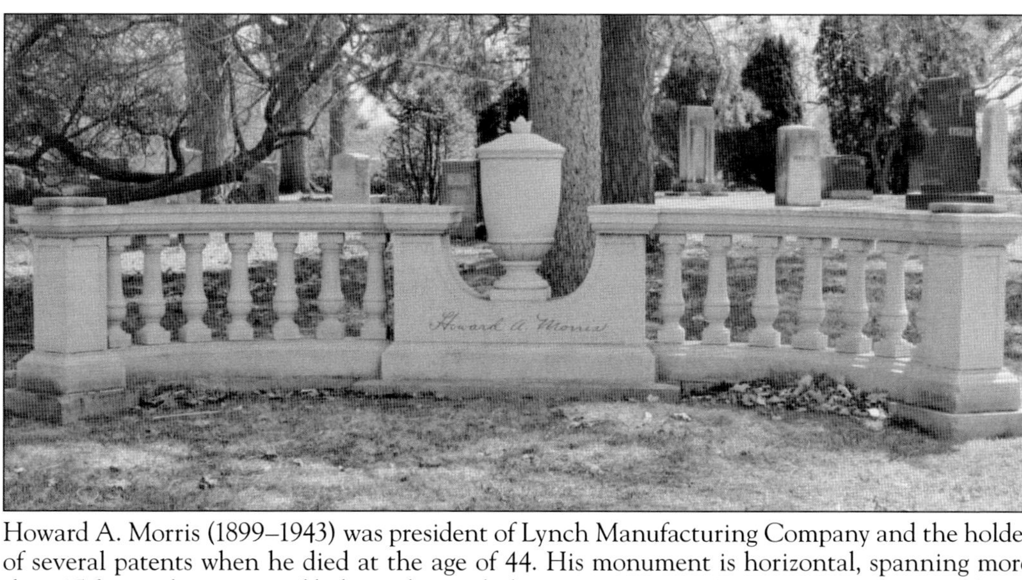

Howard A. Morris (1899–1943) was president of Lynch Manufacturing Company and the holder of several patents when he died at the age of 44. His monument is horizontal, spanning more than 15 feet with two curved balustrades symbolizing protection. Morris's signature is reproduced in the center, under the urn.

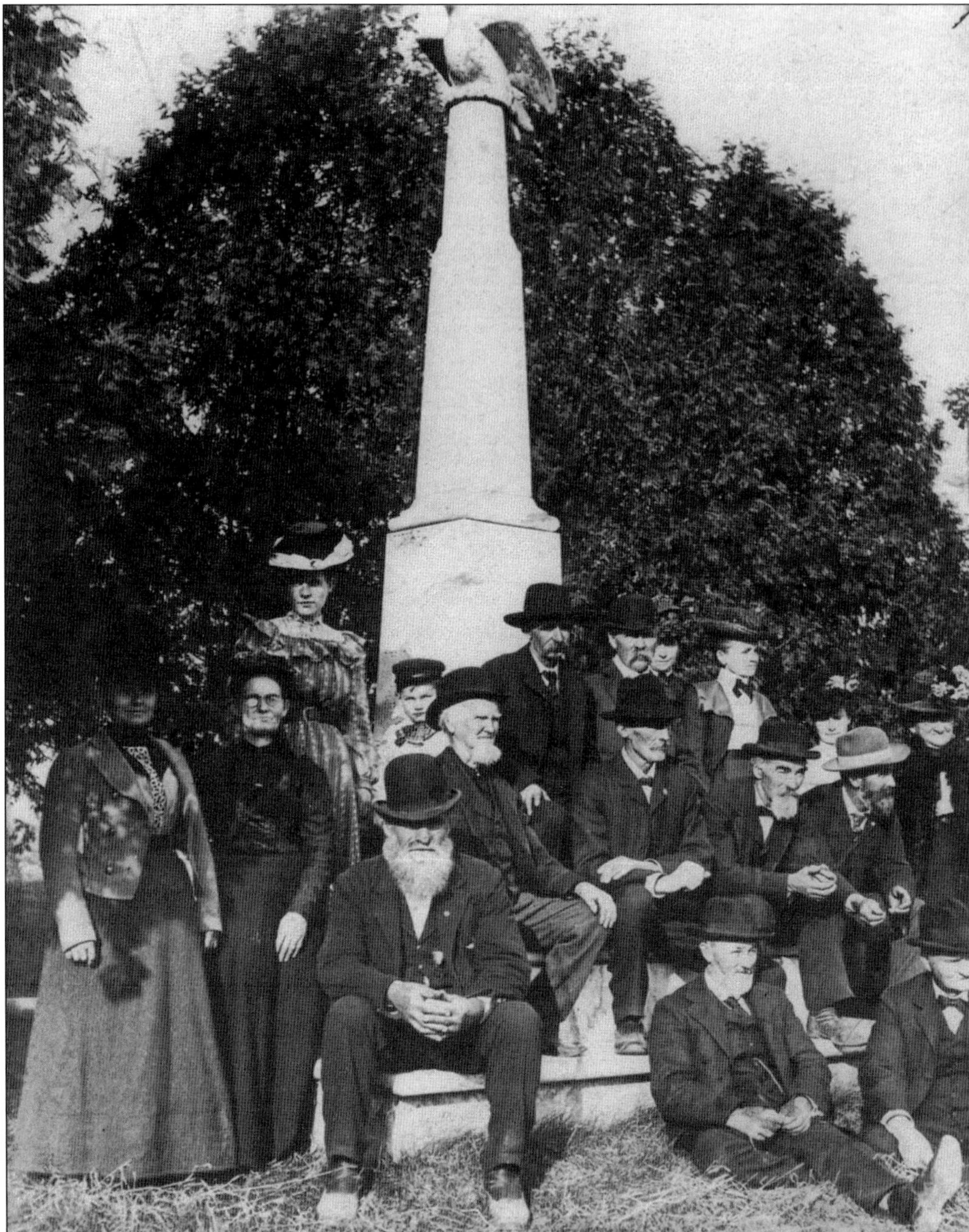

Swan Creek Cemetery is home to a Civil War monument created by Lloyd Brothers and erected in 1870. The stone lists the names of those from Monclova Township who died in the Civil War. The names of four of the six Ruckel brothers who served are a poignant reminder of the devastation of the war. George died on June 11, Philip on June 17, David on June 23, and John on August 6, in the summer of 1864. (MT.)

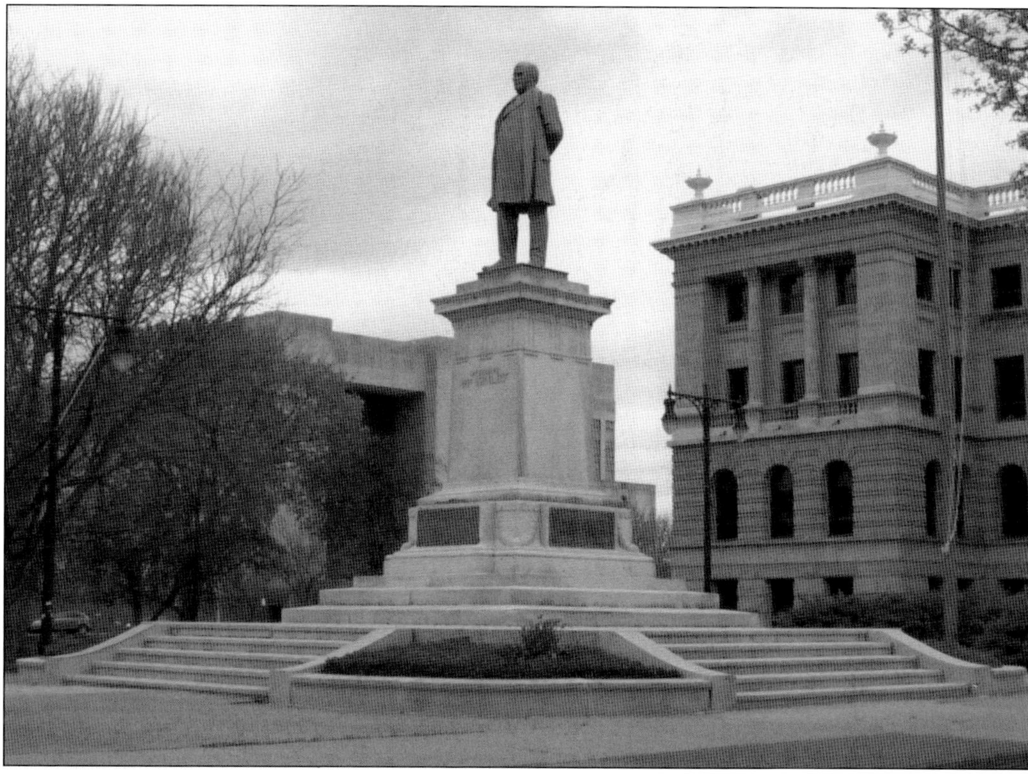

The William McKinley monument in front of the Lucas County Courthouse on Adams Street was designed by Lloyd Brothers and unveiled on September 14, 1903. It was the first monument in Ohio erected in memory of the assassinated president. One of the monument's plaques notes that 26,000 people contributed to the fund for its construction; their names are preserved within the monument. (TPL.)

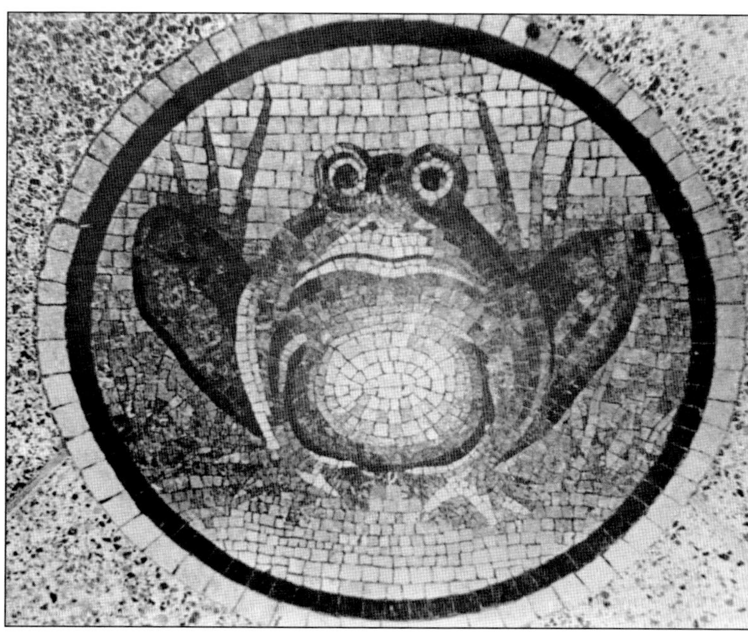

When the Lucas County Courthouse was built in 1897, a mosaic of a frog was embedded in the floor inside the Adams Street entrance. Made by Lloyd Brothers, the frog memorialized Toledo's early nickname, "Frogtown," a result of the swampy terrain of the area.

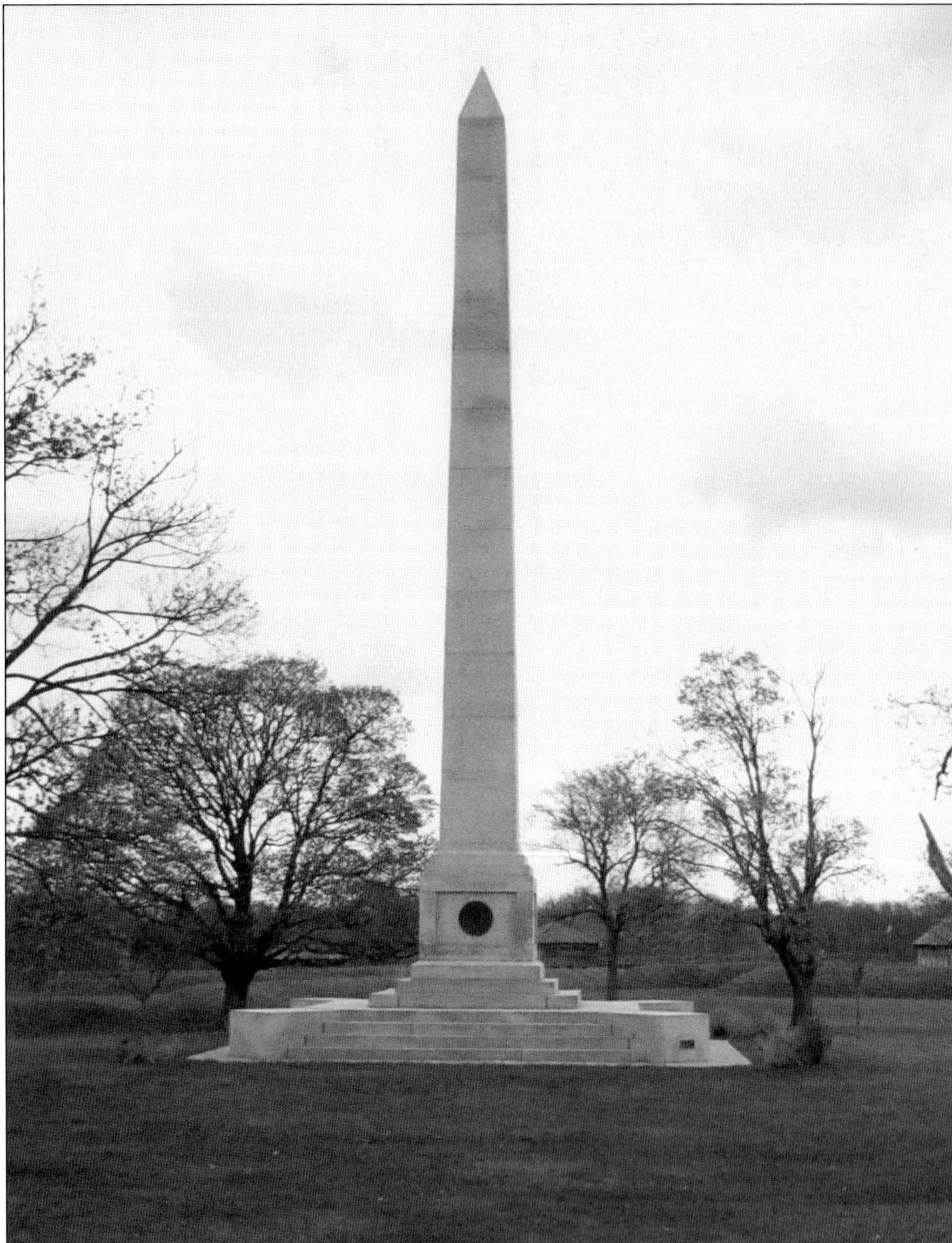

The obelisk at Fort Meigs in Perrysburg, Ohio, was built in 1907 by Lloyd Brothers. Made of granite from Vermont, it stands 101 feet tall. The monument was dedicated on September 1, 1908, and was funded by the Grand Army of the Republic as a memorial to the soldiers at Fort Meigs during the War of 1812.

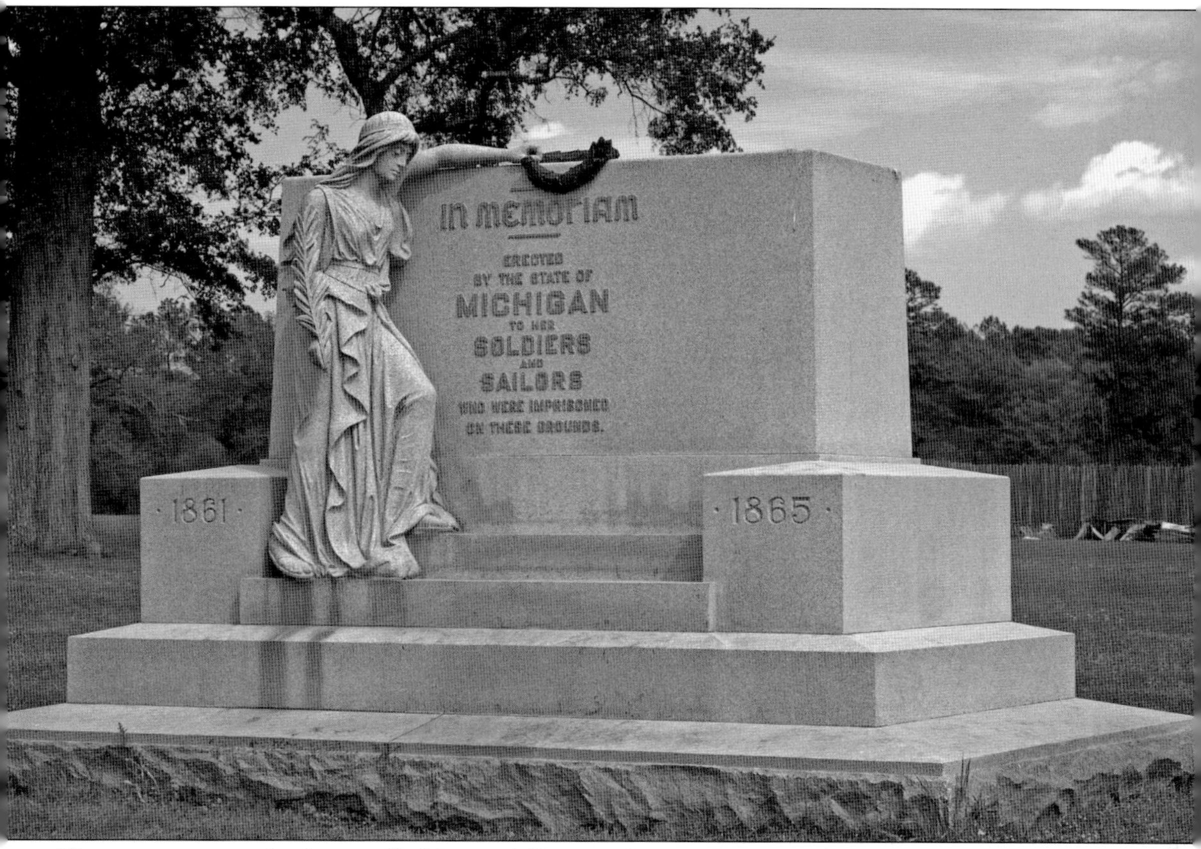

The prison site at Andersonville National Historic Site in Georgia is home to 12 monuments, most of which honor troops from the Northern states held captive here in the Civil War. In 1904, a large monument featuring a weeping angel was unveiled to remember Michigan troops. Lloyd Brothers created this monument, along with two smaller monuments honoring Lizabeth Ann Turner and Clara Barton. (ANHS.)

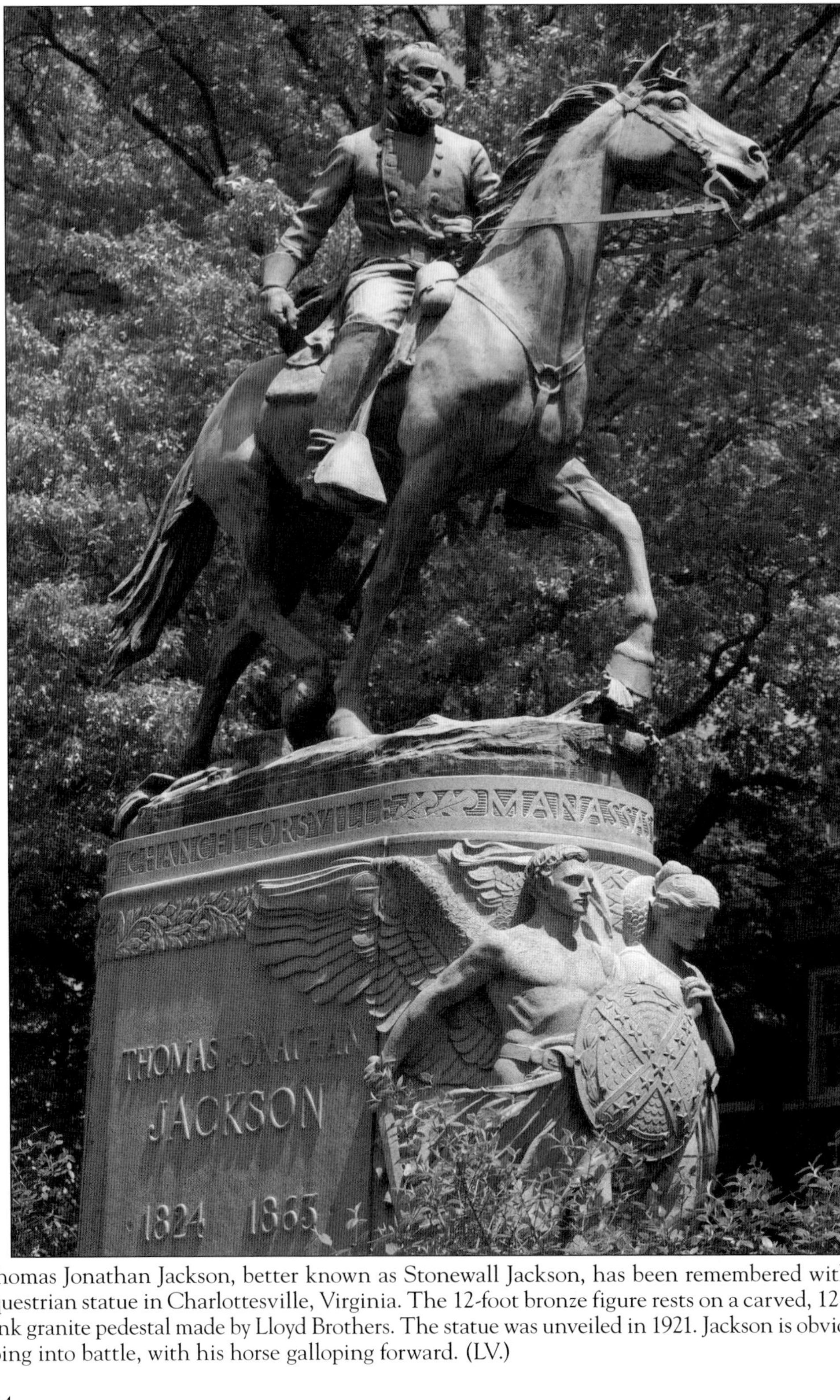

Thomas Jonathan Jackson, better known as Stonewall Jackson, has been remembered with an equestrian statue in Charlottesville, Virginia. The 12-foot bronze figure rests on a carved, 12-foot pink granite pedestal made by Lloyd Brothers. The statue was unveiled in 1921. Jackson is obviously going into battle, with his horse galloping forward. (LV.)

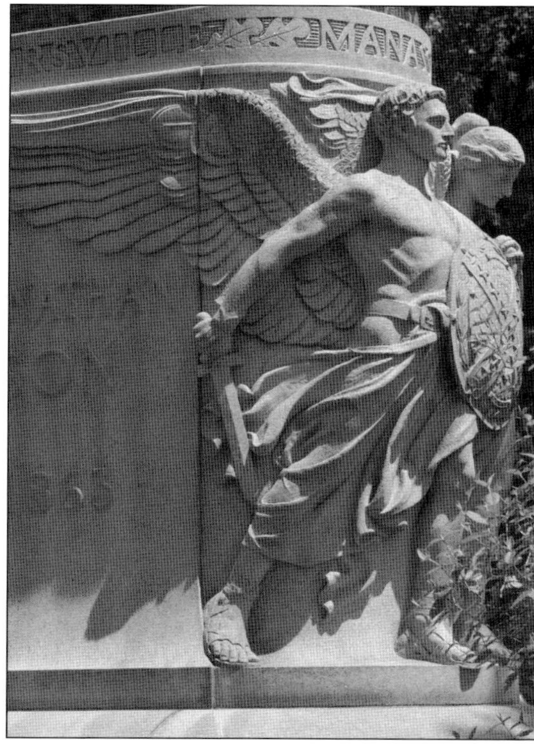

The figures at the end of the base of the Jackson monument represent Valor and Faith. They appear to be ready to leap off the base into battle. Between them, they carry a shield with the seal of the Confederacy. A list of the battles in which Jackson participated encircles the pedestal. (Both, GF.)

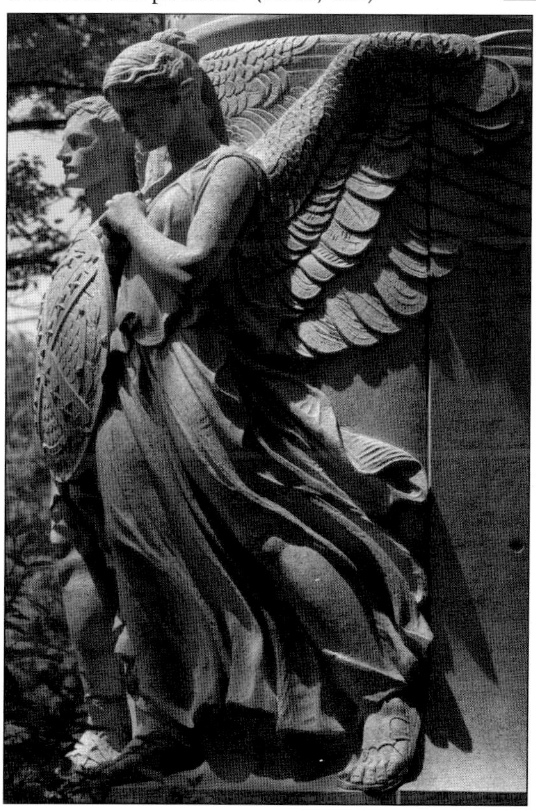

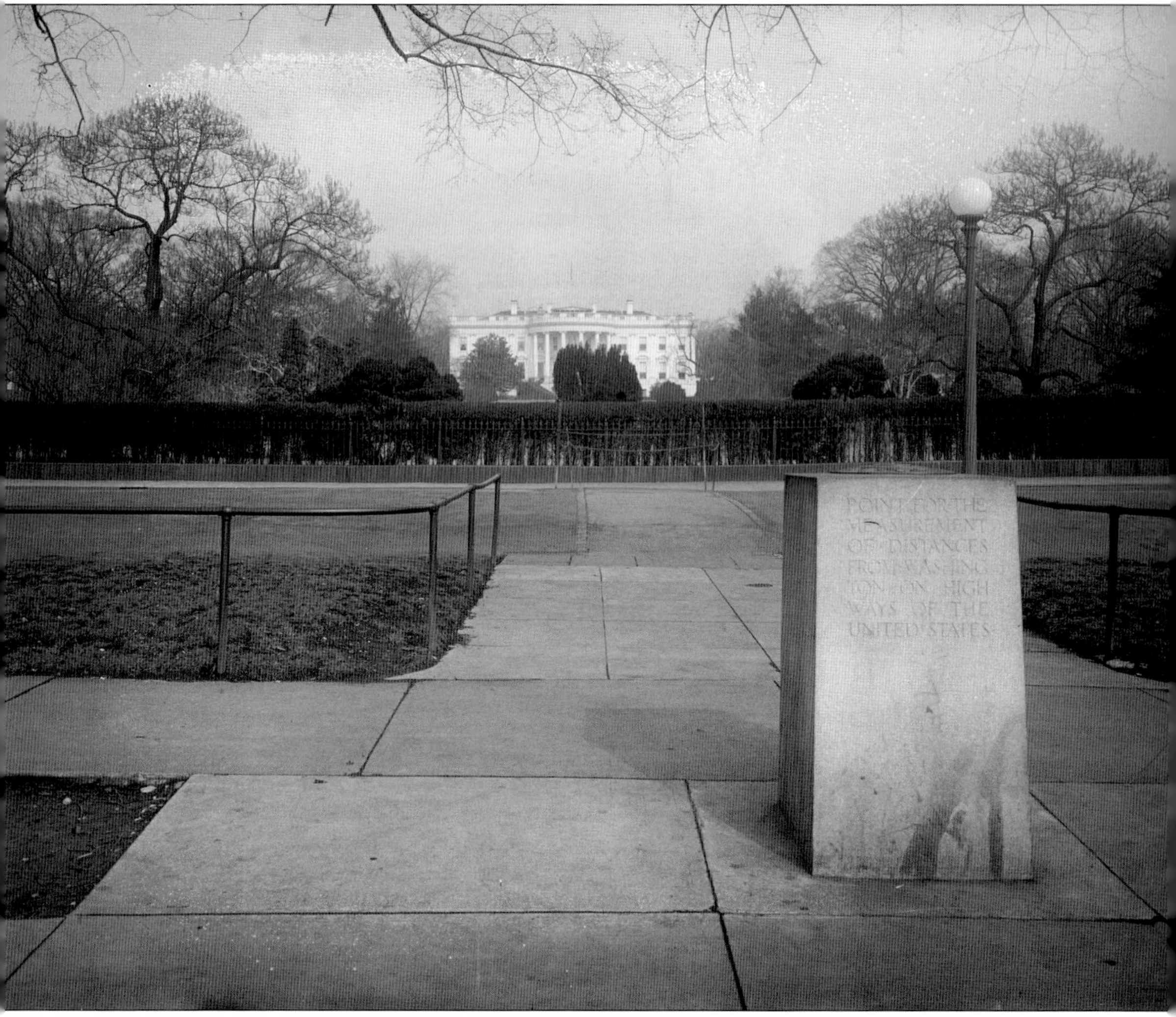

The Zero Milestone in Washington, DC, is the point from which road distances from Washington were to be measured throughout the United States. It was designed by Lloyd Brothers and dedicated in 1923. This postcard shows the marker with the White House in the background. (GF.)

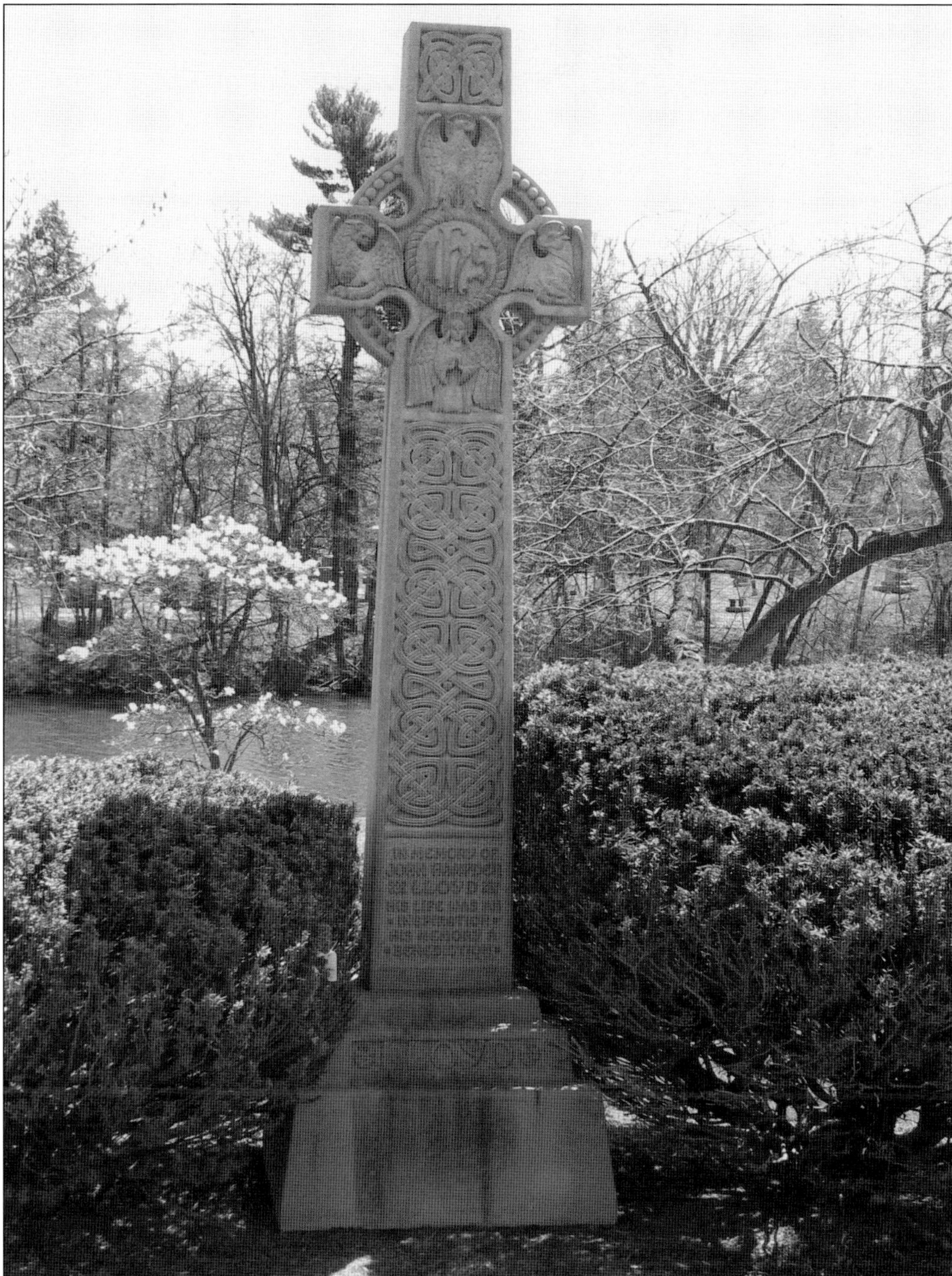

John Hampton Lloyd (1858–1938) was president of Lloyd Brothers when he died on January 1, 1938. He was 13 years old when he began working with his father, learning the skills of stone cutting. He enjoyed a national reputation for his work. His monument is a Celtic cross, possibly in recognition of his Welsh ancestry.